The Rules of Victory

THE
RULES
OF
VICTORY

How to Transform Chaos and Conflict—
Strategies from The Art of War

JAMES GIMIAN
AND
BARRY BOYCE

Shambhala
Boston & London
2008

Shambhala Publications, Inc.
Horticultural Hall
300 Massachusetts Avenue
Boston, Massachusetts 02115
www.shambhala.com

9 8 7 6 5 4 3 2 1

First Edition

Printed in the United States of America

∞ This edition is printed on acid-free paper that meets the American
National Standards Institute z39.48 Standard.

Distributed in the United States by Random House, Inc., and in Canada
by Random House of Canada Ltd

Interior design and composition: Greta D. Sibley & Associates

Library of Congress Cataloging-in-Publication Data
Gimian, James.
The rules of victory: how to transform chaos and conflict—strategies
from The art of war/
James Gimian and Barry Boyce.—1st ed.
p. cm.
Includes bibliographical references and index.
ISBN-13: 978-1-59030-085-5 (hardcover: alk. paper)
1. Success. 2. Conflict management. 3. Leadership. 4. Sunzi, 6th cent. B.C.
Sunzi bing fa. 5. Military art and science. I. Boyce, Barry Campbell, 1956–
II. Title.
BF637.S8G53 2008
158—DC22

                                                           2007024582

To the sage commanders—those men and women who have shown us how to take whole.

Contents

The Rules of Victory

Introduction

EVERY DAY EVENTS OCCUR, both close at hand and around the world, that dramatically illustrate one of the greatest challenges human beings face: finding a better way to deal with conflict and chaos. Every disaster, man-made or natural, every social or political challenge, every effort to effect change in every aspect of our lives, has these elements woven into it. And in most every situation, our failures leave us with the gnawing question: how could we have done that better?

The Art of War by Sun Tzu has long been one of the world's primary resources for working with this challenge. It emerged as a training text for generals during the Warring States period of ancient China and went on to become the most popular leadership and strategy manual of all time, in both Asian and Western cultures. Many people view it as the property of military officers and businesspeople, thinking that it's only about the logic of takeovers and one-upmanship, clever dealing and surprising the enemy. But the text's insights have gained wider application. The lessons of this wisdom tradition are relevant wherever conflict arises, which, as we know, is pretty much everywhere human beings gather to live and work, from the battlefield to the conference room, from the church hall to the school yard, and even in the "quiet" of our homes.

The text's popularity is due to the wide appeal of its central message, the oft-quoted proclamation that the leader's highest and best skill is to attain victory without battle. It then goes on to present profound methods to show how that victory—which we translate as "taking whole"—can be won. In this, the text speaks directly to the challenges faced by every person in a leadership position who has to work with resistance and conflict when trying to get something done. In every sphere of our lives, we face the challenge of bringing about a goal in a way that doesn't engender more conflict and chaos, thereby undermining our hard-earned accomplishment. The text's profound strategies show us the rules of victory—how to work with our world in a deeper way to bring about victorious circumstances that render conflict unnecessary.

The Art of War has gained broad acceptance as a strategy manual for the same reasons as most things that are adopted rapidly. First of all, it is relevant: the text speaks to our emerging worldview of interconnectedness and rapid change, of limited resources and the self-defeating effects of aggressive conquest. Next, it is effective: twenty-five hundred years of use around the world confirms that it has worked for many people. Its advice to us won't change every time the latest research findings reverse their previous position. And finally, it is reasonably easy to adopt: initially, only a slight shift in our view of the world is required for the text's practices to become helpful in our lives.

We saw these qualities in *The Art of War* when we began studying it thirty years ago, brought to it by our frustration with ineffective approaches to working with conflict. Our study led to the publication of *The Art of War: The Denma Translation,* in which we—along with our colleagues who formed the Denma Translation Group— offered a new translation of the text, accompanied by our own commentary and essays on the text's broad themes and perspectives. Our goal was to present an understanding of the text's view of the world and how to work with it as common human wisdom, accessible to all and connected to our times. Our edition spoke to all the text's users—military, business, academic, and beyond—and confirmed that this wisdom lineage was something all could participate in and learn from.

The Denma translation has gained broad acceptance and an appreciative readership. We found that people are inspired by connecting to the text's wisdom and can understand its way of approaching the world. This success brought great enthusiasm and optimism, but it also brought more pointed questions about the text's practical application. *The Art of War* is profound and rich, and places skillful action within a world that is an interconnected, whole, and complex system. The distance from the broad view to our daily lives can be great, however, and the journey to effective action can seem daunting. It became clear, then, that it would be helpful to have more guidance about how to get there from here. *The Rules of Victory* addresses the question that naturally arises next: how do we employ the skills of *The Art of War* in our lives? If uncertainty, complexity, chaos, and conflict define the new reality, then by what means can we best prepare for working with it more effectively?

This book seeks to address that next step, to help open up the profound practices in the text and render them accessible and effective. We do so in two ways. First, we deepen our understanding of the way *The Art of War* views the world and how effective methods and actions emerge from that view. Then we explore the text's famous strategies for working with the phenomenal world. *The Art of War*'s wisdom is not remote, mystical, or foreign, and we include a range of examples and scenarios to show how these practices are common in our experience.

But if this is a text for military officers, how can this be so? How does a text that talks in terms of battle and victory, armies and enemies, also apply to me and my daily life? How can the language of war help to unravel the roots of conflict and overcome the habitual aggressive approach to getting things accomplished? It is our conviction that the principles in this text speak to everyone in a leadership position, which we define broadly as anyone who has an intention to carry out some action in his or her world. If that is so, what do all the various readers and potential users of the text's wisdom—from military leaders to businesspeople to the person on the street to you in your life—have in common? Who is this text talking to?

The Art of War speaks to all people who accept leadership responsibility for what occurs in their world, who take action and seek change. Inevitably, taking such leadership will involve reaching a point in the campaign where others don't want to go along; where opinions, interests, and positions differ; and where dialogue and communication need to turn into action and things tend to get messy. This experience happens to everyone with something to accomplish, and it so often leads to frustration with the habitual means of working with conflict. That includes the stay-at-home parent and the nonprofit volunteer coordinator as well as the CEO and the military commander.

Leaders can be broadly defined as those who take action when they do not want to leave things to chance. Leadership, then, involves employing strategic thinking. At its most basic level, strategic thinking is simply having a view of your goal, assessing the situation and the resources at your disposal, and then deciding how to apply these resources to achieve your goal. This happens, more or less consciously, in any leadership campaign. Whether you think of yourself as a strategist or not, once you reflect on what you want to achieve and assess the ways you might achieve it, once you consider the resources at your disposal and decide how to make use of them, once you sense that there is a better way and aspire to learn it, you have entered the realm of strategic thinking. This is a skill required to accomplish anything in the world, and *The Art of War* offers a way of thinking and a way of being that sharpen this skill. It is the preeminent text for anyone who thinks strategically, which pretty much includes all of us.

We recognize that it is not always easy to see how the teachings and strategies of this text relate to a given challenge in life. On one occasion, we presented our work on *The Art of War* in a seminar made up of university faculty. One professor was obviously struggling with the material, and at a certain point, he interrupted to complain that he just couldn't connect to the text. He argued that the whole notion of war, battle, and enemy was contradictory to the basic philosophy of higher education. "I don't understand how this relates to my work in the creative writing department." He added that this approach to strategic thinking felt overwrought with self-conscious manipulation and that he wasn't comfortable thinking about leadership in these terms. As we were framing a reply, one of the other professors responded with a simple description of her experience of the many challenges involved in navigating departmental and university-wide politics, with its vast number of ever-conflicting viewpoints passionately argued for. Her comments produced an "aha" moment for the writing professor that fueled the conversation for the rest of the afternoon.

We are all leaders in our own sphere, and inevitably we will be compelled or inspired to take action. As we do so, we will encounter the practical realities of resources and people, which will give rise to resistance, obstacles, and challenges. We will need all the skills and faculties at our disposal to successfully negotiate these difficult times. This is the task of the sage commander, the military leader addressed by *The Art of War*. We all face the same challenges as the sage commander, and the principles within the wisdom lineage represented by these teachings apply equally to our sphere of leadership.

As we explore the teachings of *The Art of War*, we are working with a text that is short, condensed, and profound. It presents a remarkably consistent vision, but it is expressed in an often circular and ungraspable way—offering equal doses of frustration and inspiration. No book about this text can explore the whole of it or presume to be definitive. Our goal is much simpler: to create a way the modern reader can access the text—to get inside of it, so to speak—and to make an ongoing relationship that renders its skillful methods applicable in any domain. Based on our experience, we are confident that as you familiarize yourself more and more with the principles and strategies of the text, you will find opportunities to apply them appearing in all areas of your life. This occurs most readily when the deep-seated grasping for easy fixes is frustrated and you are prepared to go beyond the familiar (and usually unsuccessful) habit patterns.

The Art of War is different from approaches that prescribe very specific actions and support their arguments with historical examples. It functions more as a kind of training that seeks to change your view. As a result, it doesn't lead simply to a new way of doing things but rather to a new way of being. And out of this new way of being, new practices emerge, which give rise to more effective action. *The Art of War* is not a separate "system" of working with conflict but an orientation of mind and view that can enrich your effectiveness in whatever realm you work in.

The Rules of Victory attempts to go along with the pattern of the text. We do not present a linear argument to convince you of the effectiveness of the text's strategies. Rather, we offer an interconnected series of insights intended to spark and deepen your understanding of the text. This is a practical book, not a philosophical treatise on the nature of reality. It's about how to get things done successfully and without lots of fallout to deal with. It's about, in our experience, how the text seems to work in general and how it might work for you.

This is not a book about stunning breakthroughs and the latest research, but more about how old ideas can turn out to be cutting-edge. It will work by connecting dots for you and exploring some of the roots and antecedents of ideas currently in vogue. For example, learning about the central strategies in *The Art of War* will give you a deeper and very helpful perspective on the recently popularized concept of "the tipping point." The wisdom tradition of this text has never been about presenting a radical new thing; it has always been about discovering things that are right under your nose and investigating them deeply.

The Rules of Victory is not about an external set of guidelines that we must follow slavishly to attain our objectives. The *rules* in this sense refer rather to the underlying logic and energy of a situation, which we can work with directly to bring about our desired result. The word *rule* comes from the latin root *reg-*, originally meaning a piece of wood or rod used to mark a straight line. It then came to mean something used as a guide, hence that which is right or correct. Rules convey the sense of the governing power, what gives authority for conduct. We "follow rules" all the time in simple ways to our advantage, like when we exploit the force of gravity to ride a sled downhill. The rules of victory are about how to know and work with the natural patterns of how things go throughout our lives, and in the difficult situations we encounter.

It will be helpful to mention here a few of the conventions employed in our work. We have chosen, for example, not to use an English word for the Chinese word *shih* (pronounced "shir," with almost no vowel sound). Shih is the central concept in our discussion of the profound methods in the text, and a concept we believe could add great value if adopted more broadly in Western strategic thinking. We know that using the Chinese word creates a barrier to easy adoption. But doing so also prevents this important concept from being too easily integrated into your existing framework and thus avoids the risk of having its broader meaning diminished and its subtler meanings lost. The effort to understand shih and integrate it into effective use will help to make the concept genuinely your own. All deep learning goes through such a phase of discomfort. In our work with the text, we have witnessed how this process makes the study of the text richer and more rewarding.

Also, you will notice that, following long-established convention, we refer to the text as "the Sun Tzu," "the text," and "*The Art of War*" rather than using constructions such as "Sun Tzu's *Art of War*" that refer to Sun Tzu as a historical person. In part, that's because scholars and historians have no certainty that such a single, historical individual with that name actually existed. Beyond that, we feel that this text represents a lineage of wisdom, including human beings such as ourselves in history who have studied, learned, and contributed to the understanding. In referring to the text as the property of such a lineage, we establish the ground for you to enter this lineage and make the text your own.

The Rules of Victory starts with a review of what you need to know about the Sun Tzu text and tradition, and our approach to it. Here we give an overview of the key points we presented in our first book in order to bring readers new and old to the same ground of understanding the text and its tradition. Those who have read our first book will find that this book goes much more deeply into both the profundity and the practical application of the themes introduced there.

The Rules of Victory also serves as an excellent introduction to the Sun Tzu for those readers new to it. We present the entire text in the back of this volume as a handy reference. Those of you new to the text will benefit from taking the time to read through it, perhaps both before and after reading the first chapter. Whether you are new to *The Art of War* or a seasoned student, reading through the text helps develop a familiarity with the lines as they appear throughout our discussion.

Next, we present the pith instructions to the general about how to lead that appear on the very first page of the text: the traditional Chinese triad that we render as heaven, earth, and the general. In order to expand our understanding of this triad and apply it in our study of the text, we talk about it in terms of view, practice, and action, the three-part framework that we use throughout this book to bring the reader to an intimate, insider's view of the text. This framework is an excellent way to study and deconstruct the text because it ensures that we maintain respect for the text's wholeness and integrity. View, practice, and action is a framework that can present a holistic picture of any activity in the world. For example, the *view* of Western medicine, in general, is to cure the sick and do no harm; the *practice* is the prescribing of medicines, surgery, and other therapies; and the *action* is all of the instances where a doctor treats a patient. View, practice, and action is not an external tool so much as a way of thinking that tunes our minds in to the way the text works and views the world. It is helpful, then, to take some time to understand this framework. Thinking this way helps us enter the text at a deeper level and also provides us with a framework that can be helpful when applied to any aspect of our lives.

We then proceed to elaborate on what makes up the view, practice, and action of the Sun Tzu. In presenting the view, we expand on how the text sees the world as whole, interconnected, and ever-changing; the importance of knowing about ourselves and the world; and how all that leads to a victory we call "taking whole."

In the two chapters that make up the central section, we present the text's practices, what we refer to as the profound methods of the Sun Tzu: ways of working with the world that arise from the view and are so effective when facing the inevitable challenge of chaos and conflict. Shih is the theme here. Employing shih is the way the text shows us how to work with a part of the whole, interconnected, world—an environment, a sphere of endeavor, a workplace, a relationship—and effect change at a deep level either in a single act or over a sustained campaign. Employing shih comes in many forms, and we elaborate three: extraordinary and orthodox, forming and transforming, and deception. In so doing, we both illuminate these three practices and establish a pattern of understanding that can then be applied to the other practices presented in the text.

What naturally follows is our discussion of action. Here, rather than try to advise you about what specifically to do in a given situation, in the manner of a recipe book, we present stories of inspired and effective action. Just as with ancient commentaries, lines from the text are coupled with these contemporary stories to demonstrate how people's actions apply the Sun Tzu view and practices to the challenges in their lives. Such stories display the relevance of the text and will help to inspire your own actions. We end with some suggestions—including a basic approach to study as well as specific exercises—that will help you deepen your study and make this wisdom helpful in your life on an ongoing basis.

The Sun Tzu is about training for extreme times, for times of warfare when unique measures are required. It takes hard work to be prepared to respond with effective action in those times. When challenging circumstances are upon us, the difficult conditions have already been established, and there is seldom time to consult the manual. Studying *The Art of War* allows a certain way of seeing—and being—to seep into our minds. It reorients our view in such a way that unique, surprising, and skillful actions arise for us at times of extreme conditions.

For our study of this wisdom text to be fruitful, it has to become more than just picking up another set of tools, another way to separate ourselves from the interconnected world, create special territory for ourselves, and gain power over others. There is too much at stake. Accumulating another set of tools may well be helpful, but that in itself won't lead to actions skillful and effective enough to deal with the ubiquitous violence and aggression plaguing our world. Carving out a special place for ourselves and aggressively defending it won't work as the world gets smaller and smaller. *The Art of War* starts from the point of view that conflict, chaos, and aggression are unavoidable aspects of life, but it offers a way to engage and work with them creatively—and effectively.

The Sun Tzu offers real and practical answers to the questions readers bring to it, but it's more than just new tools or techniques. While the Sun Tzu is very practical, it is not simplistic in the sense of taking shortcuts, compromising our principles, and being expedient. The Sun Tzu's practicality relies on our ability to reflect on where we are in the world and how the world really works. It is practicality that relies on deep insight. The Sun Tzu counsels the general not to attack a heavily fortified position head-on and not to repeat the same form of attack that has failed numerous times before.

Rather, the general should await the enemy's vulnerable, open moment and move in quickly when it arises. How is this advice any less practical for us when dealing with an intransigent colleague at work or when pleading with an uncooperative teenager at home? The practices from this wisdom text work skillfully in all these situations.

We know from our work that many people come to the Sun Tzu looking for a better way to deal with conflict, often out of frustration with the shortcomings of other ways they've tried or observed. The Sun Tzu often makes an immediate impact by offering a change in how to view the world that opens endless possibilities for skillfulness. However, we know as well that the text—and its profound practices that we present here—can also frustrate readers, especially those looking for a quick solution or an easy mastery of the text. In our experience, it's like learning a foreign language, where the frustration of building up a vocabulary and conjugating verbs one day dissolves as you speak a whole sentence without first translating each word in your head. Patience, gentle exertion, openness, and a relaxation of the urge to grasp for the answers allow deep learning to occur.

The Rules of Victory seeks to make the wisdom of this text available in all areas of life, to speak about the text in a language that is as meaningful to the day-care supervisor and the AIDS worker as it is to the entrepreneur and the military officer. These profound practices need to be accessible to all and meaningful to each in his or her realm. Whether you are an experienced *Art of War* reader or completely new to the text, you will find a language and an approach here that make the pathways to enter this wisdom lineage broader and more accessible. This wisdom is not something foreign or external to you.

The Sun Tzu is a profound, systematic way of talking about and seeing the world. It offers a strategic skill set uniquely designed to be most effective in the very kind of times we live in: changing, chaotic, complex, and challenging. It is available now to all who seek a more creative and skillful approach to the challenges they encounter, who aspire to transform the conflict and chaos in their lives, and who want to gain the deeper authority for their strategic actions that arise from "going with" the wisdom of *The Art of War,* the rules of victory.

What Is *The Art of War*?
The Text and Tradition of the Sun Tzu

Some books are to be tasted, others to be swallowed, and some few to be chewed and digested.

—*Francis Bacon*

A BOOK BECOMES a classic when readers generation after generation seek it out to find fresh insights. By this measure, *The Art of War* is indeed a classic. Readers continue to learn a great deal from this ancient collection of principles, aphorisms, and metaphors about how to conduct themselves in the midst of all the chaos and conflict they encounter in their lives. While the book's title is almost always rendered in translation as "the art of war," the text is not only about making war. It is in fact a manual for how to work effectively and artfully with extreme and chaotic situations and with any kind of conflict. It not only acknowledges that conflict is inevitable in life but also tells us that we can accomplish our objective without adding to the conflict. That's why people keep coming back to it—not because it tells them how to wage war better but because it tells them that conflict rarely needs to reach the level of "war," where the highly polarized fight exhausts the resources of the parties involved, be they nations, business partners, colleagues, or friends.

When the members of the Denma Translation Group first began studying the Sun Tzu over thirty years ago, we knew that it held something we yearned for: insights about how to deal with conflict that went beyond conventional approaches. Yet we also had to ask ourselves how we could apply an ancient text from China's Warring States period to contemporary life in a way that could yield tangible results rather than simply provide intellectual stimulation or foster wishful thinking. As we started to work with the translations then available, we were frustrated, sensing that important pieces of the puzzle might be missing. The words and phrases seemed to carry cultural or historical associations that obscured the more basic, universal wisdom within. Our goal became to translate the best-known and most profound sections of the text and then explore them in seminars with others who shared our passion for finding a way to achieve difficult objectives without fighting. One part of the book led to another and another. After ten years, we had translated the entire work. Our new translation sparked the interest of many enthusiastic readers, so we began to offer seminars and workshops to explore further how the Sun Tzu can be applied in the nitty-gritty of daily affairs.

In presenting the translation, commentary, and essays in our first book, we were not trying to produce a fixed interpretation of the Sun Tzu. We wanted rather to open a path for readers to understand and use the valuable insights held in the text and the tradition of human wisdom it came out of. We were inspired to join with the tradition of the Sun Tzu and carry on the discussion in the modern day. Above all, we wanted to gather together with others and learn how to work with chaos, conflict, and complexity more effectively, aided by insights from the text. Our first book got the process started by presenting the text as a living record of common human wisdom. If the translation worked as we intended, the wisdom in the Sun Tzu would not simply be an artifact to be admired. Instead, the Sun Tzu's original power would provoke the reader's own wisdom.

Many readers have shared with us insights that emerged from working with the text and commentary in the way we had envisioned. Nevertheless, some have also told us that they found it difficult to close the gap between the profundities they encountered in working with our edition of the text and the intensity of their day-to-day reality. They experienced many "aha" moments but found it difficult to translate those into everyday actions that would help them achieve their objectives.

This message from readers has let us know that we need to go further. It fueled once again our strong desire to bring the wisdom of the Sun Tzu into everyday life. Like scientists who have made an inspiring discovery, we are eager to test it in the lab to prove it out. We are inspired to take the vision presented in our first book and show how it can be put into practice. That's what we've done in our workshops, and that is our objective in this book.

Since its earliest days, the basic human wisdom contained within the Sun Tzu has been transmitted from generation to generation through study, contemplation, discussion, and commentary—and when one knows this wisdom as if "by heart," it is reflected in day-to-day actions in a profound way that sets an example for others. That's what keeps it alive. Otherwise, it would be nothing more than wisdom from a foreign place and a distant time, an antique to appreciate and discuss but not to use. Any tradition that maintains its integrity is continued by this same method. A would-be architect begins as a student of architecture, and only when the tradition and essence of architecture have become her own does she become a full-fledged architect, producing something that is creative and new in the moment and yet strengthened by its roots in the past. The same is true for a chef, a surgeon, or a potter.

Most readers of the Sun Tzu today have had the same question at the outset that people in our Sun Tzu workshops have had: how can the distilled wisdom of ancient Chinese military leaders be relevant today to anyone in any walk of life? To address that question, we ask you to consider the following scenario:

Imagine a big world, filled with lots of entities, maybe fifty to seventy-five, of various sizes from smaller to larger, each of them powerful in their way yet having a unique makeup and claim to fame.

All of these entities are vying for control or position, motivated by a vision. Everyone is on uncertain ground. Each one is very ambitious because there is tremendous opportunity for gain. Each one is also very fearful, for it could be wiped out at any time, for so many reasons.

Each entity is made up of lots of people who all have their own hopes and fears, their lives, their families, for whom everything is riding on this constant shift of power and control and territory. They have a great deal of allegiance to where they are, but at the same time,

allegiance
loyalty
devotion there is lots of shifting back and forth, and movement of people and material among these entities. There are constant forays into others' space or territory, and everybody must decide how to deal with gain and survive loss.

It's all very confusing. There are no helpful reference points anymore; it's all new territory. The old rules of the game have been changed forever, they continue to change all the time still, and there are no set guidelines to follow.

At the end of a period of time, after the constant shifting of the balance of power, control, and territory that comes from the victories and defeats of conflict, the entities reduce in number and increase in size until first there may be fifteen to twenty of them, then maybe seven or eight left, and then finally two or three with one dominant, all established in their place, controlling all the ground.

Does this world sound familiar? Does this not very nearly describe a scenario we see played out today on an international, national, local, and even personal scale? Every time we present this scenario in our workshops, we hear a chorus in response: "That's where I work!" "That's my industry." In fact, this is the classic description of the conditions during the Warring States period that brought the Sun Tzu text into being. The people living in that time saw individuals, communities, and whole societies being damaged or lost because they were unable to deal with the clash of conflicting aspirations. Time and again, participants we've worked with have told us they find a high level of confusion and difficulty arising from the conflicts in their lives. We live in the Warring States period. At times, we ourselves are in what could easily be described as a state of war.

Our worldview in the West has evolved over the past fifty years. We view ourselves less in isolation today. We are often able to see the world as an interconnected web. In a time when enemies and friends alike from anywhere on the globe can communicate instantly with us and affect our lives directly, we are acutely aware of our interrelatedness. The scientific models and technologies developed over the last century have reshaped our view of the world, allowing us to see it less as a collection of entities than as a vast set of processes. The limitations of top-down command and control in emergent situations have caused many people to explore diversity and broad-based consensus leadership models. Many leaders can now see how each person in an organization influences the entire decision-making mechanism and can at any point play a pivotal role.

This view of the world as a dynamically interconnected whole is the view that prevailed among leaders in the Warring States period. They may have known little about what lay beyond the regions they were familiar with, but they experienced their world as one where each piece was distinctly affected by and had an effect on every other piece. From that point of view, it is impossible to regard anyone or anything as isolated. Now that the entire world has "become smaller," entities bump into one another much more and much more frequently. As a result, the interconnections have become more obvious and unavoidable. If we come to view the world as so utterly interconnected and interdependent, we stand on the same ground as those who first used the text. The Sun Tzu opens up to us and becomes a wisdom tradition we can readily join. It is tailor-made for these times.

The Crux of the Sun Tzu

What is at the heart of the message about chaos and conflict that emerges from such a dynamic worldview? How can we sum up the basic message of *The Art of War*? To begin with, the Sun Tzu regards conflict as an inevitable part of being alive. Where there is life, there is conflict—whether you experience it simply as resistance or friction, or as an obstacle in the way of what you want to do, or as a pitched battle between armies. From the Sun Tzu perspective, avoiding conflict is futile. It will find us in the end.

The Sun Tzu also puts forth the message that leadership is inevitable. Leadership in our times has come to mean many things, and on any given day, hundreds of seminars are devoted to teaching leadership skills. The great leader who guides his people (organization, team, army, and so forth) through the battle and on to the promised land is a celebrated archetype. Leadership in the Sun Tzu, though, refers to something more fundamental that applies to any person in any station of life. Simply put, each one of us is the center of our own world, and whatever sphere we operate in, inevitably we will have an intention or a vision that motivates us to take action. There will be consequences to taking the lead, though. However benign and well intentioned our motives may seem, our actions are bound to encounter resistance at some point. When we begin to take a step forward, other people might not want to go along, and that will give rise to conflict. The conflict can take the form of inaction, ongoing resistance, or organized opposition. The course of action we contemplate may even create conflict within our own mind, before anyone else has even entered the picture.

For example, consider the story of Ted, a midlevel employee at an engineering firm. Ted's firm had doubled in size in three years, and office space had been added quickly and haphazardly to keep up with the increasing size of the staff. Ted felt inspired to work up a proposal for a more rational design of the offices to solve problems that his coworkers were complaining about. However, word leaked out before he even had a chance to present his ideas, and he quickly found himself faced with a torrent of complaints, rumors about his motives, and alternative proposals. Ted was so discouraged by the response in the office that he put it aside for a time, and thought twice the next time he felt inspired to take the initiative to help. This is not an uncommon experience for those who try to accomplish something they care about.

Conflict is not always a bad thing. It often can be creative; it shakes up what needs to be shaken up. When in conference, creative teams like comedy and advertising copywriters will often disagree strongly and even harshly with one another, but that very friction can pry loose creative ideas that are hidden behind shyness and inhibition. Conflict—in the sense of the interplay between polarities—seems woven into the very fabric of life, and yet it so often can lead to wanton destruction. Nonetheless, whether we regard it as positive or negative, when a conflict emerges, it forces us to work with the friction, change, and chaos in our lives. We inevitably ask ourselves how we can work with these situations in a more creative and effective way. The answer within the Sun Tzu is that it is possible to come through the other side of conflict, having gained our objective, without blood on the floor. It is possible to achieve victory without battle.

This pivotal notion of achieving victory without battle is both one of the best-known and least understood premises in *The Art of War*. Most people assume achieving victory without waging war is just about a more clever or ruthless way of winning, about getting the upper hand, which is why the Sun Tzu shows up on Tony Soprano's bookshelf. But this central principle is about much more than that; it's about something the text calls "taking whole."

From the perspective of the Sun Tzu, once you see the world as an interconnected whole, taking whole becomes the only option. Taking whole is essentially about including the perspectives of others in your victory. It's not about "I win, you lose." It's not simply about bringing the other person over to your side but bringing him or her to something larger than either side, such as a solution that neither side envisioned at the outset of the conflict. In that way, there's no residue from the conflict, and you can build something greater from that victory.

When leaders are unable to see the whole or lose sight of it, an apparent victory may mask simmering unrest that presages the resumption of conflict. When the victors of World War I drew lines in the sand to create the modern country of Iraq, they laid the groundwork for a series of conflicts that would play out over the course of a century. Conversely, an action taken by a leader that comes from the viewpoint of taking whole can be quite powerful. In recent times, a ruling by the Supreme Court of Canada conferred on aboriginals special rights to harvest fish stocks, which put them into direct conflict with existing fishing communities. The ruling led to harsh rhetoric, vandalism, and violence in a number of fishing communities on the Atlantic seaboard. In one of these fishing villages, however, the chief of the local aboriginal band requested a gathering for all native and nonnative fishermen. At the meeting, he did not initiate negotiations. Instead, he simply asked each attendee to talk about his grandparents and tell his story. People began tentatively, but as more and more people from both sides told their family stories, it became clear that there was the beginning of common ground, the possibility of creating new relationships in the midst of conflict. It was apparent that people at the different poles of the conflict had valid aspirations that needed to be respected. The conflict did not vanish, but the intensity lessened and participants on both sides began to learn how to coexist in the new reality created by the court's decision.

If taking whole becomes a way of working with the world, the text suggests, we can go beyond the habitual pattern of responding to conflict with aggression and one-sidedness, which only escalates the conflict and results in a cascading chain of events that leads to more destruction for everyone. Conflict is notorious for enticing us to see things in a partial and biased light. Because we see only parts of the picture, our ability to act or lead effectively is impaired. The Sun Tzu shows us the wisdom of not succumbing to this smaller vision.

But how do we go about doing that?

Through knowledge, the Sun Tzu tells us. At the heart of the ability to take whole is a deep kind of knowing that becomes habitual, a part of who we are. We know the details of a situation, we know the other we are encountering, and very important, we know ourselves.

> *And so in the military—*
> *Knowing the other and knowing oneself,*
> *In one hundred battles no danger.*
> *Not knowing the other and knowing oneself,*
> *One victory for one loss.*
> *Not knowing the other and not knowing oneself,*
> *In every battle certain defeat.*
> [CHAPTER 3]

Knowing does not stop at collecting information. It involves employing all of our rational faculties as well as the intuitive grasp we have of a situation. This kind of full-bodied knowing enables us to arrive at an accurate appraisal of a situation, one that is not limited by a polarized point of view. Operating with a detailed and accurate picture of the events before us, we can act more effectively, which means acting in such a way that we include everyone's perspective. That's what taking whole means: acting on the basis of seeing things in their entirety, seeing from the perspective of the whole. To be able to take whole, then, an effective leader requires a more encompassing way of knowing.

Knowing, or cultivating knowledge, is not a onetime event, or even the culmination of a long process. It is a continual process, a mode of being. We can speak of it as a path, but this path has no final destination. Certainly there are destinations, but they become the starting point for further paths, so in the grand scheme of things, the destinations are merely way stations. This is not a mystical concept. If you learn to play a musical instrument, or to write or sing or play golf, when are you finished? At what moment do you say, "It's all over now. I have nothing more to learn"?

The path of knowing, in terms of the text, does have a beginning. It begins when we appreciate the fact that as human beings, we are endowed with leadership—the impetus to take action in our world. It begins when we appreciate the inevitability of conflict that arises along with taking actions. It begins when we appreciate both the subtleties that lie at the heart of all conflicts and the need to "take whole" rather than grasp at partial victories. It begins when we realize what we don't know, and we desire to know in new and different ways. The path of knowing helps us to learn something profound about ourselves and the world around us and why they don't always get along—and what we can do about that.

From knowing in this way, we are able to achieve victory, but the Sun Tzu turns the conventional notion of victory on its head. Normally, victory is what we attain after a struggle. From the point of view of the text, though, struggle is the mark of "the defeated army," which seeks victory by doing battle. By contrast, the victorious army is "first victorious" and after that engages. In the conventional approach to victory or winning, conflicts and adversaries stand between us and the victory we seek. We feel we lack something, and we have to strain and fight to get it. By contrast, in the Sun Tzu, the leader assumes the perspective of victory, and adversaries and conflicts become simply opportunities to engage and take leadership. They show us the path ahead and what is required to travel on it.

Inspired by an understanding of the interconnected nature of events, it is possible to engage conflict and chaos from the perspective of taking whole—instead of seeking a one-sided victory. In so doing, we will be compelled first to know rather than fight, and thereby discover ways to attain an objective without resorting to the destructive power of aggression. That is a real victory.

How the Sun Tzu Works

When you look at the Sun Tzu text itself, you find a loosely linked set of observations, models, and injunctions with only the barest argumentation connecting them. Doctrines are not laid out in lengthy, logical arguments. They are presented almost brusquely, through analogy and metaphor. The thirteen chapters do not unfold in either a narrative or an analytical order. They resemble poetry more than prose.

This collection of thoughts is more than likely not the product of a single author. It is bound together under the title *Bing fa,* which could most literally be translated as "Military Methods." (Our title, *The Rules of Victory,* could easily serve as a gloss translation of this original Chinese title.) As we argued in our first book, *military*—in the broadest sense of the word—refers to the organized application of force, and its most common example is the army. Force, which is neutral—not for or against anything—is the simple exercise of strength, a feature of almost all physical and mental acts. For anything to occur, a force must be applied. Power is the ability to apply force and produce an effect. The military, then, is an intensification of this common human activity.

This meaning of *military* encompasses every campaign that involves marshaling and focusing our resources to achieve an objective, whether it be erecting a day-care center, starting a business, dismissing a difficult employee, or running for city council. *Military* also implies a certain sense of urgency and extreme circumstances, and the risks and dangers attendant upon such a situation. Given infinite time, perhaps we would resolve all our conflicts to everyone's satisfaction. In the long run, everything will be fine, but as the economist John Maynard Keynes said, "In the long run we are all dead." The military, and organizations that have a similar degree of training and readiness to act on a moment's notice—such as hospital staff, firefighters, and rescue teams—must work with conflict that is emergent. In fact, we all have to do that. The circumstances may not be as dire on a day-to-day basis, but they are deeply meaningful and can have long-term effects. We study the Sun Tzu to learn to work effectively with the most highly charged conflicts, where time is of the essence, which enables us to work more effectively when conflicts erupt upon us without warning. Military implies a habitual yet relaxed vigilance and a readiness to act.

The other part of the title refers to "methods," which means that the concepts in the book are there not only for reflection and edification; they present us with ways to act. "Method" is one of the core principles laid out on the first page of the text. These principles present the means by which a leader assesses a situation and thus knows how to attain victory. Method, then, has central significance for appreciating what the Sun Tzu offers. The Chinese word translated as "method" originally referred to something that could be copied, like a small clay model used in the building of a house. From this it came to refer to standard forms of measurement. More generally, it came to indicate any set of standards and, eventually, the proper way to do things. In the Sun Tzu, methods are presented so that we can use them to work with conflict more effectively, which is to say, with less damage to all concerned while still effectively achieving our objective.

"Military methods," then, does not presuppose war; it only presupposes the means necessary to deal with conflict. In the particular historical context of the Sun Tzu, the conflict addressed is the conflict among the warring states, but the principles and methods set out apply to conflict wherever it arises. Conflict is conflict, wherever and in whatever degree we encounter it. The Sun Tzu's teachings, then, are not limited to any single realm of activity. They can apply at every level and in any sphere: international, national, societal, commercial, familial, and personal.

Translating *The Art of War* presents many challenges. This loosely collected set of observations derived from an oral tradition does not resemble an existing genre of literature in the West. Far from a book as we now know it—a solid entity with an identifiable author—the

Sun Tzu text is a collection of teachings recorded and edited over many centuries by a lineage of its practitioners. When the text was first written down from the oral tradition, books in China took the form of a series of thin bamboo strips, each with a few characters written on it, bound together by a silk thong. As strips were broken or lost, subsequent editors had to piece the missing lines back together. Over time, this editing process shortened the text from as many as eighty-two chapters to the thirteen we have now. But since the text was not concerned with argumentation but with establishing a point of view, the wholeness was retained by how the view manifests in every passage and from a variety of perspectives.

As if the form of the book didn't present enough of a challenge to translation, there is the very nature of the Chinese written language, wherein a single character expresses a rich field of meanings. This has led to translations that seem compelled to spell things out a little bit more clearly than the text itself may do, in an effort to clarify what appears obscure. The result in many translations is a long, discursive set of words standing for a single Chinese character, as well as a different set of words standing for that character when it recurs in the text.

We chose to keep the number of words in English very close to the number in Chinese, so that we could maintain the succinct, poetic power of the original, which derived from its roots in the oral tradition. Based as it often is on song and chant, a text derived from an oral tradition can have a haunting character. It enters the mind deeply and imprints itself. Thus, it is easy to remember and inspires in the conscious memory deeper realizations, even when one is not reading or reciting the text. This was the way that the Sun Tzu had first been transmitted, before the time of written texts. We felt that preserving this oral character would enhance the learning process for modern readers. Had we chosen to add words by paraphrasing or expanding on the original, the translation would have lost some of the lithic character of the original—the feeling that the characters had been chiseled, each having its own weight. The quality of a translation with too many words reminds one of Emperor Joseph's comment in *Amadeus* about one of Mozart's pieces: "Too many notes!"

In addition, wherever possible, we chose to render a given Chinese character with the same English word throughout. Even though it might have been more convenient for us and less demanding for the reader to use a variety of synonyms for a basic term like *victory* or *enemy* that would appear many times, we chose to retain the focus and simplicity of the original text. If we had used a variety of different words in English for the same Chinese character, we might have produced more free-flowing English, but the reader would no longer be able to tell that the same idea was being rendered again and again. Terms like *victory, advantage,* or *Tao* act as motifs within the text. Their repetition is critical to the way the text weaves and builds meaning throughout the various passages. Seeing the same term in a variety of different contexts allows us to plumb the depths of its meaning. It helps us to learn by repetition.

The single words that we chose for a Chinese character were the ones that held the broadest meaning conveyed by the character we were translating. Take, for example, these important principles of leadership presented at the very beginning of the text:

> *Heaven is* yin *and* yang, *cold and hot, the order of the seasons.*
> . . . .
> *Earth is high and low, broad and narrow, far and near, steep and level, death and life.*
>
> *The general is knowledge, trustworthiness, courage and strictness.*
> [CHAPTER I]

Many translations render the characters for "earth" and "heaven" as "terrain" and "weather," respectively. In so doing, the translators have decided that since this text is rooted in the military tradition, the military application of the broader term is most important. However, heaven and earth hold meaning that is simultaneously more profound and more simple. Paying attention to that which is above and around you (the heaven of inspirations, ideas, and views of the nature of things) and that which supports you (the earth of practicalities, vicissitudes, and ways of working through them) is much different, deeper, and on a much larger scale than simply paying attention to weather and terrain. In addition, heaven and earth hold philosophical significance in the Chinese worldview that relates to the understanding of the interconnected and interdependent nature of existence. *Weather* and *terrain* do not necessarily convey this breadth and subtlety.

In the Denma translation, we chose to hew closely to renderings of a given character that carried the full field of meaning, so that the power of the direct, earthy language could come out. At the same time, a more encompassing term like *heaven* does not exclude weather from its range of meaning. Using the more encompassing term does not mean that the reader must think only in lofty terms; it simply does not cut the reader off from the full range of meaning. The broader and deeper the reader's understanding of the meaning in the text, the more effectively the lesson can be applied to the range of unique challenges in his or her own life.

Naturally, the translation principles we applied to *The Art of War* do not apply to every translation effort, but they allowed us to fulfill our goal of creating the same relationship to the text for a modern-day reader as a member of this lineage in Warring States China had. There is no question that translating the text in this way places more demand on the reader. One important way it does that is by frustrating the tendency to interpret the text to confirm one's existing viewpoint. If we are to disrupt our habitual responses—a key to attaining knowledge and unlocking the power of taking whole—we need to confound the impulses of our apprehending mind. The fact that a given line may not yield its truth except by deeper examination is part of its power.

To go beyond simply "getting" something from the text requires taking a step back to view the bigger picture, which is the first step in the process of contemplation, the deepest form of study. By contemplation we mean creating an open yet protected space for observation. In this context, we are not speaking of contemplating any specific thing but simply creating openness to consider whatever arises. When we come to understand something by contemplating its meaning beyond our habitual framework, the truth comes not from the text alone or from our own internal resources. It arises from the relationship between the two. We mix our mind with the text, which sparks genuine insight and conviction, which we can then test in the field of action.

To aid in this process, we offered commentary in our first book—in running form and in essays—which many readers found extremely helpful. In our workshops, we employ a study method we have called "reading practice."[1] In this method, the reader recites a line aloud, considers and contemplates it silently for a few moments, then reads it aloud again before beginning to ponder and probe its meaning. This method has worked extremely well to bring out the powerful meaning inherent in the text. For example, if we use reading practice with the line "Attain both hard and soft" from chapter 11, which upon first reading appears tough to understand, it can begin to resonate deeply and say things about many different areas of our experience. One reader's response is likely to be quite different from another's and will reflect that individual's unique temperament, circumstances, and orientation to the text. However, each of these readings provides insight into the text that is valuable for us all, as our experience in seminars over the past ten years has repeatedly confirmed.

How to Be

The Sun Tzu text is a deeply interconnected and intertwined set of themes, lines, and meaning. Using the reading practice to gain insight into one line can provide us with an understanding of the whole, and the text begins to open up. Critical passages begin to sink in and take on a life of their own, becoming part of our subconscious mental landscape and reshaping how we observe and relate to challenges that arise in our daily lives. This is learning from the inside out. It is a type of learning that has long been used by people who try to understand what a wisdom text or a sacred text is saying. It is not that different from how we learn common things throughout our lives, like a new board game or home electrical repairs, which seem difficult or abstract until we "get it." What at first seemed foreign and unfamiliar begins to sink in and make sense. With the Sun Tzu, what does not appear to us on the first or second reading can appear to us on the fifth or sixth reading or as the lines emerge in our minds as we take a shower, ride a bus, or close our eyes at the end of the day.

We are pleased that this approach to the study of our translation of the Sun Tzu has helped many people to discover an inner understanding of profound insights about conflict and more creative ways to work with it. We know this from what readers tell us and from what has happened in our workshops. However, while contemplating lines in the text and beginning to make them our own yields quite powerful insights, we are still left with the question of how to actually *be* or behave the way the Sun Tzu implies is possible. How is it possible to engage conflict and chaos in our lives and achieve our objective without engendering further conflict? And how can we actually employ the compelling insight of taking whole when our teenage child is screaming that we're the world's worst parent or our boss is once again mistakenly blaming us for that missing report? We inevitably must ask, "So, now what?"

As we presented in our first book, this view of the Sun Tzu opens up the text's profound insights for the modern reader. In general, the view is a critical perspective to understand and is most often the best place to begin. It can also be quite lofty, however. If we climb a high hill and look down on a village or even a city, events can appear so orderly. All seems to be well; everything in its place. One can see the fire truck racing to put out the fire. How well put together it all seems. However, when you descend from the hill and enter the fray and see the fire spreading to your house, your well-ordered and contented view is put to the test. Many an insight formed at the seaside or on the mountaintop has evaporated within a day of our returning to home and office.

For the insights offered by any tradition to have powerful effect, even the most profound view must be aligned with practices—disciplines, broad strategies, and ways of being—that strengthen it and extend it effectively into the real world. If these two are well matched, then these practices will result in skillful actions in the world, successful applications of the view in a particular situation shaped by unique events here and now.

A cabinetmaker has a view of what a good cabinet needs to look like and how it ought to function, informed by history, style, tradition, and materials. To actually create a cabinet, he or she must be adept at all the cabinetmaking practices and disciplines required to build a good cabinet and be continually honing those abilities. In the end, the cabinetmaker must take action and create a cabinet in response to the unique needs of a certain client on a certain day, with materials available at the time and with a view to where that cabinet will go.

Just so, one might have steeped oneself in the view of responding to conflict without fighting, but without a way to apply the insight through discipline and adapt it directly to the situation at hand. We seek to address that next step in *The Rules of Victory*. First we explore further the view of the Sun Tzu as presented in the first book, to deepen our understanding of it and see more of its dimensions. Building upon that foundation, we can elaborate in greater detail on the practices presented in the text—shih, extraordinary and orthodox, deception, and so forth. Then, to illuminate creative ways to apply these teachings to specific situations, we recount stories of people whose actions demonstrate principles from the Sun Tzu.

We have learned a lot about how the Sun Tzu becomes relevant and helpful from people in our seminars. One day during a session of reading practice, a woman who had decades of experience working on the front lines in a major metropolitan fire department was elaborating on the line "Make bravery uniform" from chapter 11. In general, this line refers to using training that allows troops to express their bravery in a way that is synchronized with others rather than relying on the uncertainty of individual heroics. The notion sparked insights and questions for the female firefighter.

Working in a physically demanding job within such a male-oriented culture was not easy for her. During the workshop, she spoke about how difficult it had been to work with the entrenched habits and traditions within the fire department. Members of the department received daily reinforcement for their habits, including bonding rituals that led to ongoing tension for those who did not fit the mold. At the same time, the fire service demands an extraordinary level of camaraderie and dedication to one's fellow workers. Facing death together calls for nothing less. As she spoke, it became apparent that the interpersonal difficulties on the job outweighed the difficulties caused by the fires themselves.

We opened the floor to discussion, but others simply wanted to probe her experience further. It became apparent as she continued to talk that the same phenomenon that caused the team to work together to fight fires might be transferred to working with the interpersonal relationships. It turns out that so-called firefighters do not actually "fight" fires. They use their knowledge, training, preparedness, and teamwork to put fires out. Fires are not "bad" for those who belong to the fire department. In some sense, fires (and their prevention, of course) are their business. Those who are inexperienced lunge at and run from fire. They don't know it well, so they fight with it, and it usually overtakes them, with fatal results.

We all started to make connections as she turned the discussion to how we deal with the fires that rage in our lives. This metaphor took on a life of its own. It became clear to us why putting out fires is not a matter of fighting. In the same way, someone said, in dealing with others, if we fight fire with fire, everyone gets burned out. We got the point. A very pleasant moment or two of silence overtook the room as we appreciated something at once as simple as a cliché and yet so profound.

Then somebody broke the silence with a half comment, half question: "I'm the superintendent of schools for my city and have a very stressful job. So I'm really appreciating what I learned just now. It's very satisfying, and I know that tomorrow I may bask in the afterglow of an insight like this, and that may even last for a while. Eventually, though, I'm going to find myself in the heat of battle fighting parents over a school closure, and I'm going to end up doing what I've always done. And the fact that I once had this profound insight is not going to give me comfort. In fact, knowing that it once seemed so clear will probably annoy me. I feel in my bones that the vision of the Sun Tzu makes sense and it is what I need, but how can I learn to base my actions on that vision rather than just trying to avoid or neutralize conflict? I realize that there will need to be a journey, but how exactly do I start that journey?"

Good question.

2

View, Practice, and Action
A Framework for
Understanding the Sun Tzu

Walking one evening along a deserted road, Nasruddin
saw a troop of horsemen rapidly approaching. He
quickly sized them up and ascertained that they meant
to do him harm. In his mind's eye, he saw himself captured, robbed, or killed. Frightened by this thought, he
bolted, climbed a wall into a graveyard, and lay down
in an open grave to hide. Puzzled at his behavior, the
horsemen—honest travelers merely passing through
town—sought him out to assuage their curiosity. They
found Nasruddin stretched out, tense and shaking.

"We saw you madly running away. Are you all right?
Can we help you? What are you doing in that grave?"
they asked.

"Just because you can ask a question does not mean
there is a straightforward answer to it," said Nasruddin,
who now realized what had happened. "It all depends
upon your viewpoint. If you must have an answer, however, I will tell you: I am here because of you, and you
are here because of me."

—from the Sufi tradition

THE PROFOUND WISDOM in the Sun Tzu cannot be
learned, and employed to meet the challenges in our lives, by using
a cookie-cutter approach. When the common question "What do
I do when . . . ?" jumps to our minds, we won't be able to turn to

page 62, line 5, to get our answer. Even if we had the time to do so, the Sun Tzu text would defy and undermine such attempts. Yet if the text is to be valuable in helping us to achieve our objectives, it must be able to satisfy the essential need to bring insight and inspiration from the Sun Tzu into effective action, the very need that our school superintendent friend so strongly expressed at the end of the last chapter.

From our experience in working closely with this text, when people look to the Sun Tzu for direction or an answer to a question, the question and the questioner are also inevitably included in the inquiry. It is true that many people have heard one of the famous sayings from the text, read something about it in a magazine or on a Web site, or even purchased a book in the hope that it would contain ideas and techniques that would help them to win whatever it is they want to win or gain whatever it is they want to gain. But too often in the search for a bit of wisdom that will bear on the immediate predicament, they lose the perspective of the bigger picture, the environment in which the question is asked. In the case of the Sun Tzu, famous lines such as "win without fighting" are part of a bigger whole that must be understood to capture the saying's power. A genuine connection to the deeper viewpoint of the text, which comes from a rich and profound wisdom tradition, has the power to transform the very question itself.

A wide variety of students of the Sun Tzu—including business dealmakers, military officers, various kinds of strategists, and even criminals—have attributed their successful actions to using the Sun Tzu. A real estate sales Web site quotes Sun Tzu in order to encourage realtors to understand that "opportunities multiply as they are seized." The founder of an infamous prison gang schooled himself in Sun Tzu (as well as Machiavelli and Nietzsche) in order to extend his reach far beyond the prison walls. In speaking of the initial strike policy in the second Iraq war, dubbed "shock and awe," an analyst attributed the policy largely to Sun Tzu, citing a story (widely thought to be apocryphal) of Sun Tzu's ordering the heads of unruly members of the king's concubine army cut off to ensure the submission of the rest of the troops. On more than one occasion, including in the middle of a Sun Tzu seminar, we have heard

Sun Tzu's name attached to the famous dictum "Keep your friends close, but your enemies closer," which is not from Sun Tzu at all. In fact, it is best known as a line from the movie *The Godfather, Part II*. Since the Sun Tzu can be treated as a collection of aphorisms, many of which are cryptic and dense, the text can be readily oversimplified or even trivialized, reduced to a bumper sticker.

In fact, the impulse to fashion such a set of prescriptions to make the Sun Tzu one's own contains a certain wisdom. We all yearn for more skillful ways to work with the challenges and conflict in our lives, so it is natural that we would want to boil a large amount of wisdom down to a few things we can use during difficult times. And we can, in fact, carry the Sun Tzu into the heat of battle, without having to stop and leaf through the book, but to do so requires first apprehending and understanding the broad perspective embodied by the text.

In the tradition that the Sun Tzu comes out of, we are encouraged to make the text's wisdom our own through understanding and internalizing it, and then operating from inside its perspective. This comes first and foremost from understanding and assuming the view of the Sun Tzu, as we presented in our first book. Then, we can arrive at effective solutions by seeing our everyday occurrences in the context of these broad principles of how things work. It is difficult to get to the depth if we too quickly pick off a piece and try to make it apply to a given situation. But we can get to the depth by respecting the integrity of the text. The text's central notion of "taking whole" is a principle that, not surprisingly, applies to the Sun Tzu text itself. It, too, must be taken as a whole. The Sun Tzu can be applied in our lives, and it can be employed to develop a kind of mastery. Doing so relies on not taking parts of a whole system out of context in the hope that we will obtain its benefits.

For example, the Sun Tzu is often quoted to the effect that one should not attack walled cities, which can be extended to mean that we should never attack the secure, fixed positions held by those we encounter, whether they be a deeply entrenched business adversary, a screaming child, or a stubborn life partner. In fact, however, the Sun Tzu simply presents this as the least desirable of a series of options available to the skillful leader:

And so the superior military cuts down strategy.
Its inferior cuts down alliances.
Its inferior cuts down the military.
The worst attacks walled cities.
[CHAPTER 3]

There is a subtle but important point here that says something about how the Sun Tzu works and how to work with the Sun Tzu. In the very first chapter, the Sun Tzu says that "victories . . . cannot be transmitted in advance," which means that there are no absolutes, nothing determined beforehand, and no superficial prescriptions. A snippet of the Sun Tzu wisdom converted into a maxim like "never attack walled cities" can become, particularly when taken in isolation, a fixed position in itself, and thereby out of keeping with the strategic themes of flexibility, formlessness, and unpredictability at the core of the Sun Tzu. There may well be a time to attack walled cities.

If respecting the wholeness and integrity of the Sun Tzu text itself means that we are not able to simplify it into prescriptions, how can we evoke its wisdom and power in our lives? How can we penetrate beneath a superficial understanding and apply its profound methods to the conflict and chaos we experience here and now? To do so, we need to take the Sun Tzu's view of the world as our starting point and then look more closely at the lines and sections that present the text's profound practices and extend its view—including shih, extraordinary and orthodox, deception, and others—and consider how they may be applied to our circumstances. And we have to do this using an approach that gets us thinking in the way the text does and preserves the integrity of the text, and presents and respects its wholeness. Only in this way can the pith instructions and practical directions from the Sun Tzu come through to us with the view that empowers them and leaves them intact.

The Sun Tzu shows us such a "holistic" approach on the very first page of the text. It appears in the form of directions to the sage commander about how to evaluate the nature of something before taking action. The central elements are the well-known, traditional Chinese triad of heaven, earth, and human that we introduced briefly in our discussion of our translation in chapter 1. Presented in the text as heaven, earth, and general, this simple, logical framework builds on the way the mind naturally sees things to form a powerful tool for understanding their underlying meaning.

In this framework, heaven represents what is above, the big view and all that comes from it. The vast sky overhead holds limitless possibilities and potential, some part of which we choose and express as our aspirations. Heaven could manifest as a torrential downpour making troop movement difficult in a military campaign, which is why most translations render this Chinese character as "weather." Or it could manifest as a brainstorm of ideas in your organization's board meeting, both inspiring action and setting the parameters for it.

Earth is what is below and what we stand on. It holds the practicalities—both obstacles and supports—through which any vision must travel to reach actuality. In military terms, it usually refers to the terrain—the mountains, rivers, and flat ground that constrain and create possibilities for movement and defense. In the broader sense, earth is the ground of any situation that we face when taking action.

The general is the human element standing between the two, representing the principle of leadership. This is the agent of action that brings the aspirations of heaven and the practicalities of earth together to produce the desired outcome. The general leads the army in warfare; every one of us marshals our resources in campaigns each and every day.

Heaven, earth, and general is a model presented to the general as an approach to assessing the situation. This kind of logical framework gives the leader the best of both worlds: it is possible to look at key individual elements, such as the aspirations and obstacles, while also looking at the whole, since each element is understood in relation to the others.

The school superintendent in our workshop was facing the same kind of challenge as the general. He was motivated by a deep longing for more effective action in the face of the conflict and aggression in his workplace. He wanted to know how the principles from the Sun Tzu that so inspired him could emerge in the form of actions.

He had flashes of insight about the Sun Tzu—the beginnings of assuming the view of the text—but was uncertain about how to put them into effect, as he said, "in the heat of battle." The text's essential messages were not second nature to him; therefore, the profound actions from the Sun Tzu could not readily arise. He knew it would involve a process.

The challenge of putting ideals into practice, of joining insight and vision with effective action, is a common and routinely frustrating aspect of the human experience. From diet and exercise plans to corporate leadership training schemes, from social welfare programs to foreign military interventions, the path of high-minded intention is littered with our failed campaigns. For principles and ideals to lead to successful action, we need more than wishful thinking or good-hearted intentions.

What connects our view to our actions, or allows our ideas to have impact in the world, is the practice of our regularly repeated behaviors and ways of interacting with the world. These can be accidental or deeply ingrained habits, or actual methods, specific practices, or disciplines. Principles, intentions, and viewpoints show up in our actions by following regular pathways, trails that have been blazed through effort and training. We could read the classic text on good writing *The Elements of Style,* but the "elements" laid out in the book would only show up in our style after much practice and reinforcement.

One reason that joining vision with action is such a great challenge is that even the clearest view can be expressed in different practices, and thereby lead to different actions that result in similar outcomes that nonetheless vary in important ways. For example, if the police hold the view that there is a serious speeding problem along a particular highway, they could employ two different methods to effectively slow motorists down and decrease loss of life. One method would involve hiding patrol cars and setting up speed traps, which would lead to the action of many people being pulled over and punished. It would slow down traffic but could also result in the problem of increased courtroom time taking officers away from more pressing duties. Another method would involve placing their patrol cars in plain sight along the highway, serving as a caution to drivers, causing people to slow down in response. This method would lead to the action of not doing anything, which takes a highly trained professional, prepared for action and geared up for dangerous situations, and directs them to sit idly by for hours at a time. The result, while again slowing down traffic, could have the side effect of depressing the morale of the force. In both cases the police methods fulfill the view and slow down traffic, but the different actions result in very different sets of problems the police force will have to deal with next.

The elements of the approach we can use to get inside the wisdom lineage of the Sun Tzu are emerging from this discussion and beginning to form a model. It follows the same pattern as the framework of heaven, earth, and general that we discussed above and is closely related to it. We start, as always, with the *view*—the heaven principle of how we see the world, what we believe about how it works, what we take for granted. We then have the *practices* or methods we employ—the earth principle of the ways, most often habitual but also chosen, that we extend, express, or enact our view through the practical realities of the world. And these give rise to *action*—the way we as leaders interact with and engage our world to bring about success in our campaign.

These three—view, practice, and action—are inseparable parts of a whole way of looking at things, like appreciating a single precious stone by its different facets. The views we hold become the source of future actions, and therefore our views can be imputed from our actions. And what connects the two are our methods, the regular pathways we follow that translate how we look at things, what we strive for, and what we intend, into what we actually end up doing or producing. We have the inspiration of a favorite Chinese food dish we want to make for our best friends; we prepare the wok, shop for the vegetables, and brush up on our stir-frying techniques; and come Saturday night, a steaming plate of ginger beef delights our guests. All aspects of this experience fit together as a whole, and the wholeness of this way of looking at reality makes it an excellent means for considering the parts of the Sun Tzu while ensuring that the text's integrity is respected.

Connecting the view of the Sun Tzu to skillful action by means of its profound practices provides us with the most direct path to understanding and applying the text's principles. Approaching the Sun Tzu in this way already places us in the midst of this wisdom tradition and orients us as members of its lineage. The framework of view, practice, and action is a natural expression of how we think about and see the world. Immersing ourselves in this framework will not only enter us deeply into the text, but it can also help us to relate more effectively with all aspects of our world. So, in order to employ this framework to study the Sun Tzu more deeply, we will explore the full meaning of each of its aspects—view, practice, and action—and how they work together.

View

When we first open our eyes, or when we enter a new environment, we try to ascertain where we are. We establish our outlook or perspective. We orient ourselves in relation to the ground we're walking on, the atmosphere above and all around, and the inanimate objects and living entities occupying the space. If, for example, we are standing in a meadow, the horizon itself, where the earth meets the sky, defines where we are. This very basic act of mind-body coordination is played out over and over again constantly.

Our field of experience is so rich and multifaceted; it would be laborious to construct a "reality" from scratch with each new encounter, so we naturally rely on past associations and predetermined models to figure out how to fit into the scene. Philosophers, linguists, cognitive scientists, and neurologists have long been interested in our process of putting our world together time after time. Today, sophisticated technology such as functional magnetic resonance imaging (fMRI), which can create a visual record of brain function, tries to chart the pathways we are creating as we go about making a world for ourselves. But long before these technical advancements, philosophers and artists appreciated the fact that our perspectives define what we perceive. Anyone who has looked at an

M. C. Escher poster can appreciate the importance of perspective. The artist and founder of MIT's Center for Advanced Visual Studies, Gyorgy Kepes, in his 1944 book *Language of Vision,* demonstrated in a variety of easy-to-grasp illustrations how the language of our visual perception is influenced by the perspectives we have been taught to view things from: what we see is what our eyes have been taught to see. You can see in the illustration (below) that, as Kepes says, "two parallel lines are perceived as one unit if they are close enough together. Because the space between them is enclosed, it appears separated from the surrounding space. If one adds two more parallels outside of the first two, the figure that was made by the interval between them loses its quality as a coherent whole, and serves only as a background for the two new units."[1]

As the cognitive neuroscientist Steven Pinker points out in his book *Words and Rules,* thinkers since Aristotle have noted that how we look at and think about things relies on carving up the world and placing its pieces into categories, but as helpful as they are, they break down. "People aren't quite sure," Pinker says, "whether

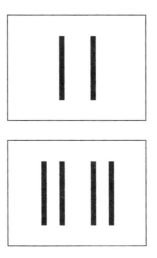

This illustration shows how easily context alters our perception. The two parallel lines in the top drawing are no longer associated with each other once we add two more parallel lines on either side.

garlic, parsley, seaweed, or edible flowers should count as vegetables." He goes on to ask, "If a clamp is a tool, why not a ball of string? Is a scorpion a bug? Is a sport utility vehicle a car or a truck? Is synchronized swimming a sport?"[2] What something is depends on how we decide to view it.

Neuroscientists and artists alike know that in reality, there is no static form. An image is a temporary event, molded from the need to find balance and order. What we consider to be a whole thing, as Kepes points out in the illustration, is merely created from the principle of nearness. We form wholes by perceiving elements that seem near to one another as interconnected. For millennia, humans have used star patterns to orient themselves and understand the order of things in the cosmos, but as we now know, the stars in the patterns are not all that close to one another.

We constantly play connect the dots, just as you are doing with the dots of ink and the letters on this page. Kepes illustrates the point that "spatial organization is the vital factor in an optical message" by showing that the same units with a slight alteration in their nearness to one another become gibberish, which we nevertheless attempt to make sense of: "sp atialor gani zationist hevital fa ctorin an op ticalme ssage." Kepes writes that "light rays reaching the eye have no intrinsic order as such. They are only a haphazard, chaotic panorama of mobile, interdependent light-happenings. As soon as they reach the retina, the mind organizes and molds them into meaningful spatial units."[3]

It is view that creates order out of the chaos of light messages.

Our view is what determines how we will move through space. If we have developed a view of a city as made up of a variety of sections and neighborhoods but we don't have an overarching view of how they connect—by means of a map in our head or an actual map—we may suddenly be surprised when we cross into another section. How did we get here? People walking around in cities like London and Paris, which are not set up using a grid method, commonly have this experience. It shows what can happen when we hold a partial or limited view. We can get lost.

When we move beyond the visual and spatial to the psychosocial, we also find the pervasive power of view. If we are a parent and we enter our family home, we may quickly assume our role as mother, father, or spouse and act from that perspective, shouldering certain responsibilities, communicating with those around us from within that perspective. If we go to our own parents' home for a reunion, we are now child and sibling, aunt or uncle, nephew or cousin. The changed perspective can have potent effects. For example, a man in his forties who was the youngest sibling in a very large family was treated like a child at large family gatherings, despite being a father himself. His wife was always taken aback at seeing her husband transformed into a child, but such is the power of the perspectives we hold. They govern how we see and how we are seen.

We aggregate all our many smaller perceptions and perspectives into a larger whole, which is what we are calling "view." It exerts a governing influence on our individual lives and throughout the larger spheres that our lives occur in. We inherit our view from others, and we can also actively train and shape it, which is exactly what the Sun Tzu text seeks to do. In order to deepen our understanding of what we mean by view, it will be helpful to look at various terms we can use to describe view. Each shows a different facet, and each has a slightly different contribution to make to our understanding. All of them taken together will help us to understand and appreciate the nature and power of view in greater depth.

Paradigm

The concept of "paradigm"—which was once esoteric but has been a popular term for some time now—is one of the oldest Western expressions of the principle of view. The original Greek word came from a verb that meant "to compare," which itself came from *para* ("alongside") and *deiknunai* ("to show"). A paradigm, then, is a pattern or model we use, often nearly unconsciously, to organize our views and experience. It could also be described as a collection of beliefs and assumptions that govern how we see the world and how we act in it as a result. The power of a paradigm can be so subtle and pervasive that we barely perceive it. It's the water the fish swims in.

In 1962, in his book *The Structure of Scientific Revolutions*, Thomas Kuhn used the now widely known phrase "paradigm shift" to demonstrate that science advances in "intellectually violent revolutions" where "one conceptual worldview" is replaced by another. In scientific terms, the earth-centered Ptolemaic system was replaced by the Copernican system, which in turn gave way successively to Newtonian physics, relativity, and quantum physics. In economic terms, America moved from a frontier and agrarian paradigm through manufacturing and on to high tech. In international relations, the country has moved from a paradigm of isolation through alliance and on to a nearly imperial model. As paradigms change, lingering notions still pervade our worldview. The frontier ethic, for example, still holds great sway in America, despite the fact that there is very little genuine geographical frontier left.

Traditional training in effective public communication respects the power of paradigms, by encouraging public speakers to address an audience's commonplaces. If the audience's worldview is dominated by a fear of communism or by the thought that their country must be a beacon of freedom in the world, the speaker regards those commonplaces as being as real as the ground we walk on. If she hopes to persuade, she must either reinforce those commonplaces or redirect them—depending on her purpose—but ignoring them is a prescription for speaking over people's heads.

Culture

What we call "culture"—the sum total of all behavior patterns transmitted to a group of people and expressed in belief systems, patterns of social interactions, arts, and many other institutions and modes of behavior—is a form of what we are calling view. In the past few decades, it has become commonplace to describe the totality of behavior patterns within a given organization as a "corporate culture." Think Apple and IBM. Whether the totems and taboos that compose these cultures are made explicit or not, they exert a tremendous influence on action.

In her book *Dark Age Ahead,* the late urbanist Jane Jacobs demonstrated how culture represents a view of the world that is translated into actions with potentially far-reaching and long-term consequences—for good or ill. Jacobs expressed the concern that these "overriding cultural purposes" are never examined sufficiently and only seen after the fact when one is dealing with the outgrowth of such deeply ingrained views. The Great Depression exerted such a strong influence on the American ethic, she postulated, that it made job creation and job retention into virtues that trumped all others. It was largely job creation, for example, that motivated the building of the Interstate Highway System, which has shaped communities in ways that are very difficult to undo. To be cultured, it would seem, is to be deeply inculcated into a view that connects one to others in a group—and by habit, one will act in accord with the prevailing dictates of the culture and thereby reinforce one's connection to the culture.

Theory

Yet another dimension of view is expressed by the term *theory,* which comes from the Greek word for "spectator," *theoros,* which itself comes from *thea,* meaning "a viewing," and *oros,* meaning "to see." In modern times, it refers to a set of statements or principles that has been repeatedly tested or is widely accepted, and that can be used to make predictions. Theory is essentially a picture that allows us to fit instances into a large whole. At a very simple level, a fire investigator develops a theory of a fire's origin and then sets out to show, based on the available evidence, that the fire could not have started from any other source. At a more sophisticated level of theory, when someone gets sick, one avenue of investigation, according to germ theory, is to determine whether he or she has been infected by an outside bacteriological agent. Without germ theory, there are no outside bacteriological agents per se. They become defined as such within the context of the theory. It's a seeming abstraction, but of course, without germ theory, many people would have died.

The domino theory that influenced American foreign policy in the 1950s and 1960s, simplistic as it may have been, purported to predict what would happen as various individual societies adopted communism. It also demonstrated how theory and ideology can go hand in hand. The theory creates the ideological truths and beliefs that are held to be inalienable. A theory allows one to see something that might have been missed, but it just as easily allows one to miss what might easily have been seen. The domino theory, for example, allowed political and military leaders to look beyond individual national characteristics to a greater underlying "evil," at a considerable cost in human lives. Many would argue that this same use of theory and ideology to overlook individual characteristics has dominated America's approach to the Middle East in the past several decades.

Context

The last dimension of view we will consider is context, which comes from a Latin term meaning "woven together." All modes of communication require context to function. For example, a given set of syllables, such as *rang tong,* will appear meaningless in one context, like nonsense syllables in a children's song. In another context, such as among Tibetan religious scholars in this case, this phrase may connote a very sophisticated philosophical principle, namely that all phenomena are "empty of inherent existence." In what are called "high-context" situations in communication theory, a few small gestures or expressions may communicate a great deal. In Japanese society, which is very culturally homogenous, a little bit of communication can go a very long way. The way someone bows to you when you meet in that society can communicate a range of levels of deference and respect. In American society, which is much more heterogeneous, two Americans may share so little context that each can barely understand what the other is saying, much less what they are hinting at through small gestures. A resident of International Falls, Minnesota, may have to repeat himself several times to be understood by someone from rural Tennessee.

It is the power of a shared view that enables communication to be so strong in a high-context situation for those who are inside the context; yet the very power of that shared view can create an insularity that becomes very hard to crack from outside that context.

When you enter a situation, such as a corporate board meeting, an airport departure terminal, or high school basketball practice, it is often quite easy to detect the context that people share. Everyone knows why they are there and what they are doing. The shared view has a shape or a gestalt, something that is very difficult to put into words perhaps, but it is there nonetheless, just as much as the room and the furnishings. In fact, not only is a group's shared view something that is detectable and almost tangible, but figuring out and understanding that view is often as important as, if not more important than, listening to the words people are saying—particularly if you are trying to get to the heart of what people care about and what moves them to act in the ways that they do.

View is how we see things. The "view" that an individual or a group holds refers to something more than their superficially known beliefs; it is their whole orientation to the world. View is deep-seated and not easily altered. It interprets reality and affects our perception of things. It is what we take for granted. It involves norms, models, and paradigms that govern and order the world. Just as a culture unites and joins people, view has the power to cohere, but it also has the power to limit, and it is important to appreciate both of those aspects of view. View is neither a good thing nor a bad thing, but it is important that we understand what it is and how it leads to actions. Understanding the view of the Sun Tzu, in as much fullness and detail as possible, will help us to understand its practices or methods and apply them in a way that will result in successful actions.

Practice

Bing fa, the Chinese title for *The Art of War,* means "military methods," as we discussed before. The phrase "in general, the method of employing the military . . ." occurs repeatedly in the text. "Method" is one of the core principles laid out on the first page of the text that counsel the general about how to attain victory. The principle of method conveys the understanding that each time we act, we rely to a certain extent on practiced modes of behavior. Each time we make a left turn when we are driving, we do not need to make up the procedure on the spot. While each left turn is unique, *the* left turn is a standard form.

In every area of our lives, we have skills, habits, and practices that have been formed through education, training, emulation, and repetition that help us to carry out specific actions. In terms of our threefold framework of view, practice, and action, the principle of "practice" describes ways of doing and being in the world that bring a given *view* to bear on any particular *action*. Practice makes the link. However, in this context, it is not thought of as an expedient or means alone. Its qualities emerge from the view. To elaborate on an example introduced earlier, a cabinetmaker who has the view of producing fine furniture will acquire and develop woodworking practices that are in keeping with that overall view. She will school herself in the selection of woods and learn how each of them takes to sandpaper and the aesthetic qualities of their grains. She will learn time-honored techniques of joinery and make them her own, enabling her to be not only skilled but also creative. By contrast, someone trying to produce inexpensive furniture quickly will employ practices in keeping with that view—using pressboard, nail guns, and spray paint.

To appreciate the principle of practice, just as with view, we will look at various ways to understand its facets and get a sense of its broad implications.

Method

The Chinese character we have translated as "method" appears frequently in the Sun Tzu, introducing many of the injunctions in the text, such as "the method of employing. . . ." When it is discussed directly in the Sun Tzu in the first pages, "method" is presented very straightforwardly:

> *Method is ordering divisions, the Tao of ranking,*
> *and principal supply.*
> [CHAPTER I]

It connotes establishing order and systemization. Our everyday English usage of the term *method* contains these same connotations. To approach something "methodically" contrasts with approaching it in an ad hoc or a haphazard way. When faced with a challenge, such as buying a new car, we can approach it through caprice and whim, or we can develop or borrow a method for arriving at an acceptable purchase. Frequently, trial and error leads us to our method, but often, particularly in complicated situations, such as fertilizing difficult soil in a garden or shingling a roof, we seek authority. We look for a method with a record of success.

Freedom and creativity stem from going beyond the bounds of method, but to be successful, they generally rely on a grounding in it. For example, the best free-form poetry is crafted by people who have a good sense of form and rhythm. In fact, good poetry emerges from the marriage of inspiration and method. Inspiration without method produces mush, and method without inspiration produces a mechanical simulation.

Method permeates our everyday encounters with the world. Knowing how to drive a car, how to manage finances, how to cook risotto, how to program a computer, how to teach a class—all require method. Method often contains or channels wild energy, abandon, and impulse. It's fun to sing in the shower, but singers who want to perform for a living, and share their passion with large audiences, need to learn breath control, pitch control, phrasing, and a variety of other skills. Those with a method at their disposal will often act coolly, with a sense of command. Method, in fact, can spell the difference between life and death. If we return to our firefighters from the last chapter, let us imagine if they approached a fire with no methods but rather improvised on the spot, taking suggestions, reaching consensus on the fly, and learning by trial and error. They could hardly merit the appellation "fire department"; they would simply be a group of people taking a shot at putting out a fire. For this very reason, the Sun Tzu speaks of the value of "preserving method" and of "method's rewards." Method is often what quells the madness.

Human beings are often defined as the tool-using species, and a tool is nothing more than a physical manifestation of method. Technology, the logical extension of the human propensity to use tools, derives from the Greek term *techne,* meaning "skill" or "craft." It is reason applied to action. Aristotle and many other ancient Greeks held *techne* to be one of the highest virtues. Someone without *techne* had little worldly worth. It was regarded as a type of knowledge that led one to be productive, to successfully reach a conclusion or a desired outcome. Homer celebrated Odysseus's *techne* when he recounted the clever means the hero developed to outwit the powerful forces arrayed against him, and in so doing held craft up as a quintessential human virtue.

Practice and Practices

The term *practice* elevates and enlarges the notion of method. For example, one speaks of the practice of medicine or law. The notion of practice, then, seems to involve having a collection of methods that extends a particular view. From the view of healing the sick and promoting health, doctors are able to practice medicine when they have an arsenal of methods and devices at their disposal. Any complex and challenging enterprise—medicine, education, government, architecture, law, manufacturing, the military, and so forth—cannot rely on instinct alone. Some repeatable approaches and procedures are required.

The notion of repeatability gives us another meaning of "practice": to do something over and over and over again in order to attain mastery, such as practicing the piano. In fact, in the arts and athletics, the time spent on practice far outweighs the time spent performing or competing, and for many practitioners, the time spent practicing is deeply rewarding. To practice meditation is a similar kind of notion. While meditation practitioners don't necessarily practice meditation to become better at the practice of meditation, they do practice encountering the workings of their mind straightforwardly over and over again.

The notion of a practice (and practices) as a panoply of techniques that can work to extend a view and the notion of practic*ing* as a means of deeply embedding a way of approaching the world are both integral aspects of practice as the link between view and action. In fact, these two types of practice go hand in hand. We master a practice by practicing. As is said by sources as varied as our Spanish teacher and the *I-ching,* "It is only through repetition that the student makes the lesson his own."

Routine

The theme of repetition leads us naturally to the notion of "routine." When we do an activity repeatedly in much the same way, it cuts a groove in our psyche and in our muscle memory, creating a neural pathway, for good or for ill. Practice in some way has to do with habits and routines, following a tested route to the destination. Certainly routine behavior can be no more than monotonous, nonthinking drudgery. Many of us are stuck in habitual routines that create difficulty for us and those around us. On the other hand, we could not live without routine. Just as our blood would be of no use without vessels to travel through, we need pathways to guide our actions.

Of course, to say we travel along a pathway can make it sound a little easier than it really is to marry our view and our actions successfully. If we are not careful, we can treat the practices and methods we adopt as a fixed route, a set of rigidly repeated approaches, missing the nuances in the ever-changing situation that require a unique response each time. Every time our children do something wrong, we give a lecturette. These seemed to work so well when they were younger. Meanwhile, we've stopped noticing that our children are tuning out. "Blah, blah, blah" is all that registers with them no matter what brilliant and cogent wisdom we may be imparting. They hear the same old intonation, the telltale sign that our route has become a rut that we are stuck in.

It's also possible to treat methods and practices as mere expedients and overlook the consideration, care, and attention we need to put into developing and enhancing practice. A strong view can be so compelling to us, so inspiring and exhilarating, that it seems as if it ought to be simple to make the view manifest itself in action. As a golfer looks out from the tee, she envisions how her shot will fly straight and drop softly in the landing area she has chosen, just as it does for her instructor and those golfers on television. It all seems quite simple. But then after the swing, the ball careers into the woods. The practices that would make the view manifest were not deeply enough ingrained. Practice is the middle piece that requires patience and exertion and takes us through the *earth* of the experience—obstacles, missteps, uncertainty, and hard work.

Practice is not a one-shot deal. It evolves. It takes time for a set of practices to become our own and develop even further into something entirely new and utterly flexible. Practice generally begins with imitation. A teacher or an expert, someone we trust and admire, demonstrates how something is done and we try to copy it. If the skill is simple, such as tying our shoe, we may quickly make it our own, but if it is subtle and complex, in the early stages we will usually miss the mark.

In rhetoric, the classical form of teaching writing and public speaking, students memorize long passages and speeches and then create their own work almost as an exact replica. This kind of imitative technique can be tremendously helpful in creating pathways for someone to follow in his or her writing and speaking. It is a matter of looking at the external form of something, its image (which comes from the same Latin root as *imitate*), and trying to replicate it.

Of course, with something as subtle as writing and public speaking, or working effectively with chaos and conflict, the power of imitation will break down eventually. A copycat cannot produce a fresh response to the needs at hand. At the point when imitation—working from the outside in—reaches its limit, we need to emulate, to work from the inside out. Emulation involves coming to know the view behind the practices, understanding where they arise from, so that we can generate fresh responses that nevertheless have the power and integrity of the person, people, or tradition we wish to follow. The practices that emerge from the view of the Sun Tzu are of the very subtlest kind. To apply them will require imitation, but ultimately we will need to emulate the Sun Tzu to follow the path it sets out.

Practice is *how* we are and how we do things; it is what connects our view with our actions. It also extends and reflects view. The practices of a fine craftsperson emerge from the view he or she has of creating high-quality products or works of artistry. Practically speaking, practice is a pattern of behavior and a disposition of mind that may incorporate many methods, such as "the practice of law," or to extend the terminology a bit, "the practice of the Sun Tzu discipline and tradition." Practice also involves repeated performance that enhances and more deeply embeds a skill, such as practicing guitar or archery. The more we do it, the closer we get to the target.

And yet, as we develop our practice through practice, at some point simple repetition and imitation will not suffice. We will need to come to understand more deeply what makes one a virtuoso guitarist, a skilled archer, a fine cabinetmaker, or a practitioner of the Sun Tzu. When we cross from copying into trying to make something our own, we begin to discover not a finite set of techniques and procedures but rather an inexhaustible well of skillful means. At that point, practice transcends the notion of simply having methods to apply to external situations. At that point, our practice and our practices become an unending path of discovery, out of which our actions naturally and even gracefully emerge.

Action

> *And so one who knows the military*
> *Acts and is not confused,*
> *Initiates and is not exhausted.*
> [CHAPTER 10]

When Chinese philosophers speak of "the ten thousand things," they are referring to the relative world, the world we live in day to day with its multiplicity of forms and its many vicissitudes. No text that purports to offer wisdom about how to work with challenging circumstances involving conflict and chaos can shrink from the complexity of the world, the myriad details and possibilities that both inspire us and threaten to overwhelm us on many a day. Each action in the world, no matter how practiced or routine, takes place in a context of uniquely interconnected elements, so no one can tell us ahead of time precisely how to act and how that action will work out. We can, however, try to discover what path we need to follow to make our actions appropriate to the situations we find ourselves in and effective in attaining our objectives.

Of view, practice, and action, action is the simplest to describe. An act is a "doing," a focused energy intended to accomplish an objective. Action is more than having ideals, aspirations, ideas, and plans; it is doing something. The very need to act is what brings the Sun Tzu into being and makes it so relevant for us. In encountering the world, we feel the need to act, but often we don't quite know how. We would like our actions to be guided somehow—and to be successful.

Action also contains the notion of result, or effect. The actions we see on the surface of the world do not spring from nowhere but are the result of causes, intentions, tendencies, and so forth. In the terms we are talking about here, actions spring from views and practices. And actions cause things to change, either by the exertion of an intentional force or power or by a natural process. Actions are both the result of previous events or causes, and create the causes and conditions for further actions. And we are the agent, the general that the text is talking to, the leader taking these actions in the world.

In the context of the Sun Tzu, action includes the intention to bring about change, to achieve an objective based on a certain vision or view. But it is often very difficult to change things because doing something different goes against the grain of the established momentum, the habitual patterns that people are mired in and that create inertia. Effecting change is a manual rather than automatic process, so it takes a focused energy. This is the application of force, the broader understanding of military we discussed before. And this is the place where the Sun Tzu has its roots, which is why it is such an important reference point for taking action to achieve an objective in the midst of difficult circumstances.

Action as an application of force is often a natural process. While a single leaf in a river may seem too small to have much of an effect, a mass of leaves could change the way that the currents flow and where the logs get stuck, and therefore result in the river's applying its force in a different way somewhere downstream. The mass of leaves rearranges the many interconnected things and thus gives rise to changing possibilities. This, too, is action. The relationship and interplay between intentional, organized action and natural processes will be more fully explored in our upcoming discussion of the text's profound methods such as shih and deception. Skillful actions capitalize on the conditions that occur, often as simply as a sailboat uses the prevailing winds, and they nurture conditions that will support skillful actions in future opportunities.

Action is *what* you do. It is the arena where theories are tested and fall apart or are borne out. It is the point at which we all get the feedback—when the cabinetmaker delivers the piece to the customer, the firefighter faces a roaring blaze, the student turns in the assignment, the parent tries to adjust a child's behavior, the player strikes the ball, the general moves the troops. When actions respond to the uniqueness of the present configuration of things, then every moment is fresh and it is possible, in Sun Tzu terms, to "initiate but not be exhausted." The ten thousand things, rather than overwhelming us, provide us with the opportunity to put our view into action.

View, Practice, and Action Working Together

View, practice, and action can be helpful as a framework to look at every aspect of life, from macrocosm to microcosm, from the level of nation-states and global systems to family dynamics and simple biological systems. We have explored each of the elements of this framework individually. Now we will consider how they work together so we can make this way of thinking more fully our own, and then go on to apply it to the text.

First, view, practice, and action are not three separate elements cobbled together but three inseparable parts of a whole way of looking at things. Each part contains the other two, and each is a gateway to the whole. Because this framework is a cohesive whole, it helps us to understand the cohesiveness of what we are looking at—a particularly important feature in approaching the Sun Tzu. View, practice, and action isn't a system for aligning things to achieve a forced consistency, as if we were looking at something from the outside and trying to give it labels and handles. Rather, the framework helps us see and understand the internal coherence of a thing, how it works viewed from the inside, as it were. And it is applicable in all realms—personal, societal, and natural.

An instructive example from the natural world is the relationship between the seed, the plant, and the flower. The seed (view) holds within it the entire plan for what the plant and flower will become. The plant (practice) extends that potential into the world in relationship to the planting zone, weather, soil, and so forth. The flower (action) is the *result* of what was potential in the seed and how the plant realized that potential, while itself also adapting to the elements affecting its particular environment. In most cases, the flower holds within it the seed for the next cycle. Likewise, the backyard gardener has a view of the display of flowers he would like to bring about through the summer and fall; he employs the mulching, watering, and weeding practices that work best for the raised-bed plantings in his zone; and the next-door neighbors enjoy the burst of colors flooding their breakfast nook as they have their morning coffee.

When we focus on one part, the other two are present; how can they be separated? This is the nature of a whole. It has no beginning point and no end point, and each part is vitally important. As it says in the Sun Tzu,

Of the Five Phases, none is the lasting victor.
Of the four seasons, none has constant rank.
[CHAPTER 6]

View, practice, and action is not only an interconnected whole. It is also a loop, a learning process continually feeding back upon itself. Whether a practice or method works or not, and what is learned from that success or failure, will inform the view. An ineffective action will eventually call for a reconsideration of the view and practice that it arose from. The golfer who continues to pull her drives to the left goes back to the club pro and the driving range.

Views are very complex, and thus their internal inconsistency is not always apparent. This can give rise to conflicting methods that lead to different actions. The results of these actions may appear similar but they can lead to very different consequences in the future. We saw this in our example of a police department's different options for enforcing the speed limit. Sometimes, methods are not in keeping with the view and the values it represents. This results in actions that send confusing and counterproductive messages that give rise to doubts about the purported view. Long-term detention without trial and severe interrogation techniques are examples of methods that, while regarded by some as justified in extreme conditions of terrorist threats to public safety, are considered by many to be out of keeping with the view and values of a democratic society. The public is, not surprisingly, disturbed by this disjunction between view and action.

Views are also constantly evolving, and methods and action can sometimes seem to have one foot in two different worlds. The model of leadership in the corporation, long based on a vision of strict hierarchical command and control, is a cogent example. As the limitations of this leadership model became evident in many settings, a transition to a more inclusive, collaborative approach to decision making emerged. Often, though, the corporate decision to become more collaborative is itself made in the corner office, and the methods and actions for carrying out that plan are selected there. The new strategy's practices and actions still carry the old view embedded within them, which is transparent to all who are subject to them. The leadership is left to wonder why the initiatives failed to gain traction. In another corporate-world example, a few years ago analyzing business processes carefully at a minute level to find inefficiencies became a popular practice, and it was supported by a robust and lucrative consulting industry. In some organizations, it took on a life of its own, such that analyzing processes spread like a virus through the company and became extremely time-consuming and counterproductive. The attempt to hunt down inefficiency became itself highly inefficient. When the view and practices are not aligned, the effectiveness of the action is undermined—and those involved get the message. Yelling at people to "calm down" rarely works.

While all parts of the whole are important, it is critical to begin with an accurate view, which is why the Sun Tzu emphasizes knowledge to such a great degree. A particular practice or action may be deemed successful without taking into account the view that lies behind it, but an accurate view is necessary for us to know which practices and methods will lead reliably to consistently effective action.

The widely used formation of a strategic plan is a good example both of the importance of establishing a commonly held view and also of the shortcomings of this approach when employed improperly. In general, a strategic plan brings all stakeholders together to create a blueprint to guide future decisions and action based on shared view and understanding. It employs a disciplined method to discover shared values and goals—the view—and then builds the plan that future decisions and actions will flow from. One shortcoming of this approach is that future decisions are always developed and assessed according to a plan and an understanding established in the past, which is further away with each passing day. Such strategic plans can work well in static or slow-changing situations, but even then they have the limitation of grounding the decision maker's mind in a previous reality, which may or may not still be relevant.

In an emergent, changing, and difficult situation, a static plan—however brilliant—can be extremely limiting. In highly changeable environments, it is critical to establish a deeply shared view in all stakeholders, which allows them to respond to local circumstances in the moment. Creating the ground for effective action must take place at the level of view and practice; by the time action happens, it's too late. Seeing the view clearly is often sufficient to give rise to the most effective and skillful action. In these circumstances, establishing a well-developed strategic *view*—out of which many plans, practices, and actions can arise in the moment—is more effective than working out one strategic *plan* with the hope that it will encompass all future events.

While view is the critical place to start, it has no significance without action. It is empty and untested. As actions are initiated in the battleground of the world—the world of the ten thousand things—

views and practices are tested, adjusted, and refined. In fact, views and practices that are unresponsive to the messages from the world of action become stagnant and unworkable. The messages we receive from the world and the people in it are the only way we have of knowing how well we are emulating the ideal embodied in our view.

The Sun Tzu is about working in those environments and on those occasions when things get tough, when difficult actions must be taken—often without enough time or as much information as you would like. Simply working on improving surface actions alone, such as making safety rules and enforcing them, establishing accounting procedures, or making house rules, can have important benefits. It can give people a common reference point and help create order and regularity. However, in highly charged or intensified situations where chaos and conflict abound, operating merely on the level of action without also operating on the level of view and practice will result in limited effectiveness. If the actions you take in response to events arise from a deep view and well-honed practices, it is more likely that everything you've developed and invested in will have a stronger impact on how your action works in the heat of battle. If you rely on superficial training and thinking, operating at the level of action alone, your resources may become wasted on actions that miss the mark.

United States Army general Norman Schwarzkopf described leadership as "a potent combination of strategy and character." He added, however, that "if you must be without one, be without strategy." [4] The reason for that, he further explained, quoting an old military adage, was that "no strategy survives contact with the enemy." Actions can emerge from either character, something deeply ingrained, or strategy, a plan one has developed. When things become very intense, as they do in battle, his experience has shown that it is what is deeply ingrained that will determine action. Likewise, David Keithly, who teaches at the American Military University, points out that a lack of reliable information means that combat leadership tends to be highly instinctive. "Leaders employ the textbook analytical method to decision-making perhaps one time in ten," he says, "while relying in the main upon intuitive evaluation." [5] He goes on to argue that, for both military commanders and business leaders, trying to make reasoned decisions based on an excess of information often falls short.

When we observe someone's actions, we can discern the views and practices that lie behind them. If someone is continually carrying a backbreaking load in his arms, we can guess that he has a view of trying to get the work over with as soon as possible and a practice of taking shortcuts. If a safety engineer observes the process closely, she might try to adjust the person's view and train him in practices that will lead to different results, different actions. Looking at any situation, we can ask: What view of reality does that action or practice arise from? Or, conversely, given a particular view, what is the action or practice that will emerge from it? To conclude, let's look at a couple of examples.

In eastern Canada, where we live, forests cover a large portion of the landscape, and wood and other forest products constitute a significant part of the economy. But there are two strikingly different ways that these products are viewed, processed, and brought to market. Most of the landowners take the view that their product is wood and their woodlot is the place where their product grows. Since wood is their product, the woodlot owners have adopted practices for harvesting as many of their trees as possible and doing it as cheaply and quickly as possible. The industry has developed large, mechanized tree harvesters, called feller bunchers, that grab trees—sometimes up to five or six at a time, depending on their size—shear them off near the ground, strip off the limbs, and "bunch" them in a pile for later pickup. One effect of using these highly efficient machines has been to greatly reduce the workforce in the harvesting process. Finally, the "action" is to get this high-volume product to the marketplace as quickly as possible, so it is mostly sold at low prices as saw logs or to pulp mills. One of the shortcomings of this process for woodlot owners is the long recovery cycle for the forests: once you cut down all the trees in a woodlot, it takes nearly sixty years for it to grow back to a harvestable state.

An alternative to this is the approach taken by a small group of woodlot owners promoting a forest stewardship approach to woodlot management. They take the view that the forest is their product, and that through careful and limited harvesting of trees, it can be turned into a sustainable business. Their woodlot management practice, then, is to select trees for harvest based on maintaining the overall ecological balance and health of their forest. These practices include harvesting trees using horses so that heavy machinery doesn't damage their "product." Since they harvest a smaller quantity of trees, their "action" is to convert their harvest into high-value-added products such as flooring, architectural trim, and musical instrument components.

Another example comes from recent trends in the business software application industry. By far the biggest share of this market is controlled by companies that view their product as "enterprise" software—that is, programs that they create and sell to businesses that then load the software program onto their own computers. Their practice is to develop desirable software products, and their action is to sell these products, as well as ongoing support and software upgrades, to as many businesses as they can. The purchasing business faces a high capital outlay for the software as well as the costs of an internal IT department and ongoing upgrading of its computers.

A different view of this industry may be emerging as a trend. Some companies now view their product to be business services. Their practice, then, is to sell Web-based access to their software application for a monthly fee, eliminating both the high up-front capital investment and in-house upgrading of computers. Their action is relentless attention to customer service to ensure that the Web-based applications function effectively and fulfill the business needs of their clients.

Any role that we assume in life takes the shape of a campaign, and that campaign will necessarily have a view that governs it, practices that extend the view, and day-to-day actions that result. A school superintendent, such as the one in our workshop, might regard the view of his campaign for successful schools as providing the broadest possible education for the vast diversity of students under his jurisdiction. His practice would be to use methods that support teachers, students, parents, and administrators in their pursuit of the best possible education for the largest number of people. His action would be to hear as many suggestions, complaints, and queries as he can from all parties and make decisions based on what he has heard and the unique perspective he has as the person who sees all aspects of the mission.

In the end, view, practice, and action is a powerful method for seeing the wholeness as well as the parts of any activity, so that we can learn. In reality, the boundaries between each of the elements will blur, and in the heat of battle, there is not always time for fancy categories. But the framework of view, practice, and action is an education and training tool that allows us to more closely observe the components of our actions, how they hang together or don't, and where they came from. In this way, it is a great aid that helps us to see how to emulate the ideal of the sage commander that is at the heart of the Sun Tzu.

Now that we can see in this way, we can immerse ourselves more deeply in the view of the text. The more we appreciate the view, the more we get inside it and make it our own, the more that view will shape our minds and how we see the world, and thus inspire in us the kinds of skillful practices and actions that are the riches of this wisdom tradition.

3 _____

The Big View
How the Sun Tzu Teaches Us
to See the World

> The size of the moon, as seen by people on earth, is no
> larger than a big ball, but a moon-dweller would see it
> as a colossal world. The perception of the moon as a
> ball, or as a world, does not increase or decrease the size
> of the moon itself. When it is seen as large, its largeness
> is revealed and its smallness concealed, and just so the
> other way round.
> —*Ch'eng-kuan*

> There are no whole truths; all truths are half-truths. It is
> trying to treat them as whole truths that plays the devil.
> —*Alfred North Whitehead*

ANY METHODOLOGY we use to accomplish our aims
is only as good as the context in which it is born and the context in
which it is used. Context, here, is the web of understandings, back-
grounds, prejudices, inclinations, and implications—both ours and
others'—we find ourselves in at any given time. As much as we would
sometimes like to break completely free of the context we find ourselves in, its gravitational pull is sure to exert its force on our actions. For the Sun Tzu, context is king. All action is considered in
view of the context in which it will occur, the terrain and the atmosphere that will determine its usefulness.

In the months following the attacks of September 11, 2001, the
United States government created the Department of Homeland Se-

curity. Shortly thereafter, the new department instituted the Homeland Security Advisory System, which consists of a series of color codes corresponding to the various levels of terrorist threat and what should be done to respond to the threats at each level. Citizens soon found themselves living in one of a series of five threat conditions—from green, the lowest, through blue, yellow, orange, to the highest, red. It became something like a weather report.

Using color codes to identify conditions of threat—and the corresponding levels of awareness required to work with the threat—has proved quite effective for individuals working in security, and for military and police units. Cooper's Color Codes, for example, is a simple system of four codes, where white is a state of almost non-awareness, yellow a generalized awareness, orange a focused awareness, and red an intense awareness instantly ready to be converted to action. The system teaches those who are on a security detail that the level of awareness needs to be keyed to the level of possible threat, because as one moves higher up the scale of awareness, one can maintain a state for a shorter period of time before fatigue sets in. It is not possible to remain on red alert all the time and be effective.

When the same methodology was applied to public information about the security of the nation, large numbers of people responded with confusion, anger, and disorientation—precisely the opposite of what awareness color coding was created to accomplish. Whereas military and police units have extensive training and procedures that enmesh them in a tightly woven context that allows them to act almost as a single body, the populace at large operates in a much looser context (thankfully). Given how poorly the system was received, department officials were forced to take into account the fact that the population is not organized by training and tradition to operate as a unified force at a moment's notice. Wisely, the department toned down its approach to the codes, placing most of the emphasis on informing key players who had more context to make use of the information. Color coding, an excellent methodology in one context, is dubious at best, and dangerous at worst, outside of that context.

As we discussed, the Chinese title for the Sun Tzu translates as "military methods": it suggests methods, from the simplest to the most sublime, that can be employed to bring about an advantageous outcome when we engage with the world. Like all other methods, they derive their power and effectiveness from the detailed context out of which they arise, what we have been calling "the view" of the Sun Tzu. In this chapter, we will explore the critical facets of that view, which will enable us to better understand the practices that emerge from it and the kinds of actions that may result. Just as we wouldn't use a baseball mitt while handling a bow and arrow (or use a bow and arrow during a baseball game), we can't make valuable use of any of the text's injunctions to skillful action until we have understood the context, or view, from which they arise.

In the very first page of chapter 1, the text establishes a context for what the Sun Tzu is pointing us toward by proclaiming:

> *The military is a great matter of the state.*
> *It is the ground of death and life,*
> *The Tao of survival or extinction.*
> *One cannot but examine it.*
> [CHAPTER 1]

It is not happenstance that the Sun Tzu is valuable when applied in so many areas in addition to the formal military. As we have defined it, the "military" describes the application of force in the world to achieve an aim. While an army may be the most focused manifestation of this principle, it has much broader implications. As human beings, we all exert this energy one way or the other. In employing the wisdom of the Sun Tzu, we are being asked to examine the nature of applying force from a position of leadership: when we find ourselves needing to apply some kind of force to achieve results, how do we go about doing that in the most effective and least damaging way?

At the core of the Sun Tzu is the general, or sage commander, the person to whom the Sun Tzu is speaking. If we think of ourselves as the general—the person in the center of the action with a goal to achieve—our very first question may well be "What am I supposed to do when I am in charge?" Some form or another of this question strikes us whenever we have an important objective and find the need to exert some kind of force, to lead, in the midst of chaos, uncertainty, and resistance.

But this turns out to be the wrong question. Trying to figure out exactly what to do ahead of time, trying to arrive at the ultimate recipe book for effective action, has frustrated everyone who has tried to lead others to the achievement of an aim. We can receive advice from a friend or colleague, a great book or seminar, but it so often turns stale when we face a real-life situation. We are left trying to employ a half-truth as a whole truth, and that plays the devil with us, as Whitehead pointed out in the quote at the beginning of this chapter.

The way out of the trap of needing to know "what to do" is to learn instead "how to be." Again, we turn to heaven, earth, and general, the principles of leadership presented in the beginning of the text. The general exists surrounded by the great forces of heaven and the vast support system of earth, and must learn how to be in that context. Whenever we have truly learned how to do something well—fly an airplane, make a delicious pot of soup, write a report, hit a ball, climb a mountain, give a speech, swim the butterfly stroke—we do not think of the activity merely as the sum of a myriad of techniques. At a certain point, the individual elements coalesce into a sense of wholeness; we have an intuitive feeling about whatever it is we are trying to accomplish. The ingredients in a pot of soup become something more than items on a shopping list. In the same way, skillful action becomes more than a combination of learned techniques; it can become second nature.

There is nothing mysterious about this process; it is a common, ordinary experience. The fact that knowledge transfers into effective action through this experience of wholeness, what we are calling "being," is simply a fact of the human psyche and its environment. We are interrelated, integrated whole systems functioning in larger interrelated, integrated whole systems. Rayona Sharpnack, the founder of the Institute for Women's Leadership, speaks pointedly about what our focus ought to be when we find ourselves in the role of leader: "Leadership isn't about doing. It's about being. You are more likely to succeed if you concentrate on transforming your mental framework rather than on memorizing mechanics." Sharpnack is an avid baseball player, so she likes to talk about what makes it possible for her to move so quickly to field a ball, almost as if she moved to the ball before she could see where it was headed. She, and others engaged in such highly concentrated activity that they have learned well, are able to perform not by adhering to a set of rules but as a result of, she says, "a state of being—a complete focus and presence of attention. . . ." Sharpnack's conclusion is that for companies and individuals to accomplish their aims, they need to "explore their views of the world . . . and how those perceptions shape their behaviors and opinions."[1]

This is what the general in the Sun Tzu is seeking to learn—not simply a set of methods that corresponds to a predetermined set of challenges. And a more powerful and encompassing view of the world will allow for more powerful action. If our view of the world is as simple as, "If I obtain more money and things, that money and those things will bring ultimate achievement and satisfaction," such thinking will dictate a certain range of actions and the results that come along with that. If we take the opportunity to reflect and our view therefore takes in a larger sphere of actions and results— such as the impact of actions on family, friends, colleagues, community, and world—then we are in the realm of the Sun Tzu. We are exploring "the great matter of the state." And for that, we need a very large view.

In the coming pages of this chapter, we will examine that view in terms of the key elements that make it up, that are woven throughout and repeat themselves as motifs in the text of the Sun Tzu. They follow one after the other in a logical chain and point to the basic and broadly applicable wisdom that animates this classic work. Getting to know them will allow us to better understand the skillful actions they give rise to. They are:

Interconnectedness—the dynamic and interdependent web of causes and effects that make up our world, the "heaven and the earth" that we operate in, whole and ever-changing, giving rise to chaos and challenge

The inevitability of encountering conflict whenever we engage the world

Taking whole as the overarching way of responding to conflict

Knowing as the essence of taking whole and the source of how to be

Victory, inclusive and without aggression, as the mark of the actions of a sage commander

Interconnectedness

While traveling in Africa with singer Bobby McFerrin, world-renowned cellist Yo-Yo Ma asked an elder in the village they were visiting to sing one of the important songs of his tribe. As the haunting melody filled the air, Ma furiously scribbled down the tune, but the music went by too fast and he was unable to catch it all. When the song was over, Ma asked if he could hear it a second time so he could fill in the missing notes. The elder agreed and began his song again. But as Ma listened, he noticed that somewhere in the middle, the song had changed slightly. When Ma asked why the song was different this time around, the elder pointed out that the second time he sang the song, birds were flying across the sky in a different direction.

The heaven and earth presented on page 1 of the Sun Tzu are not regarded as something separate from ourselves. The view that we are part of a vast continuum, an infinite web of interrelationships, central to the Chinese worldview at the time of Sun Tzu, is an understanding that is hardly uncommon today. Even if we didn't have chaos theorists telling us that one little event way over here can have profound effects on something way over there, our everyday experience in modern society constantly reinforces the notion of interconnectedness. With the Internet and global communications and rapid travel, it is simply very hard to be isolated. There are countless stories of people watching an unfolding disaster on a television screen at an airport only to receive a cell-phone call from someone in the middle of it.

We also stand today atop a mountain of data that has been collected, organized, and distributed in all sorts of forms that allows us to obtain a very big view. On the same home computer you can use to balance your checkbook, pay your credit card bill, or buy the complete works of Shakespeare, you can look at satellite images of the earth, survey the Western Hemisphere, then the Northern Hemisphere, and then zoom in on your city or town, your neighborhood, and then the very house you live in.

A visit to the Hayden Planetarium at the Rose Center for Earth and Space in New York City provides a good example of one form of experiencing the kind of spacious, even cosmic, framework we find ourselves in. Sitting in your chair, you can watch on the rotunda screen above you as solar system gives way to galaxy to the Local Group of galaxies (33 in all) contained within the Virgo cluster of galaxies (150 large and over 1,000 small) contained within the Virgo supercluster of galaxies, and on and on.

When you leave the planetarium theater, you emerge on the balcony, where astronomers have used great calipers to take the measure of heavenly bodies. You are told that the known universe extends to 10^{26} meters. As you walk along the railing, the exhibit uses models to give you a sense of scale. If the huge sphere over there is the known universe, then the incredibly tiny ellipse you see before you is the Local Group of galaxies, which the Milky Way is part of; and if the great sphere is the Local Group, then the very tiny ellipse is the Milky Way; and if the great sphere is the Milky Way, then the teensy ball is our solar system—and so on and so on until you've made your way around the "ball" that represents the tiniest subparticle that has been encountered at 10^{-14} square meter. It's a trip from the infinite to the infinitesimal.

If that is not enough, you can travel along a spiral ramp representing the progression of time since the Big Bang. Each normal stride represents about seventy-five million years. Recorded human history is a hairbreadth at the end of the spiral. You feel small and large at the same time. And then you leave and find yourself standing amid the crowds and traffic of Central Park West. You flip open your cell phone, and before you know it, you are connected to your brother, who tells you what he just heard on the news about a bombing in Asia. You raise your hand, and just like that, a cab pulls right up to you. Before long in the cab, the driver is talking about the same bit of news your brother just shared with you, expressing concern about his family in that troubled area. From outer space to the city street, we are tied into a web of connections that is not simply the backdrop for our world. It is our world.

Interconnectedness, and the awe that can be associated with it, have become clichés, which makes it possible for us to take interconnectedness for granted and think of its implications as trivial. "So what if everything is connected? I still need to finish this report by Friday and get to my daughter's soccer game by six o'clock." From the point of view of the Sun Tzu, interconnectedness, known in Chinese philosophy as "the Tao," is important not because it is mysterious or cosmic. It is important because apprehending things in a linear way is incomplete and ineffective, and the consequences are often harmful. How many managers have focused immense attention on what they want one person to do, only to ignore how that one person fits into the whole system? Rather than working with the system as a whole—the web of interconnectedness that the employee fits into—the manager treats her as an isolated entity, with all the possibilities for alienation and dissatisfaction that such isolation can produce. The same situation occurs so often with parents who see their children frozen in space and time and cannot see the whole context that parent and child are sharing. Think of the parent who missed the soccer game, only to find out that the report wasn't really needed so badly by Friday, then learned how the damage to his relationship with his daughter began to hamper his productivity at work.

In a completely linear world, one cause would only have one effect and there would never be unintended consequences, clashing priorities, paradoxes, and dilemmas. However, we know that any time we act, we set off not one isolated reaction but a pattern of chain reactions, and we live within—and to a certain extent, are created by—the chain reactions set off by others. Like a good chess player or a good strategist, we may try to observe and plan for as many of the consequent occurrences as we can, but it is impossible to include them all.

It may seem like a great accomplishment to observe the interconnectedness of things, perhaps we could even say to "enjoy the Tao,"
but this is still only a partial victory. We, too, are part of the interconnectedness. While the world changes around us, we are changing right along with it. Whitehead was fond of pointing out that we
are not only observers of nature: our very bodies are nature, and
they rely for their survival on regular nourishment supplied by the
surrounding environment. We are part of the process, and we can
only understand the fullness of the Sun Tzu if we include ourselves
fully in the equation.

From the perspective of the text, an important corollary of appreciating interconnectedness, and our place within it, is accepting
and appreciating chaos and change, not merely as unpleasant by-
products but as vital and even helpful.

Chaos is born from order.
[CHAPTER 5]

Conventionally, chaos strikes us as the clustering of myriad details
beyond our control that appear to be random and to bear no relation to any pattern. We just seem to be getting hit with one thing
after another all over the place. But this definition of chaos takes its
meaning only from the point of view of the fixed order that we
would like to impose on events, the plan that we hope to carry to
fruition unaltered. Events seem random when we cling to limited
perspectives that don't allow us to see the greater patterns they may
be part of. When a passing acquaintance drops by unexpectedly in
the middle of a very busy day, it seems a random act to us, but it
is part of a pattern of ordered events in his or her life that led the
person to our door. Great movements have been born of seemingly
chance meetings and chance occurrences.

From the point of view of the Sun Tzu, chaos is not something
to be avoided but is an expression of the power of interconnectedness. It is only frustrating to the extent that we try to obtain a fixed
point outside of it. Certainly, there are times when we can ride on
the plethora of details, and there are times when the details swal-
low us up, but there is never a time when the mass of details is not

there. It is no surprise that "God is in the details" and "The devil is in the details" are both popular sayings.

Of the Five Phases, none is the lasting victor.
Of the four seasons, none has constant rank.
The sun shines short and long.
The moon dies and lives.
[CHAPTER 6]

Resisting change and seeking permanent security seem almost to define what it means to be a human being. And yet they also seem to be based on a fundamental misconception about the way things work and turn out to be very problematic approaches. The Sun Tzu text repeatedly counsels us to avoid solidity and a fixed position, except when it is a strategic response to particular conditions. In general, holding a fixed position denies the reality of change and interconnectedness and thus separates us from the way things actually work. And, in particular, fighting solid positions with further solidification is an approach fraught with danger. Martin Luther King Jr. knew that if he attacked the solidly established white power structure head-on with the solid and justified resentment at his disposal, only senseless conflict would ensue. Likewise, trying to change our partner's firmly held opinion through direct argument only solidifies the resistance. The Sun Tzu therefore encourages the sage commander to not rest in any particular fixed, predictable form but rather to emerge in the form that the dictates of time and place and adversary indicate will be successful. To take action using change as an ally requires us to transcend a linear approach.

The Sun Tzu is a book about becoming a leader in whatever sphere we find ourselves in at any given time: the sphere of our family, our friends, our colleagues, our nation, our world, our own mind. The text's view of how to do this is very similar to the teachings of the mandala principle, represented by the geometric designs symbolic of the universe used in Hinduism and Buddhism as an aid to connecting to reality on a deep level and found in the works of Carl Jung and modern artists. The mandala principle teaches us that there is always a center and a fringe, and we are in many centers and fringes.

From the point of view of leadership and taking action, however, we find ourselves at the center of our personal interconnected system—our mandala—where inner and outer, subject and object, are interconnected, dynamic, and ever-changing, and where apparent chaos gives way to an underlying order apparent from the bigger view. The Sun Tzu presents methods for how to conduct our lives while seated in the middle of a system so rich and complex that it could easily appear to us as a maelstrom that could overwhelm us.

Change produces daunting chaos if it threatens what we seek to hold on to or to build. When we fear loss or hope for achievement, change may seem a threat. But the same change and chaos can also produce opportunity. Things that were solid and resistant to our efforts can rearrange themselves to produce openings without our discernible direct action. The seemingly monolithic and impenetrable Soviet bloc dissolved due to internal conditions rather than political or military bombardment from Western powers, leading to numerous opportunities for influence and development. A leader who sees change as the way things are—sees that situations, conditions, relationships, are always in flux, that no moment is ever exactly like the last one—is in a state of relaxed readiness and able to capitalize on openings as they arise. Being part of the interconnectedness and present in the midst of the inevitable change is the first step to being able to take advantage of the unfolding of occurrences.

In the view of the Sun Tzu—based on interconnectedness, chaos, and change—leadership is not about controlling and manipulating the environment as if it could be owned. You cannot truly own something that is always changing, but you can be its steward for a while. The effectiveness of the leader, then, comes not from power over other people and things but from *being part* of the interconnectedness, not merely observing it. It's not like being a baby staring at a mobile rotating above the crib. It's being a part of the mobile itself.

The Chinese classic *Tao-te Ching,* by Lao-tzu, presents the Tao—the totality where all polarities merge and that we find ourselves part of—as a governing principle that is itself ungovernable:

Man follows the ways of the Earth.
The Earth follows the ways of Heaven.

Heaven follows the ways of Tao.
Tao follows its own ways.[2]

If we limit ourselves to a dualistic view, we are always pitting ourselves against something. Man is pitted against evil, man is pitted against nature, man is pitted against man. From the point of view of the text, there is nothing to be against. We cannot enslave the Tao and bend it to our ends. We cannot hive off a part of it and make it our own wholly protected domain. But by paying close attention to the matters at hand and the context they arise in, we can follow the tendencies, clusters, and patterns. As a result, it is possible to encourage beneficial results within the sphere of our stewardship.

That is what the Sun Tzu is suggesting we can do. It is suggesting that we can incorporate a view of the world as a whole and its interconnectedness as an integral part of our sense of being—quite simply because it already is. If we seek to change things to meet a preconceived notion, we will be frustrated, but if we are willing to be part of the change and ride it with attention, we can bring about beneficial action.

However, the moment we engage, when the parts of the whole come up against each other, there is friction. Appreciating that friction, which we generally call conflict, is an important part of the overarching view of the Sun Tzu.

Conflict

Nothing is more difficult than an army contending.
[CHAPTER 7]

Although the view of the Sun Tzu starts by seeing our world as intimately interconnected—each of our actions sets off a chain reaction, and we are subject to chain reactions set off by others and by the world at large—the text fully acknowledges that we still always have a perspective and a goal. Our race, gender, culture, and nationality give us a perspective. Our roles in life—boss and employee, parent and child, vendor and client—are all perspectives. Once we have a perspective, it is inevitable that there will be others with perspectives that don't agree with ours. This oppositional nature of things leads us into the realm of differing views, disagreements, polarity—the realm of conflict that the Sun Tzu addresses.

In addition to perspectives, we all have goals and objectives we strive to accomplish, from the simplest to the most grand. We sometimes call these our *aspirations*, a word that also means "to breathe," so it is rooted in the most common and critical aspect of human existence. For a human being, if there is no breath, there is no life. So, extending ourselves into the world begins with the simplest gesture of breathing out. The road to conflict begins with this most basic human function.

We share the same space with others—in a home, a business, a school, or a country—and so we will express our aspirations in that shared space. Inevitably, however, we will differ regarding the plans and courses of action these aspirations might take and, indeed, very often in our analysis of the situation itself. Parents will disagree with other parents and with the architects when an expansion is proposed for a school. Suburban voters will disagree with urban voters over development and transportation plans. The sales department will disagree with engineering over the importance of a product feature. Two countries will have differing plans for their joint border.

While a disagreement arises from holding a view, contention and conflict arise from taking a course of action. We are operating from and bringing our perspective to bear on the situation. In the human realm, having views and acting on them is unavoidable, and doing so involves leading and influencing others who are affected by our action. This is what it means to take leadership. In the Sun Tzu, this human activity is the province of the general, the sage commander.

The process that results in conflict begins simply with some kind of contact. A possible action is about to take place, and we make contact with others in the world (or simply the world itself). The course of action we envision comes into contact with other people and what they would like to do and how they would like to operate. Often this kind of contact leads to an easy cooperation, like two friends meeting for lunch who readily find a mutually agreeable place to eat. However, when contact does not lead to a mutually agreeable conclusion, we start to experience friction, which easily turns into contention. Facial expressions change. People squirm. Voices are raised. Others' viewpoints, objectives, and habitual ways of acting come to be seen as obstacles or impediments to getting what we want. They may respond in kind, seeing us as an obstacle to what they want, and contention becomes the gateway to open warfare. For the Sun Tzu, this opposition or contention seems to be inevitable; out-and-out conflict, particularly its most extreme manifestation of war, is not.

Conflict is the most common term in English to describe this interaction between parties on opposing sides of an issue. Conflict (from the Latin *confligere,* "to clash together") can be a very bad thing. It is uncomfortable. It does damage to everyone involved. This is what most of us think most of the time. Consequently, we tend to avoid it. Occasionally, we might decide to indulge in it, even then regarding it as something bad, or alternatively feeling that it is the only possible way to engage a particular situation. Sometimes conflict can be good, as when competition between companies vying to bring a new product to market inspires innovation beyond either company's initial vision, or when the earth's tectonic plates collide and form Mount Everest or the Rocky Mountains.

The most simplistic analysis that we can apply to the experience of conflict is to conclude that we are right and others are wrong, and *they* are the ones responsible for conflict. This school yard logic—He started it!—recurs an astonishing number of times in daily affairs from the personal to the international level. Daniel Gilbert, Harvard psychologist and author of *Stumbling on Happiness,* reports research that shows that because our pains and our reasons for doing things are more obvious to us than the pains and reasons of others, we are more likely to blame others, causing us to take actions that lead to an escalation of mutual harm. "Research shows that while people think of their own actions as the consequences of what came before, they think of other people's actions as the causes of what came later."[3] But looking to others as the source of conflict avoids getting to the genuine source of conflict because it increases the polarity that is the heart of warfare.

The Sun Tzu does not present a moral standpoint on war but rather a frank acknowledgment of the shortcomings of open warfare in serving either side's needs. The text speaks pointedly about the suffering—before, during, and after—that both soldiers and ordinary people experience in a war. Several poignant stanzas from the text make clear that even the warrior class does not truly relish war or the rewards of war.

On the day that orders are issued,
The tears of seated officers moisten their lapels,
The tears of those reclining cross their cheeks.
[CHAPTER 11]

Wrath can return to joy.
Rancor can return to delight.
An extinguished state cannot return to existence.
The dead cannot return to life.
Thus the enlightened sovereign is careful about this.
The good general is cautious about this.
[CHAPTER 12]

So the sage commander does not seek war or the use of force but acknowledges that at times it is the only option. He avoids "the calamity of attack." In fact, in its most famous lines, the text proclaims that fighting, doing battle, is not held in the highest regard: "One hundred victories in one hundred battles is not the most skillful. Subduing the other's military without battle is the most skillful."

This is a distinctly different viewpoint from one that values avoiding conflict at all costs. It is also a distinctly different viewpoint from one that enters into conflict easily, with no real appreciation for the great costs involved, supported by a sense of the romantic glory, heroism, and self-righteousness of the fight. The Sun Tzu points to a path between these two extremes of avoiding or indulging, the passive and aggressive responses to potential conflict.

Conflict avoided can often be conflict postponed. Whatever remains unresolved through inaction can fester and revisit us in some form in the future. We find ourselves in opposition, facing resistance, for a reason. It is not necessary to aggressively tackle the resistance head-on; at the same time, pretending it is not there can be like ignoring a stone in our shoe. How many times has someone left a job or a relationship in order to get away from confronting something, only to see the same situation re-arise in the next job or relationship? How often have we been part of a group rendered dysfunctional when the presence of the elephants in the room is not addressed in order to avoid the "negative experience" of conflict? The passive approach to conflict avoids by suppressing, creating a false sense of peace and harmony that masks turmoil beneath.

The aggressive approach still manages to avoid the root cause of the conflict, in this case by denying the needs and perspectives of the other and simply seeking to obliterate those. As with avoided sources of unresolved conflict, those overcome by force will also return to confront us another day. World War I was known for a decade or so as "the war to end all wars," and yet the peace that was established in Paris in 1919, and took shape in five separate treaties, drew borders and boundaries that would ensure future wars, including in the Middle East. Even though the shooting war was over, the brokering and bullying at the peace table ignored the needs and perspectives of people in many places. As bloody as the conflict from 1914 to 1918 was, much more blood has been shed since then over the borders established at that time.

The Sun Tzu starts with acknowledging conflict as a natural part of life rather than a problem. It addresses the moment when alternatives seem exhausted and things get dicey. Its lessons apply to the continuum of the basic human activity of taking action—from aspiration, contact, contention, conflict, to pitched battle. Conflict may be unavoidable in life, and no doubt a most considerable obstacle to bringing about our aspirations, but how we deal with it determines what happens.

Acknowledging conflict means acknowledging the need to genuinely and thoroughly relate to the positions that others present to us. To do otherwise, from the point of view of the Sun Tzu, is to resist the reality of the interconnectedness that forms the basis of the view, to imagine that we could attain a kind of one-sided victory whose effect on others could be disregarded. These two vital aspects that form the ground of the Sun Tzu view—the interconnected web that all action takes place within and the fact that entities will find themselves in continual poles of opposition—have to be reconciled.

Taking Whole

The effective action at the heart of Sun Tzu arises directly out of the text's view of the world as whole and interconnected; if you see the world that way, then taking whole becomes the only option in response to conflict. The phrase "taking whole" describes the basic orientation of the Sun Tzu:

> *Taking a state whole is superior.*
> *Destroying it is inferior to this.*
>
> *Taking an army whole is superior.*
> *Destroying it is inferior to this.*
>
> *Taking a battalion whole is superior.*
> *Destroying it is inferior to this.*
>
> *Taking a company whole is superior.*
> *Destroying it is inferior to this.*
>
> *Taking a squad whole is superior.*
> *Destroying it is inferior to this.*
> [CHAPTER 3]

In these few simple couplets, the Sun Tzu puts forward its most profound message to all who seek to be accomplished leaders in any sphere of activity: when responding to conflict, leave whatever you encounter intact as much as possible. In every case, destroying is inferior.

The text doesn't shy away from telling us that there are times when destroying is necessary, but even then we are counseled to do the least amount possible. The Sun Tzu clearly acknowledges that at certain times, extreme force is the only option, such as when greater damage and suffering might come from not acting in that way. In July 1944, a high German military official, Count Claus von Stauffenberg, in collaboration with other conspirators, planted a briefcase bomb in Adolf Hitler's Wolf's Lair. Although members of his staff died, Hitler was only slightly injured. It has been argued that had the plot been successful, over five million lives might have been saved on all sides of the conflict, which did not end for another ten months. In our own lives, we may not have such dramatic examples, but nevertheless, there are clearly times when extreme force is necessary. If we are a parent, we must at times sharply say "No" to a toddler about to run into danger. As a manager or business owner, we may have to let someone go who is creating chaos in the workplace, in order that other jobs may be spared.

Having acknowledged that the use of extreme force could be necessary, the text directs the general to, when employing force, create the *least* amount of destruction possible. The greater the destruction, the Sun Tzu tells us, the greater the obstacles and resistance to one's objectives that will arise in the future. Whatever is destroyed must be rebuilt, whatever lives are lost represent lost human productivity and creativity, those who are ill will need to be cared for, those who have died will be mourned over, and those who have been beaten down will harbor resentment and live to fight another day. Something must be left to build on, or one's "victory" is no victory at all, just as when two children fighting over a piece of clothing tear it beyond repair. The text presents a hierarchy based on this principle:

> *Therefore, one hundred victories in one hundred battles is not the most skillful.*
> *Subduing the other's military without battle is the most skillful.*
>
> *And so the superior military cuts down strategy.*
> *Its inferior cuts down alliances.*

Its inferior cuts down the military.
The worst attacks walled cities.
[CHAPTER 3]

To overcome opposition and resistance without battle is the most skillful. The glory and heroism of battle, the excitement, may be given up, leaving in its place more life and power preserved. At the other end of the spectrum is the worst possible outcome, the destruction of a city, the center of community, life, and culture. All that power and vitality is ruined. Occasionally, it might have to happen, but the overriding goal is always to "take whole."

And so one skilled at employing the military
    Subdues the other's military but does not do battle,
    Uproots the other's walled city but does not attack,
    Destroys the other's state but does not prolong.
One must take it whole when contending for all-under-
    heaven.
[CHAPTER 3]

"Taking whole" is not an arcane or artificial principle. It's the step that naturally follows from appreciating the interconnectedness of life and the opposition, resistance, obstacles, and conflict that arise from that. It is the action that resolves the disconnected and contentious quality of conflict with the overall interconnectedness of things. In order to take whole, the leader looks to the larger perspectives of both space (all the relationships affected by the outcome of the conflict) and time (what kind of repercussions will be felt in the future and for how long). The adversary's perspective must always be included, as must the leader's own hopes and fears.

As we come to know taking whole, we begin to appreciate that it is not a trick, ploy, or stratagem. It is a *way of being* that comes out of relating to the world as a very big and connected place, and seeing the conflicts and obstructions as encompassed by that larger space. The general sees problems that arise in the midst of the campaign as an important part of the process and something to learn from. The orientation of taking whole keeps options open by including possibilities, even ones that seem remote. As a result of this way of being, the leader can see the big picture and act with the interests of the greatest number of people taken into account. Taking whole is an ongoing orientation.

A more limited view of conflict sees *this* (whatever we are seeking to keep secure) opposed by *that* (the monolithic force that threatens to destroy it). As long as we are trapped in this limited view, our alternatives are reduced, and the default more often than not is to fight aggressively to vanquish that which opposes us. The broad view of conflict embodied in the principle of taking whole knows that all perspectives must be included, that positions will change as a result of the interaction of opposing forces, and that the highest aim is to arrive at a resolution that accommodates the needs and aspirations of everyone. The new day will arrive. The question is how much damage will be left to clean up and how much strength and life will be left to build on.

In Tony Judt's history of Europe from 1945 to 2005, *Postwar,* he discusses how groups in Allied countries demanding vengeance and retribution from the defeated Germans wanted to remove almost all productive capacity and reduce Germany to a vassal state. Justice and reform were needed, in the form of the Nuremburg trials and denazification, but would a policy that led to decades of privation and hardship also be required? Stalin surely hoped so, because he was poised to exploit the certain collapse of Western Europe. Fortunately, a few farsighted people were able to see that the two wars exposed underlying problems with the economic systems and relations among countries that were leading to instability and war, and that rather than trying to settle a score and re-create a bygone era, the rebuilding would have to usher in a new era and force new kinds of economic relationships. The Marshall Plan and the Bretton Woods reforms to the international economy operated from the larger perspective of all parties and transcended the boundary between victor and vanquished.

In the same way, when we witness a child break a precious vase in a store and then be harshly and very publicly disciplined by his or her parent for this reckless behavior, we can feel the parent viewing the child's behavior through the narrow lens of the parent's own embarrassment and discomfort. Certainly children break things due to a lapse in the kind of paying attention to their surroundings that parents may have to help them cultivate. But children's "reckless behavior" also occurs because they are energetic, rambunctious, spunky, and inquisitive—all qualities that can lead to success in school and later life. If the parent's corrective measure does not take into account the whole of this picture, the punishment may well dampen the more positive qualities contributing to the "reckless behavior," and with far worse effects for both the child and the parent in the future.

In taking whole, the Sun Tzu presents pith instructions for leaders in all spheres about how to move their objectives successfully forward through the thorny field of opposition and conflict they will surely face. This central principle tells us that the way through is by including the perspectives and goals of the opposition. Taking whole is about how to work with chaos and uncertainty and preserve the possibilities, how to embrace the interconnectedness and the conflict, and move forward. This kind of action is very demanding. It requires a sound grasp of all the details that make up a situation and the patterns they form, as well as the shape they give to events. It requires us to know deeply.

Knowing

We live in an age when knowledge rules. It has become the new capital of our time. In the knowledge economy, knowledge industries have replaced factories. One reason the Sun Tzu speaks so directly to us nowadays is that it tells us that knowledge plays a central role in our efforts to work more effectively with conflict and chaos in our lives. And while taking whole is a natural outgrowth of appreciating interconnectedness, it is knowledge that takes it from a mere ideology to a way of being that informs our actions.

> *And so in the military—*
> *Knowing the other and knowing oneself,*

In one hundred battles no danger.
Not knowing the other and knowing oneself,
One victory for one loss.
Not knowing the other and not knowing oneself,
In every battle certain defeat.
[CHAPTER 3]

In the Sun Tzu, knowledge begins with the mundane. It starts with simple, patient gathering of information from direct observation, counting and calculating, studying, learning how things are done, what works and what doesn't. In general, there is a temptation to circumvent this step. We are often willing to establish an impression from a little bit of observation and let this suffice for research. Without a doubt, we all possess the faculty of rapid cognition, the seemingly intuitive leap as discussed in Malcolm Gladwell's *Blink,* where whole pictures come to us in a flash, but even those are based upon having the right data input. Knowledge of all kinds rests on a foundation of details.

Young news reporters are prone to reporting their impressions as facts and are quickly taught to follow the dictum "Show me; don't tell me." When a reporter says that a *large crowd* showed up for the mayoral candidate's rally, he is *telling* us. When he says *six hundred people* showed up, he is *showing* us. When he says the car was traveling *at a high rate of speed,* he is telling us; when he says that Officer Smith estimated that the car was traveling *160 miles per hour,* he is showing us. When he says that teenage pregnancy has become a *significant* problem, once again he is telling us, but when he says it has *increased 14 percent in the past three years,* he is showing us, and we can decide whether it is significant or not. Helpful knowledge, for the Sun Tzu, involves the tedium of counting and calculating, and the application of metrics to determine size and shape and the relationship of one thing to another.

The raw data we accumulate, however, cannot be blindly trusted. It is only as good as the lens through which it is seen. For the facts to be truly accurate, they must be gathered by a clear-seeing mind; otherwise, the input becomes distorted by wishful thinking. The reporter who dutifully counts the number of people at a rally may do a better job than the one who merely creates a rough impression, but if he cannot see the whole picture as he is counting, he will overlook pertinent details that reveal something critical about the numbers. He may not discover that one-third of the crowd has been bused in directly from the candidate's headquarters. When we gather facts, we are all prone to the tendency to note what we think is significant and overlook or discount much of the rest. To patiently observe from a vantage point beyond our own hopes and fears, self-interest, and impatience to resolve matters can be exceedingly difficult at times, but it forms the only true basis for knowledge.

One of the most common ways of gaining knowledge is inference, reaching conclusions based on logical connections between bits of information already at hand. But even this is often unreliable. Logical fallacies show us the many ways that bias in such judgments can lead us away from knowledge. One common fallacy is "post hoc, ergo propter hoc," believing that simply because one event preceded another in time, it is the direct cause of the subsequent event. Another is "misleading vividness," where a few dramatic events (two downtown shootings) are taken to outweigh statistical evidence (an overall decrease in the crime rate). And there are dozens more. What many people regard as knowledge is merely a collection of weakly drawn inferences.

This is one important reason that the Sun Tzu tells us that knowing ourselves is as crucial as knowing the other. If we don't know our own hopes and fears, our prejudices—what we are most attached to, what we are willing to lose, and what motivates us—we cannot see how we may distort information. The same dispassion required to collect information is doubly required when drawing conclusions based upon it. We cannot look down from above; we can only look across at the other from the limited vantage point of our own compulsions. One who willfully or unconsciously distorts the data to perpetuate preexisting beliefs or wishes will be guilty, as *New York Times* columnist Maureen Dowd puts it, describing the behavior of Cinderella's evil stepsisters, who cut their feet to fit them into the glass slipper, "of butchering reality in order to make the fairy tale come out their way."[4] And in that, knowledge is lost.

Obviously, the most common way to gain knowledge is through direct experience, but humans rely heavily on what we have seen, heard, understood, and assimilated in the past as a pattern to overlay on new events. We are always trying to fit what we see into a preexisting schema or pigeonhole. Beyond the personal hopes and fears that affect knowing, there is the basic view or framework that we can never shed. Current neuroscience research shows that sensory data, such as light bouncing off a flower onto the eye, is relayed to successively higher brain functions as it goes through the process of identification. In the case of the flower, the light begins in the primary visual cortex as a pattern, then the next "higher" brain function establishes color, and then the functions higher than that establish identity and other associated information about that particular flower. This direction of flow is called "feedforward." Researchers were surprised to learn that more of the bundles of nerve cells dedicated to carrying this sensory information were traveling in the opposite direction, from top to bottom in a direction called "feedback," by a factor of ten times. In what the neuroscientists call "top-down processing," the framework built by experience interprets the raw data coming in. What you see is almost never what you get.

This particular obstacle to knowing is also referred to as "confirmation bias," the cognitive error we make when we find what we expect to find by selectively accepting or ignoring information. The study of cognitive errors—the mistakes we make in the way we come to know things—provides us with many other examples that ring true in our experience. In "anchoring," for example, we fix on one bit of information and rely on it too heavily when making a decision. We make the "representativeness error" when we are overly affected by what is typically true and fail to pay attention to anything outside of that. Research in cognitive errors confirms how often what we know turns out to be what we *want* to know.

Nowhere is the discussion of cognitive errors as obstacles to knowing more interesting and vitally important to us than in Dr. Jerome Groopman's book *How Doctors Think*. In pressured environments from their offices to the ER, Dr. Groopman tells us, doctors rely on shortcuts known as diagnostic algorithms to help them determine the nature of an illness and the correct treatment. Such algorithms outline a decision-making tree that seems indispensable when treating patients. But, as Dr. Groopman points out, all of us when confronted with uncertainty—what doctors face when they try to diagnose a patient—are susceptible to unconscious emotions and personal biases. So, we are more likely to make cognitive errors. In describing the cognitive errors that he and other doctors make, Groopman reports that "part of what caused these cognitive errors is our inner feelings, feelings we do not readily admit to and often don't realize."[5] No doubt the framework of the diagnostic algorithms is helpful, but if the doctor is too faithful to them she might miss important information—at the patient's peril. Decision-trees that should lead to correct diagnosis and therapy are not necessarily good for those times when we need to be, as the Sun Tzu says, "going beyond what everyone knows," when the situation is unclear or uncertain.

The Sun Tzu starts with the assumption that the general has goals and objectives, important frameworks that should not easily be given up. Indeed, being perfectly free of frameworks or goals is not possible. However, they are not a hindrance to knowledge as long as the general doesn't cling to them as the final conclusion but rather is able to suspend them when need be. In the review of the Sun Tzu text and tradition in chapter 1, we talked about this process beginning when we take a moment to reflect on our experience to gain perspective. This "suspending" process can further develop into what we refer to as a contemplative approach—creating a protected space of openness and attention that allows for clear seeing. This is an approach that comes quite naturally to the human mind, which we experience when our mind is stopped by a moment of awe and appreciation, or made crystal clear by fear in the face of an insurmountable challenge. One manifestation of this faculty is the creative source of the literary and plastic arts, and another is what performers and athletes experience as "the zone." This faculty can also be cultivated. In his advice to doctors, Dr. Groopman suggests adding the simple gesture of a moment's reflection into the diagnostic process to create the open attentiveness and nonjudgment that is the key to seeing beyond expectations and projections.

The Sun Tzu puts much more of an emphasis on knowing as an active process than on knowledge as an accumulation of information. In fact, what Malcom Gladwell calls "rapid cognition"—the ability to decide quickly when need be—is overwhelmed and breaks down when confronted with too many facts. To borrow from the lines in the Sun Tzu on taking whole, gleaning the few critical highlights that help one to see the whole is superior; merely accumulating information is inferior to this.

Knowing in the Sun Tzu is an openness to and accommodation of the steady stream of new inputs, without feeling the need to latch onto any of them. It is being attuned to discovery, which allows things to come to us in their own time. When we allow knowledge to become static, once we have collected as much information as we like, we begin to solidify "reality." That fixed reality becomes our own possession, which we juxtapose against other realities. This hardens positions and makes for easy targets. The puffed-up know-it-all colleague at work who doesn't allow the space for his friends to confuse him with the facts is one painful recurring example.

Knowing in the Sun Tzu comes back to rest on the basic reality that the view is built upon: in an interconnected world, the sage commander is not separate from what she knows. The sharpness and precision of intellect is joined with the insight and profundity of intuition. In this way, we transcend the problem of too much information and overmeasurement, not being able to see the forest for the trees, where reliance on information actually clouds our ability to clearly decide and act. We can see beyond what is there and make leaps. A master politician of the last century, Speaker of the House Sam Rayburn, who had a reputation for being keenly attuned to the activities of the 435 members of the U.S. House of Representatives, used to say to those who served there, "If you can't feel things that you can't see or hear, you don't belong here."[6]

Indeed, knowing in the Sun Tzu appears to involve that kind of mystical perception, but it's really a normal human faculty. It's about how we "get" very complex things—things that have a lot of context, like a joke or a piece of music—in one shot. We might start our learning by following steps of logic or a recipe, but in the end, we get the whole thing. It's about learning by immersion rather than explanation, as in the teaching style of great masters with their apprentices. It's the palpable way we understand the wholeness of ordinary things.

Once established, no principle appears more prominently in the Sun Tzu than "knowing." It is a hallmark of what is unique about the Sun Tzu: it bases its approach to action not on techniques and tricks but rather on a deep and abiding quality of knowing that grows out of an appreciation of the interconnectedness of people, phenomena, and events, from which the general is inseparable. It constitutes the alternative to relating to the world as a collection of opposing forces of good and bad, victor and vanquished. In the view of the text, it is knowing that allows the sage commander to pierce superficial appearances. It is what makes profoundly effective action possible.

Victory

While knowledge is a central notion in the text, the Sun Tzu is all about victory. The sage commander—and each of us in our particular sphere—is a leader who has goals that get mired in conflict and who needs to overcome opposition and bring about success. In nearly every chapter, the text describes, defines, and discusses victory but stops short of promising to deliver it, since it tells us at the outset that victory cannot be "transmitted in advance." What are the qualities of this victory that forms the final stage of the view of the text?

The best-known and most often quoted line from the Sun Tzu sets out the key objective for the sage commander, which also happens to be one of the text's most intriguing messages for readers today and throughout history: how to be victorious without going to war.

> *Subduing the other's military without battle is the most skillful.*
> [CHAPTER 3]

Winning without fighting is not just code language for a more clever way to beat the other guy. It is a serious strategic position, and it has proved to be effective. It acknowledges that the destruction and devastation that result from battle leave a residue, not just for the defeated but for the victors as well, and this provides the basis for future conflict. The sage commander seeks the victory that is ongoing, beyond the aggression and impatience that lead to battle in the search for short-term solutions.

Further, the Sun Tzu tells us that the skillful action that will give rise to such a victory "can be known. It cannot be made." The conditions for victory can be encouraged, but victory itself can be neither manufactured nor manipulated; victorious action arises as a direct result of knowing. This knowing is the open and accommodating orientation the sage commander maintains in relation to the ever-changing, interconnected world. It both creates the ground for victory to arise and provides the awareness to catch it in the unique conditions of the moment when it does.

The sage commander is able to recognize and "capture" victory as it arises because he has already assumed the perspective of victory in his own mind, prior to engaging on the battlefield:

> *One skilled at battle takes a stand in the ground of no*
> *defeat*
> *And so does not lose the enemy's defeat.*
> *Therefore, the victorious military is first victorious and*
> *after that does battle.*
> *The defeated military first does battle and after that seeks*
> *victory.*
> [CHAPTER 4]

This point in the text is often misunderstood to mean a false confidence or bravado, or only engaging where a winning outcome is guaranteed. But the Sun Tzu is far more subtle than that. It describes how the battle is first won in the mind. Assuming the perspective of struggle invites conflict; an orientation beyond struggle at the outset attracts the conditions of victory.

Not surprisingly, the Sun Tzu tells us that a victory of this nature is only possible through profound action that is often mysterious to those who witness it:

In seeing victory, not going beyond what everyone knows is not skilled.
[CHAPTER 4]

Deep and lasting resolutions to thorny conflicts rely on measures beyond habitual patterns, common knowledge, or obvious gestures. One interesting example is how some researchers are paying increasing attention to eccentricities and aberrations in phenomena rather than to the consistencies in a data set, the seeming norm. To find a more complete victory, the text tells us, requires a leader capable of both extreme exertion and farsightedness.

In the end, the Sun Tzu seeks a victory that arises out of knowing and does not perpetuate further conflict:

Know the other and know oneself,
Then victory is not in danger.
Know earth and know heaven,
Then victory can be complete.
[CHAPTER 10]

The text is grounded in the brutal reality of the Warring States period in China, where complete victory seemed an elusive goal. Even so, the text tells us that the conditions for it may well be present in the conflict in front of us. To attain complete victory, the sage commander goes beyond the superficial to the source of conflict. This requires actions based on knowing heaven and earth, and thereby finding a larger resolution based on the practical realities that affect both sides of the battle. A victory is complete when it includes the enemy—and renders further conflict unnecessary.

Now we have "the view," the way in which the Sun Tzu sees the world, the way the sage commander in the text can be skillful in the face of conflict, the way we can view the difficulties we face as leaders. It is the heaven principle, the starting point we need in order to apply our framework to the more detailed workings of the text while still respecting its wholeness. We described each of the stages of the view at length in order to establish a deeper understanding, so it will serve us well as we explore the practice stage, the text's profound methods and practices that follow from this view. It's really a simple sequence of stepping-stones describing the path, each step following from the previous.

The view of the text begins with understanding the world as an *interconnected* whole, a dynamic and interdependent web of causes and effects that we live in, which gives rise to chaos and change. As leaders in that world, we will inevitably face opposition and contention, which will easily turn into *conflict*. If we see the world as whole, we can only respond to conflict with the effort to *take whole*—that is, to preserve the possibilities, to achieve our goals while leaving as much intact as possible. Such action is only possible if we *know* this world as deeply and intuitively as possible and can thereby respond to challenges with skill. Acting in the world that way, we can achieve *victory*, which for the Sun Tzu does not generate further conflict.

With this view, we can now come back to the question posed by the school superintendent in our workshop. If we are inspired by the Sun Tzu, if we are oriented as leaders to working with the world from this perspective, what subtle practices does the text have to share with us to make it possible to translate view into action? What methods can we discover and learn that will allow us to extend this skillful action into the world of conflict and chaos? What are the rules of victory?

4 _____

The Basic Practice
Learning How to Employ Shih

Technique is necessary to start with, but it is also necessary at some stage for the technique to fall away.
—*Chögyam Trungpa*

Master the instrument, learn the changes, then forget all that shit and just play.
—*Charlie "Bird" Parker*

Great improvisational tango dancers are not thinking "ocho, ocho cortado, molinete with a swirl close. . . ." The great dancers have internalized the information to the point they no longer have to think about much at all. They have learned how the steps, figures, patterns and structural elements feel on a crowded dance floor. On a crowded social dance floor, intuition is an important part of improvisation. With spaces appearing and disappearing, dancers have a relatively brief time to react. Consequently, navigation relies heavily on intuitive decision making, rather than a deliberate sorting through the possible options before making a decision.
—*Stephen and Susan Brown*

BEFORE EMBARKING on their long-anticipated journey, many tourists have carefully studied the guidebooks and maps of Paris, made all the necessary transportation and lodging arrangements, bought the proper electrical adapters, purchased the traveler's checks, readied the cameras, and studied the phrasebook only to find themselves with a crumpled, sweaty map dangling from their hands and mouths agape, standing in the Trocadero or the Tuileries awestruck and immovable. The map is not the territory. The book is not the story. Nothing completely prepares us for acting on the ground, in the field, in the terror and the magic of the moment. Moving from view to practice means starting to enter the perilous—and promising—realm of action.

The view of the Sun Tzu holds out the promise that it is possible to "take whole," to act decisively in the world in such a way that conflicting perspectives can be included. We can talk—and we have talked—at length about what that means, but at some point for taking whole to be *meaningful,* for the view of the Sun Tzu to materialize in our everyday lives, we need to know what to do and how to do it. We need to understand the methods referred to in the original title of *The Art of War,* "Military Methods," how they arise from the view of the Sun Tzu, and how we can practice them.

In the framework of view, practice, and action, practice is the earth principle. It is that which links our overarching perspectives and motivations to our specific actions. In chapter 2, we defined practice as a behavior or a set of behaviors—ways of being and working with the world—that extend our views into action, that bring a given view to bear on any particular action. The view takes shape as a way of being, and that way of being reiterates and elaborates the values inherent in the view. It also becomes the birthplace of specific actions. If we have the view of being an excellent tango dancer and enjoying that art, we learn all the methods and techniques that allow us to look and act and feel like a tango dancer, and then when we are on the floor and the music starts, we dance.

It will help to begin with a brief review of our discussion of practice in chapter 2. "Practice" refers to a pattern of behavior and disposition of mind that can encompass many discrete and interrelated methods. In every area of our lives, we have skills, habits, and practices that have been formed through education and training, imitation, repetition, and emulation that help us to carry out specific actions—driving a car, writing an e-mail, managing a household, cooking a meal, skiing, playing golf, running a meeting, dealing with the objections of a difficult colleague. Authentic practice relies on method as a way to contain and channel wild energy, abandon, and impulse, which enables that energy to be creative and responsive. It makes it possible for us to act coolly and with command in difficult situations.

Practice also relies on routine, repeated performance that enhances and more deeply embeds a skill. It is not, however, limited by rote repetition and never treats methods as mere expedients. In practice, we learn and develop as we go, and therefore the panoply of methods that we employ has a living, organic quality. When we are impressed by someone highly adept—our personal physician, our favorite method actor, a neighborhood leader we deeply admire—we don't think necessarily of individual skills; we think first of the overall power of the person's presence, his or her being. Practice begins with imitation and then moves to emulation and embodiment. The methods we learn are part of us, so practicing them becomes second nature. Because we understand and are continually refreshing the view that our practice arises from, we always generate fresh approaches. Our actions have the rigor that comes from being methodical and the imagination that comes from having a big view.

The challenge of practice is to move successfully from aspiration to outcome. It is not as simple as wishing it were so. Practice implies an element of discipline and work. The advent of inexpensive digital cameras and video recorders has produced many pictures and movies that are nifty to e-mail around, but this sophisticated technology alone will not make stunning photographs or films. When people want real photography or film, they turn to those who have mastered these arts. Would-be photographers or filmmakers need to learn about light and shadow, angles, composition, and a myriad of other skills that, with practice, will yield the results they aspire to.

Simply hanging out and acting like a filmmaker won't work either. "Fake it till you make it" may be an important element in early stages of learning, but "making it" eventually requires more than mimicry. Working from the outside in, trying to parrot or copy what we aspire to rather than deeply embodying it, eventually fails and can even have very negative consequences. Major corporate scandals have been attributed to people who have faked their way to the top. Choosing style over substance, according to Professor Robert Hare, coauthor of *Snakes in Suits,* they have the outer appearance of brilliant leaders, but at the center of their being, there is "a hollow core." Leadership training and weekend management courses can often fall into the trap of emphasizing a menu of winning behaviors that do not take deep root. They wear out once the buzzwords that support them are forgotten or go out of fashion. There is an old Buddhist saying that good ideas are like patches on a garment. Eventually, they fall off.

Authentic practice implies a journey to be traveled. For practices to be embodied at a meaningful level, there must be deep learning that leads to a genuine way of being. Training and education do not simply add enhanced features to our preexisting habits. They change our behaviors. In the most heightened of circumstances—when time frames are short and consequences are extreme—we rely on what has been deeply ingrained. That's why nurses, rescue workers, pilots, and soldiers must be trained so thoroughly: how they behave in a crisis must be part of their being, not simply a checklist from a poster by the time clock. But even assiduous training in sound methods and practices is not sufficient to prevent tunnel vision from setting in, an overreliance on rote methods that can lead to a disastrous lack of creativity, as we saw in Dr. Groopman's presentation of the diagnostic decision-making tree used by doctors. In an atmosphere of chaos and conflict, unpredictability is the norm.

For this reason, our presentation of the Sun Tzu always emphasizes starting with the view. For our actions to be in line with our aims, not only must our practices be deeply ingrained but they must also be in sync with and refreshed by view. So often, in the heat of the moment—when we are trying to achieve immediate objective after immediate objective—we lose sight of the mission. In communities, the fight over parochial interests can cause us to lose sight of the greater good that binds us together. In the home, the attachments to our notions of relationship or discipline can cause us to not hear what our partner or our children are trying to tell us. In the battlegrounds of warfare or city streets, soldiers or police officers can end up harming the very people they are meant to protect.

When we find we have lost sight of the view, correcting things simply by "changing what we are doing" will not go deep enough.

At that point, the antidote is to coordinate our practices with our view. Practices that are deeply empowered by a view allow us to learn as we go. By traveling this kind of path, which requires us continually to broaden the view, we learn not how to think and strategize more cleverly but rather how to act—as we have said, "how to be"—in a way that marries view and practice.

In our whole and interconnected world, the practices we employ are not simply something we do to other people. When we take action, we not only *effect* things but we are *affected* by them. When we raise our children, they also raise us. When we manage others, they also manage us. The same applies to countries and their allies and enemies, and companies and their competition.

Practice is the critical transition from view, which gives rise to powerful and effective action. What is it, then, in the Sun Tzu that forms this kind of practice for the sage commander, that extends the view of interconnectedness and taking whole out into the world? What can serve this function for us as we face the challenges of our everyday lives?

Shih: What Is It?
A General Description

The central character in the story of strategic practices in the Sun Tzu is *shih* (again, this is pronounced "shir," with a very short vowel sound). Shih describes how a particular configuration of forces in the world can focus effective power. A simple example is water amassed behind a dam, then released to turn giant turbines in an electricity generating station. For those willing to tune in to and employ the power of shih, it can bring advantage and accomplish taking whole. In its basic meaning, it is neutral. It is not for or against anyone, nor is it anyone's possession. It is simply a norm of the world and its activities.

Shih can be likened to the arrangement of pieces on a chessboard, which establishes a pattern of force and possibility, or in a natural-world analogy, it is like a system of mountain rivulets, creeks, streams, and waterfalls that come together to form a large and powerful river,

In human terms, it can be seen in the dynamic within any squad, team, or unit within a company, where all the roles, responsibilities, tendencies, and aspirations of the individuals come together to create powerful moments of harmonious cooperation and rancorous conflict and everything in between.

Once we come to understand its meaning, we will recognize that shih is not a mystical and arcane concept—we can find it everywhere in the world—but it is subtle and multifaceted. It describes something that we are familiar with, that we always knew about on an intuitive level, but we probably have not had a name for it. And, as we consider the qualities of shih and some guidelines about how to employ it in this chapter, we can begin to see how it can work in our lives, and understand how to use it in a genuine way.

Shih may also defy conventional notions about strategic advantage, which tend to focus on the qualities of the strategizers and their use of these qualities to manipulate others. While people do have within them a configuration of forces, a shih, in its fundamental meaning shih is not narrowly defined as an attribute of a human being—like cunning, guile, or cleverness. Furthermore, although methods may be part of its makeup, shih is neither something we achieve nor something we do to someone else. It arises within the interdependent world, and we can therefore take advantage of its inherent power.

As much as the text has become famous for the principle of "subduing without battle," the key to actually doing that is to work with the world by marshaling the power of shih. The Sun Tzu is indeed a profound text about how to effectively handle conflict, but the process begins long before the moment of contact. The text stresses the importance of establishing a victorious environment, the ground for accomplishing your goal, before the sources of conflict arise. It's like going into a critical board meeting knowing that all your influential colleagues' opinions are aligned with your position before the matter even comes to a vote. Establishing such ground is based on employing shih.

Employing shih, the phrase the Sun Tzu uses to advise the general about how to work with the deep energies of the world, is a powerful means to create the ground of victory on an ongoing basis and also the way to respond when we are faced with the need to act on the spot, without relying simply on conditioned response or impulse. Employing shih is the overall practice within which the specific strategies that the Sun Tzu is famous for—such as deception, the extraordinary and the orthodox, and forming and transforming—find their place. This subtlety can often be lost if we are focused on the individual "techniques" in the text alone. Taking a larger view of the practice of the Sun Tzu has the distinct advantage of revealing an effective way to work with events at all stages of their development, from antecedent and seed to full-blown manifestation. In working with the world in this way, we may avoid the trap of waiting anxiously for moments of perfect resolution, at which point our actions may be too little, too late.

The deep methodology of the Sun Tzu offers a way to achieve objectives, whether the situation involves an immediate conflict or not. Conflict is simply the most obvious and urgent manifestation of the complex interaction of forces that makes up our world. Working with shih offers an excellent means of engaging complex, emergent situations, and the disruption, uncertainty, and chaos that occur when things are changing quickly and a new reality is coming into being. The Sun Tzu works effectively in difficult and extreme situations, but it is not a strategic text that we simply dust off when things are getting tough. It offers insight for every step of the way.

Events often have a way of unfolding that takes us by surprise. It seems a mystery to us how some conflicts in the world seem to get resolved without more bloodshed, or at least without a lot more yelling and screaming. The sudden fall of the Berlin Wall was so highly celebrated in large part because it seemed to come almost out of nowhere. The transition from an authoritarian apartheid regime to a racially egalitarian democracy in South Africa, without a protracted civil war, took most people by surprise. A teenager picking up the expensive clothes you've bought her and hanging them up neatly, without the lecture and the usual eye-rolling and groaning response—that takes you by surprise. An employee who hasn't been contributing and seems lost causes you to struggle over how to let him go, and then suddenly he decides he wants to take his life in a more fulfilling direction and is thankful for the opportunity you've given him but feels it's time to move on. These breakthrough moments have a kind of ordinary magic about them. Every once in a while, a situation that seems stuck, tense, and impossible one day now seems workable, even creative, and the outcome does not seem connected to any particular action or specific effort.

Do such sudden, almost mysterious, moments in fact arise out of nowhere?

Not really. They arise from a myriad of causes and conditions that no single person can hope to see all at once. Historians, psychologists, educators, and political theorists may try to pinpoint and argue over what is the one central and vital cause, or the several key causes, that account for a sudden shift. Who can say, however, that one cause could predominate in the absence of many others? We can list numerous reasons for the fall of the Berlin Wall or the collapse of apartheid—especially since we are viewing those events after the fact—but no one can definitively state a root cause, and no one could have predicted with certainty the timing of either event beforehand, just as a doctor cannot pinpoint the exact day of someone's death in advance. There are simply too many factors.

Working with shih means working with the world in a way that appreciates the concatenation of many factors that gives rise to events and realizing that we do not stand outside, apart from all those factors: *we are one of those factors.*

Further than that, by paying close attention, through knowing shih, we can learn to respond to the events leading to a particular conflict and to conflict itself in a more profound and subtle manner, resisting heavy-handed attempts to wrestle the world into submission. Breakthrough events can be something more than a hit-or-miss occurrence. We can help to bring them about by working with reality at a deeper, more intuitive level—by cultivating a way of being and acting in the world that can allow us to employ the power of shih.

Since shih is the gateway to unlocking a treasury of practices described in the Sun Tzu, we need to look at it in greater depth. Is shih a tool, something tangible we use, is it a feature of the world, a way of being, or all of these things? Most important, how can we work with it in our lives, and how do we train ourselves to better employ its power?

How the Text Presents Shih

Shih is a complex and subtle notion, yet it has a deep simplicity about it as well that accounts for its power. As our understanding of the subtleties of shih deepens, its usefulness increases. We will consider it from a variety of perspectives in order to build up our understanding of this central concept and not limit our appreciation of its breadth and depth. That's one reason we did not translate it into English. In various translations of the Sun Tzu text, single words used for shih include *force, energy, momentum, potential, disposition, configuration, influence, authority*. Phrases used to translate it include *strategic configuration, strategic advantage, potential energy*, and *strategic configuration of power*. Clearly, no single word in English captures it. And it is our conviction that if it is translated as a variety of different words in different contexts, the power of the underlying theme that connects those contexts is lost. It is a word like *Tao, karma,* or *ch'i* that has enough power and relevance, and speaks to enough of our commonplaces, to make the leap into English usage untranslated. It's a foreign word, but not a foreign concept.

In an earlier time than the Sun Tzu, shih meant the power of the ruler: his control over others and his ability to affect them from a distance. By the time of the Sun Tzu, people had come to recognize that the power rested not in the person but rather in his position and the entire structure that supported it. Being in the right place—on the throne—magnified his influence. The ruler is powerful because he is at the head of a complex set of relationships. This understanding gave rise to the meaning of shih employed in the text. The power of shih is relational. It arises from a configuration of forces that are both in action and existing as potential.

If you were to glance at a game of Go in progress, you would see black and white stones shaped like M&M's arrayed at the intersections of lines on a wooden board. If you knew the game, you could discern in the shapes the stones form where power is concentrated and ready to be released. Of course, as mentioned above, a chessboard would present the same kind of configuration of relational power. In a less static example, the players on a soccer field represent a particular configuration of power, and the more you know of the game, the more you will recognize it. Just so, if you enter a public meeting in a city you have just moved to or a meeting in a company you have just joined, knowing little of the players, you might not see all the interlocking configurations of power and influence. Nevertheless, they are there. You can sense them a little even when you don't know much. Once you become more familiar, you can see them very clearly. The whole world exists in this way. The power held within configurations is ever-present. The human body itself is a power-holding configuration. Indeed, the earth, the solar system, and the tree in your backyard all contain and carry power as a result of a given configuration or collection of configurations. This is shih.

Chapter 5 of the Sun Tzu presents shih in three ways. Each of these demonstrates a kind of configuration, but each imparts a slightly different intuitive feel for shih. First, it presents it as power-in-motion, where water, otherwise soft and harmless, can be transformed into a powerful force by its configuration.

> *The rush of water, to the point of tossing rocks about.*
>   *This is shih.*

It next presents it as shape, where shih is described as steep, evoking the power of troops taking the higher ground in a mountain ravine:

> *Therefore, one skilled at battle—*
>   *His shih is steep.*

Finally, it presents it as accumulation of power:

> *Shih is like drawing the crossbow.*

Each of the preceding lines is also part of a couplet that contains the idea of shih's being joined with the critical moment of its release, or application, known as the "node." (*Node* translates as a word that refers to the very small connection that separates segments of bamboo, essentially a moment of transition from one phase to the next.) Hence,

> *The rush of water, to the point of tossing rocks about.*
>   *This is shih.*
> *The strike of a hawk, at the killing snap. This is the node.*

> *Therefore, one skilled at battle—*
>   *His shih is steep.*
>   *His node is short.*

> *Shih is like drawing the crossbow.*
> *The node is like pulling the trigger.*

Abrupt, short, sudden—the node shows us how vast power can be released in an instant. It also represents the fact that power comes not through strength or force alone but through the timing of its application. An ill-timed punch line in a joke ruins it completely. A short, wiry golfer with excellent timing can send the golf ball as far as a hulking brute whose club strikes the ball at an inopportune moment in the arc of the swing. A soup served before or after its time doesn't bring together all the flavors in just the right way. Without timing, music is noise.

The interplay of shih and node respects the fact that all events have a gradual and a sudden aspect. Something that happens suddenly actually occurs as the result of many events over time. A sudden and debilitating spasm in the back seems to emerge from nowhere, but in fact, it arises because of a long series of barely detectable microtraumas. When we analyze a gradual development, we see a chain of discrete events. Good timing—which in Sun Tzu terms represents an appreciation of shih and node—is not a matter of anxiously waiting for the right moment, as if we were ambushers poised to attack. It comes from connecting with the larger picture of events on an ongoing basis and noticing appropriate moments as they arise. This leads to spontaneity, in contrast to a clumsy and contrived application of force. When our "shih is steep," the advantage of momentum and force enables us to allow situations to develop rather than chasing after our goal. And when our "node is short," there is no hesitation to release, act, or let go when the moment of effective action arises.

And finally, the closing lines from the same chapter:

And so one skilled at battle
Seeks it in shih and does not demand it of people.
Thus one can dispense with people and employ shih.

One who uses shih sets people to battle as if rolling trees
*   and rocks.*
As for the nature of trees and rocks—
*   When still, they are at rest.*
*   When agitated, they move.*
*   When square, they stop.*
*   When round, they go.*
Thus the shih of one skilled at setting people to battle is
*   like rolling round rocks from a mountain one thousand*
*   jen high.*

This is shih.

One day, we were talking together about what more to say about shih to make this elusive phenomenon clearer. Just then, water started leaking into the office through the ceiling tiles right above us. When we reached up and removed one of the tiles, we discovered that a pipe had burst at a joint and was spewing a steady stream of water. After someone from building maintenance came and investigated, he told us it was a drain pipe that had accumulated fifteen years' worth of debris. At the moment we were talking about shih, the pipe had finally clogged and burst.

We realized in that moment that "buildup" is occurring around us in all kinds of ways all the time—in natural systems, in organizations, in people, and so on. It may be hidden to us, behind surfaces such as tiles or the expressions on people's faces, but the accumulation of power is there. We can either work with and influence it, just as the bend in the pipe could have been unclogged, or we can be subject to the effects when the buildup is released.

Qualities of Shih

The lines we have just reviewed, as well as others from throughout the text on the same theme, present qualities of shih that can help us understand how it works in the world and how we can work with it. These lines are full of evocative imagery such as water tossing rocks about and drawn crossbows, and provocative statements such as dispensing with people. The images and statements can make it challenging to see how the lines about shih apply to our lives. It will be helpful, then, for us to explore in greater depth the qualities these images point to in order to see what they reveal to us about shih.

Shih is an elusive concept, subtle and profound, and thus often difficult to get a handle on. It can seem abstract and remote, and to apply only to distant scenarios. But shih is about the way the ordinary world works, in ways we see around us all the time. It is something we can learn to work with, and working with it means having a more effective impact on immediate, practical matters in our life.

To keep the practical nature of shih in the forefront of our discussion, we begin our exploration of the qualities of shih by recounting a story. This one was shared with us by a woman—we'll call her Jane—who found the Sun Tzu helpful in dealing with a very difficult transition in her family life. Like the stories in our upcoming chapter on action, here we have an ordinary person who learned to employ shih to handle an apparently impossible situation when nothing else seemed to help. Hearing this story, rich with examples of both turning points and failures, can help us learn about shih, how it works in the world, and how we can come to employ it.

JANE AND HER ELDERLY PARENTS

Jane's parents lived into their nineties, but their last seven years were full of constant physical and psychological health crises. Jane describes this period as one of the most difficult phases of her life. An only child, she lived thousands of miles away from her parents, and she had a busy career and a family of her own to care for. "Whenever I thought the situation was stable, something happened and we were back in crisis mode again," she says. "I really wanted to help, but it was pretty damn hard at times to figure out how to do it."

Her parents weren't making it easy. "They became like my children, yet I couldn't treat them like children: they would lose their dignity, making their life transition that much harder." Jane realized that she couldn't make decisions unilaterally, even when their welfare was at stake. "Any attempt I made to impose even the very best solution was futile. I had to wait until the forces at play—their health, doctors, financial situation, etcetera—were lined up or, if I was really lucky, we could agree on a decision." Jane's frustration with going head to head against "the system" soon brought her to see that she had to acknowledge and work with the forces and dynamics that were already in place.

Jane's parents, like many elderly people, wanted to stay at home. However, this became increasingly worrisome to Jane. They couldn't remember to take their medications and if either one of them had a serious problem, the other wouldn't be able to help. Unfortunately, it was nearly impossible to bring support workers into their home. In order to save money and retain control, Jane's father insisted on hiring unqualified helpers, which resulted in a string of disasters. "For months, I tried to convince my father (mostly by telephone) that home was no longer the best place for them, but he wouldn't hear of it." Then Jane's mother started falling down regularly, and when Jane's father found he could no longer help his wife up he called to say that it was time for her to move into a care facility. Seizing this opportunity, Jane got on a plane within hours. "This was the advantage I had been waiting for. I needed to act immediately so that I could find a good place for my mother before my father changed his mind."

After Jane's mother moved into an assisted-living facility and her care plan was stabilized, the situation with her father became worse. He insisted on driving his car, and Jane would get calls from friends who'd seen him barreling through stop signs. "I tried to get his doctor to tell him he couldn't drive, but it took days just to get his doctor on the telephone, and then she treated me as if I was just a meddling relative." She says that during this period, she had interminable discussions with doctors, nurses, caregivers, and insurance companies but often felt that no one was listening or, worse yet, that she was being lectured to. "At times, they even treated me like an adversary. Unless I could phrase my concern in a way that either made their life easier or fit into their rules and regulations, I got nowhere."

Then one day her father called to say that he was going to have an operation for colon cancer, and he didn't want to come back to the house when it was over. He was finally willing to make a change because he thought he was dying, a fear Jane did little to address even though the doctors told her that her father was unlikely to die from the cancer. She flew out to be with him during his operation, and during his recovery in the hospital, Jane cleared out the family home and sold his car. As soon as he was released from the hospital, Jane moved him into the same facility as her mother, thinking everything would settle down once they were together again.

"While my mother did pretty well in her new home, my father was angry and abusive from day one," Jane reported. "He alienated everyone." Jane was on the phone with the staff constantly dealing with the fallout from his bad behavior, all the while holding her breath hoping it was going to work out. She decided to throw a party for her parents' sixtieth wedding anniversary, wanting to cheer them up and do something nice for their fellow residents, whom her father had alienated. "I sent out a hundred invitations, Jane said, "and people were coming from far away to celebrate my parents one last time." Then, just weeks before the party, the owner called Jane to tell her that they were kicking her parents out, and things were so bad they couldn't wait until after the party. "I was shocked," Jane told us. "But fortunately I had come to know the staff so well over the hours of phone calls about my father that, even though they were annoyed, they convinced the owner to wait." So, while Jane was shopping for party favors she also had to find her parents a new place to live! "We had a wonderful celebration," Jane reported with great relief. The very next day Jane packed her parents up and moved them to the new location. Her father was so relieved to be leaving that she didn't bother to tell him that they actually had been kicked out.

Not long after her parents moved to another group home, Jane's mother died. She continued the struggle from afar to make all the elements of her father's care come together. She says she was just beginning to get the knack of making it all work when he developed a serious respiratory illness and soon thereafter died.

Jane said she learned that caring for elderly parents "is a campaign with its own timing and rules" and that you can't "prevent people from going through it themselves." She added, "When my friends talk to me now about their problems with their parents, I can see how they are so focused on the immediate crisis, as I so often was, that they can't hear anything from me about how looking at the bigger picture can help them with the conflict right in front of them. But as hopeless as it was for me at times, a solution always seemed to open up."

Jane's story is a succession of challenges in a long campaign, rich with multiple subplots, conflicting interests, shifting forces, individual and institutional needs. It has its victories and its frustrations. Her story is familiar to us whether we have cared for aging parents or not, because it expresses challenges common to us and our campaigns. With this story as background, we turn to a review of what the text tells us about the qualities of shih.

Advantage

Advantage refers to any beneficial factor or combination of factors, a favorable position. It is a critical part of the fabric of shih, because it reveals the right moment to act:

> *If it accords with advantage, then act.*
> *If it does not accord with advantage, then stop.*
> [CHAPTER 11]

When one recognizes the smaller, relative advantages that exist in any situation and adjusts their relationship in order to tip the scales toward one's objective, that is employing shih:

Having appraised the advantages, heed them.
Then make them into shih *to aid with the external.*
Shih is governing the balance according to the advantages.
[CHAPTER I]

By paying attention to what is advantageous and orienting yourself to capitalize on those advantages, you bring about a configuration of power—that is, you "make them [the advantages] into *shih*." Facing the eviction of her parents from their assisted-living home, Jane was able to marshal the goodwill she had worked so hard to build with the staff. Even though they felt abused by her father, they came to Jane's aid and convinced the owner to stay the eviction until after the party.

This principle of transforming advantages into shih applies to any type of advantage: physical, psychological, moral, experiential, energetic, or otherwise. And, as ever, the Sun Tzu bases its approach on using native human faculties, since looking for and sensing advantage is something familiar to everyone, particularly to leaders. Paying attention to things as they are in the world, their nature and relationship, enables one to take action that will rearrange existing energies and advantages and tip the balance in one's favor. Then, rather than waiting for your ship to come in or cooking up a master plan in the isolation of one's office, one can align the variety of seemingly discrete events to create a larger advantage.

It is as if one places one weight after another on one side of a beam that is balanced on a fulcrum point. What makes shih such an interesting and rich concept is that, from the view of the world as a whole with ever-changing interdependent parts, not only are the weights of advantage shifting but the very balance point of the beam is ever-changing. Determining the advantages and locating the fulcrum point, which determines how the whole beam will tip, is what "governing the balance according to the advantages" means.

Preponderance

When the weight is amassed on one side, as in the balance example, the result is a rapid falling, a collapse of one end. In the realm of action, such an accumulation of advantage leads to preponderance, a compelling force that influences the direction of all that comes into contact with it. This is the overpowering quality of shih. The text offers several images that convey the sense of building up a victorious preponderance:

How a military comes to prevail, like throwing a grindstone
    against an egg.
[CHAPTER 5]

A victorious military is like weighing a hundredweight
    against a grain.
[CHAPTER 4]

Advantage is relative; it is governed in relation to the situation and bound by time, place, position, and so forth. In the ever-changing world, advantage isn't permanent or static but must be freshly found in the new configurations that arise. Attempting to solidify and hold on to an advantage makes us deaf and dumb to the interplay of events that will give rise to inevitable vulnerabilities that we will have to prepare for. Jane had argued with her father about moving her mother into assisted living to no avail. But at the moment when a number of factors coincided—her mother's increased feebleness and repeated falling, her father's increased inability to help, the ineffectiveness of the low-paid helpers, the increased familiarity with assisted-living options from discussions with Jane—then her father saw the necessity for change and the move happened in a matter of days.

Preponderance, then, has nothing to do with amassing absolute advantage but rather is about the economical accumulation of what is sufficient to outdo or overcome. Amassing more and more can become an obstacle. Trying to be the all-powerful hero can become a weakness. Many an entity—from an individual to an organization to a nation-state—has amassed seemingly awesome power only to find itself surpassed by smaller, faster rivals and upstarts because what had been its advantage has become cumbersome, and thus it has become too slow to respond. Preponderance is when the advantages are amassed just to the tipping point.

Swiftness, Not Prolonging

The ability to move quickly is at the heart of the Sun Tzu and critical to employing shih.

> *It is the nature of the military that swiftness rules.*
> *Ride others' inadequacies.*
> *Go by unexpected ways.*
> *Attack where he has not taken precautions.*
> [CHAPTER 11]

> *Thus in the military one has heard of foolish speed but*
>   *has not observed skillful prolonging.*
> *And there has never been a military prolonging that has*
>   *brought advantage to the state.*
> [CHAPTER 2]

The text does not counsel raw speed alone—moving quickly just for the sake of getting things done sooner. This is "foolish speed," the antithesis of careful attention and knowing. Swiftness is rather being able to move decisively at the critical moment. Such swiftness enables us to capitalize on opportunities available only in the moment. We saw the benefit in Jane's story when she leaped on the opportunity to move her mother into assisted living when her father finally came up with the idea himself.

Further, it can defy the assumed limits of time and space: "Where did they come from?" "How did they get here so fast?" This upsets the other's assessment and plans, attacking the basis of their strategy. Swiftness is flexible and effects surprise, while prolonging expends valuable resources, which negates advantage.

Seeing People in a Larger Context

> *And so one skilled at battle*
> *Seeks it in shih and does not demand it of people.*
> *Thus one can dispense with people and employ shih.*
> [CHAPTER 5]

The text counsels the skilled general to "dispense with people and employ shih," which seems shocking to many in this era when people-centered leadership styles are emphasized. But the Sun Tzu hardly sees people as irrelevant; rather, it tells us that the best way to lead and motivate people is to see them in their larger context. In the same way that the power of the emperor derives from his throne or position, the power of the group in action derives from the configuration of the myriad parts that make it into a whole.

While the people who make up the group are important, to focus on the individual risks losing the momentum of the whole. A single round rock rolls downhill; a group of rolling rocks makes an avalanche. Shih goes beyond the simple fact that round rocks will roll; it is focused on the impact on the environment the rocks will make when they roll down the mountain together. And focusing on that bigger movement is the way to get that group of rocks to roll together. The text is about the power to move the whole, to create the avalanche, and to move the rock as one part of that.

In her campaign to get the best of care for her parents, Jane had to contend with formidable forces in the guise of doctors, nurses, caregivers, administrators, friends, and family members—each with his or her own busy schedules, personal styles, and "job requirements." Trying to get these people to do what she wanted through personal appeal or sheer will power proved to be an ongoing struggle until Jane saw how to capitalize on the bigger forces that shaped their response to her. The assisted-living administrators had to conform to the procedural guidelines of the head office, and the doctors and nurses could only work within the constraints of the health insurance policies.

Looking at the level of a person is like looking at a tree rather than the forest. When you look at the forest, you consider all the trees, their location on the earth, the quality of the soil, the weather patterns, encroaching development, and the practices of the forestry owner. In the context of shih, a person is one part of a greater whole.

The text points to multiplying the power of individuals through the moving of the group, thereby not having your effectiveness blunted by the vagaries of how particular individuals might perform. To "not demand it of people" refers to getting the best out of people not by trying to alter and adjust their basic nature—who they are—but by finding the context in which their greatest strength emerges.

Relying on the Nature of Things, Not Changing Them

> *One who uses shih sets people to battle as if rolling trees and rocks.*
> *As for the nature of trees and rocks—*
> *When still, they are at rest.*
> *When agitated, they move.*
> *When square, they stop.*
> *When round, they go.*
> [CHAPTER 5]

Employing shih requires knowing the nature, energy, and tendencies of things in the world and then cultivating and activating these toward the accomplishment of an objective. It's about taking advantage of the naturally existing patterns rather than ignoring or fighting with them. We have examples of this principle all around us: the damming of a river and controlling the release of the water to create electricity works because water will flow downhill, and when lots of water does it at the same time, it creates a powerful force. There is tremendous energy in the changing, interconnected world, and shih is about engaging a bit of it.

It takes lots of energy to create an alternative to how things are, to "go against it." Our actions so often fail because we feel we have to first change the way people behave and the way things happen. Trying to change things projects a not-so-subtle aggression that gives rise to resistance, which ties up resources and diverts our efforts from the main objective. The action that results from relying on the nature of things is a deft touch rather than an awkward pushing through.

Throughout her parents' last seven years, Jane's overarching objective was to allow them to maintain their dignity in the difficult transition through hospitals, care facilities, and death itself. But as she grew more and more impatient with their stubborn unwillingness to do things that were clearly "for their own good," she found herself becoming the aggressive influence in their lives, and this worried her. Her parents simply could not manage to do more than manifest as aging people frightened of the changes and loss of freedom. Realizing this allowed Jane to have the patience to await moments of opportunity brought on by their inevitable behavior, such as the deterioration of their home life that led to her father's call for help.

Inexhaustible

The ever-changing, interdependent world is an inexhaustible font of options and opportunities. From a seemingly finite number of things, an infinite number of possibilities arises:

> *Musical pitches do not exceed five,*
> *Yet all their variations cannot be heard.*
>
> *Colors do not exceed five,*
> *Yet all their variations cannot be seen.*
>
> *Tastes do not exceed five,*
> *Yet all their variations cannot be tasted.*
> [CHAPTER 5]

The "ten thousand things" are inexhaustible and therefore confer a wealth of resourcefulness. We have a richness of options to work with when we seek to employ shih that lies far beyond the limits of what we can manufacture or dream up. And appreciating this vastness of options serves to continually expand our view of how we can attain victory. It shakes us out of the habit of trying to repeat the solution that fit the last set of circumstances.

Jane was frustrated when every solution she found to stabilize her parents' lives quickly deteriorated into the next crisis. It was relentless. But then she learned how each new crisis brought help with the bigger questions, such as when her father's cancer surgery allowed her to stop his dangerous driving and to move him to the assisted-living home to be with his wife.

The inexhaustible variations and combinations of things ensure that there will always arise another opportunity, another possible configuration that can effect circumstances that bring about victory. Knowing this opens us to seeing the victorious options when they arise.

Employing Shih in the World

The text's injunction to rely on and employ shih addresses the familiar challenge of anyone in a leadership position who finds the inevitable need to take action: how do we interact with the interconnected parts of our world to effect change? In simpler terms, when it comes to taking effective action, how do we actually do it? The first step is to realize the many ways, large and small, that we are already employing shih. Whenever we do something well—from hitting a tennis serve to renovating a home to conducting a negotiation between rivals—we follow some version of this process:

> We look out at a myriad of constantly changing events and begin to see how they connect.
>
> We make a first step by applying a method or practice that takes advantage of the naturally occurring conditions and dynamics.
>
> We help to bring about small alterations that will tilt things more in our favor.
>
> We prepare ourselves to work with what results.
>
> We act, and we begin the process again based on the results.

Take, for example, the mundane activity of learning to hit a tennis serve. You have a flat, hard surface with a restricted area of fair play and a net at a certain height, a small ball that bounces and spins in a certain way, a racket with a sweet spot that projects the ball through the air, the limits of your physical condition and coordination, the teaching style of your instructor, what happened at work earlier that day, the cost of the lesson and how many you can afford, and on and on. All these factors are integrated into your approach to learning the serve. And you take your "action," which then brings feedback with every frustrating failed attempt. You adjust your next action based on what you've learned, fine-tuning also for any changes in the initial conditions, as maybe it has become windier, your wrist is sore, or the tennis balls are worn and have less bounce.

Even in a simple example like this, it's clear that you can't account for all the many variables and how they get integrated. Now think of this same process as it applies to beginning a challenging job with a new company, attending the local school board meeting on a hotly contested topic affecting your daughter's education, attempting to introduce a new product successfully into the marketplace, or commanding your military unit to take a forward position under enemy fire. Employing shih describes the process you go through when you follow the familiar set of activities you engage in when challenged to act effectively.

The Sun Tzu takes this familiar way of working in the world and helps us to improve our effectiveness in employing shih by first seeing the world as whole. With this basic and ongoing orientation to wholeness, we pay close attention to the essence of all the elements we encounter—events, conversations, people's habits, corporate cultures, prejudices, predispositions, and so on—and the patterns they form. Then we are able to benefit from the power, or shih, that emerges from the relationships among all the elements we survey. We can see the timing of critical moments and act. We eat a fruit when it's ripe, not simply because we're hungry.

Employing shih, then, is a journey that begins with broad awareness, which focuses itself into knowledge, which sees timeliness. Working with shih involves the kind of knowing that we described in our discussion of the view, knowing that combines intellect's precision and detail with intuition's ability to grok the essence in an instant.

Shih operates and can be employed at any level of activity or anyplace within a system. In a business, it is at play in how the mail room functions (where a lost courier package could have large implications) as well as how the legal department writes its contracts (where a missed comma can cost millions). At home, it functions in the realm of the refrigerator and the kitchen sink as well as at the level of the mortgage, remodeling, and line of credit. Each part of a system has its weights and measures, but no part is left out of the realm of shih.

Employing shih involves looking closely, to see the rhythms and leverage points of whatever world or system you are interacting with. If you are a surfer trying to ride a wave, you cannot rearrange the ocean currents and wind to suit you, but you can look for the best position within the existing configuration and ride the wave to shore. In the same way, in any objective you choose, the number of details involved will be inordinately complex and the energy of the whole situation will be beyond controlling, but it is still possible to take effective action.

Here shih offers a skillful option. No one can own the power and magic of the world—of heaven and earth, as the text would say it. Indeed, there is no need to control; any attempt to do so is frustrating and counterproductive. Rather, employing shih is about letting things take on a life of their own and trusting that we can find the configuration of power and the moment to release it. This allows us to play along with the world, not push it to conform to our preconceived ideas. Then, its power becomes available, and we can take advantage of the mischievousness of reality. It might seem—as with the celebrated fall of the Berlin Wall or the peaceful transition to postapartheid government in South Africa, where all the details could not be known—that we ended up there as if by magic.

The power of shih is indeed available to us, and since it is a principle of our interconnected world, it can be available to us instinctually, intuitively, even at a prethought level—and it has been many times. The same can be said for many activities—running, eating, thinking, talking, and so on—and yet all of these innate tasks can be done with more skill, elegance, consistency, and effectiveness. They can be enhanced in service of a larger view. We can cultivate our ability to run and become a marathoner, if we so choose. We can cultivate our diet, our ways of thinking methodically, our conversational and public speaking skills. Just so, we can cultivate our employment of shih, and because we are also part of the shih that we encounter, it is possible to cultivate shih itself. It is possible to alter the configuration of power in our lives, in the spheres that we have influence within and are influenced by.

One way that shih shows itself in the natural world is in how the shape and power of water change as it flows through different landforms, ranging from powerful as it rushes through a mountain gorge to gentle as it meanders through the plains and then to quiescent as it sits in a pond on a breezeless day. Similarly, shih moves through an institution, a company, or a group of people just like water, and its flow can be altered in the same way that altering a landform would alter the flow of water. Leadership is about affecting how human energy flows through a group or community, or any such system, and about how that gives rise to power, creativity, and conflict.

When our need to effect change meets with strong resistance or immovability—or simply the inability to see a creative way forward—it can be easy to fall into the despair of powerlessness or cling to the myth of ultimate control. In fact, shih shows us that neither extreme is really how things work. We feel powerless when we are seemingly at the mercy of a monolithic force, unable to find any way to take effective action. But even in these situations, we still can at least shift things, encourage disturbance, and take advantage of opportunities as they arise in the course of change. At the other extreme, we may be confused by the illusion of control, thinking we should be able to bring about our specific goal but find ourselves struggling harder and harder even as our objectives are thwarted one after another. The orientation of employing shih can free us from both extremes and place us in the middle ground, where we can see multiple and shifting reference points that leave openings and opportunities to achieve our goals.

One of the most common leadership impulses, noted in many ways in the Sun Tzu, is to try to achieve victory by "taking the bull by the horns"—that is, by overt force, direct attack, or pushing the situation. Whatever success we can accomplish with that approach comes complete with an array of commonly experienced shortcomings: aggressive responses, depleted resources, warring factionalism, endless repercussions, and escalation. How many times, whether on the world stage in the form of regional ethnic or religious "cleansing" or in our family situation in the form of sibling rivalry, have we seen the pain inflicted on others come back in a more destructive form?

By contrast, employing shih sidesteps the impulse to always take the path of direct confrontation. Instead, one takes advantage of the naturally existing patterns and energies, awaiting the right moment to arise, and then applies a little nudge. It means understanding the elements involved, their natural tendencies and how things work, seeing how things are shaping up, using every opportunity to help things to develop, and then finding the node or moment when the power is ready to be released and a little nudge is all it takes. Rather than always struggling to move upstream, employing shih is being part of the interdependence, where one can make adjustments, gain the advantage of natural momentum, and rely on things as they are.

When we are about to take action—from the mundane situations of our lives to the midst of intense conflict—the first step is to take a moment to recollect the view. All we need here is a quick reminder or flash, like taking a deep breath to gather our energies before plunging into the fray. At this point, view is being activated in practice, mixing with one's way of being in the world, and in practical ways. Remembering it will lead us to effective action.

Wholeness, interconnectedness, and change are not theoretical; they make possibilities.

We focus less on fixed objects and more on processes in trajectory. Things rise, dwell, and pass away; what goes up must come down; spring always follows the winter. The magic of the world is ordinary, not a mystical transformation. And the discontinuous quality that we call change is itself discontinuous; we can't even solidify the interdependence and change. But we can capitalize on it when we need to achieve objectives.

Conflict is the messenger of wholeness and interdependence.

Conflict is not a problem to be squelched or avoided; it holds the promise of a deeper solution. An old tale from Asia about a dog and a lion points out this difference. When a dog gets hit by a rock, it chases after the rock. When a lion gets hit by a rock it chases after the person who threw the rock. We can chase after conflict, as if we could catch it and contain it, or we can see the larger perspective it is inviting us to.

Taking whole is the only enduring solution.

Whatever we do always takes place within the larger framework of the interconnected world, and we must always look to the larger context. Stimulating economic development in order to alleviate political or social problems seems to work—until the resulting environmental damage threatens continued life on the planet. Smaller-minded solutions are not complete victories, and conflict will not subside unless and until there is an approach based on taking whole.

Knowing joins intellect and intuition: counting and connecting deeply.

When knowing becomes both a science and an art, it is possible to employ shih. The myriad details can never be fully counted, but we aspire to know them, and then to go beyond the countable things to know the larger and deeper patterns in the phenomenal world. Then we can "go with" these patterns to apply powerful and effective action, just as seafarers came to know the patterns of winds and ocean currents to chart their way across the vast featureless expanse of the ocean.

Victory can be found.

Victory can be obtained in even the most intractable situation. Our minds remain open and we never give up. How do we know victory? It goes beyond just fulfilling our own goal or thwarting someone else's; it does not leave others focusing on their own defeat. Partial victory—or a victory that is forced when it isn't ready to be found—wastes valuable resources and creates further obstacles.

Reminders for Employing Shih

From a general description of employing shih and how the view of the text becomes more engaged at the practical level, next we offer reminders for when one is actually in the middle of doing it. There's no need to treat these as any kind of system or list of dos and don'ts. They serve more as guidelines that help one to work with the world in a way that fosters employing shih. These reminders do not form a system as much as paint a picture; they are a set of suggestions loosely gathered around a theme, very much like the text is itself structured. They are obviously intertwined and they are presented in an order, but there is no hierarchy among them.

These reminders may well seem familiar; there really is nothing new under the sun. Their value may be in how they come from and reiterate the view of the Sun Tzu and how they work together. There will be much that you already know and do, and we hope this will make clear how close at hand a more skillful employment of shih really is. Based as they are on familiar human abilities and faculties, and on developing character, they can—unlike an adopted strategy—withstand "contact with the enemy."

OPEN AND ENGAGED WHETHER ACTIVE OR INACTIVE

Sometimes employing shih takes place in the foreground, and sometimes it takes place in the background. As events unfold around you, you can be taking part actively, taking part indirectly, or merely soaking things in. Nonetheless, you are part of the interconnectedness, whether you are conscious of it or not.

Being part of the whole means being passionate about contact, open and inquisitive about your surroundings, with an appetite to learn what's there. Such openness requires having a genuine interest in other people for themselves rather than for what they can do for you. At a lower level, this is what we usually call networking, going to a function, meeting, or social event to exchange business cards and turn cocktail hour stories into strategic alliances. But you can achieve this on a grander scale by being open to what's around you during the normal course of your activities in life. Networking is paying attention to the pathways and connections that are self-existing; you are building networks everywhere all the time.

As a wealth of relationships and interconnections inevitably develops, it is as if you are building capital all along the way. There are therefore no casual or irrelevant moments, and you leave no encounters unexplored. All are moments of seeing and learning, or what we have come to call knowing. Then, at some later time when it can be most helpful, the networks are triggered as part of shih, the configuration of power. This activity of openness and connecting differs from simply manipulating others through a series of threats and rewards, because you are driven forward by natural interest in and appreciation for the world.

Engaging with the world can sometimes be a way to confirm your smaller, protected version of things, operating with the naive belief that every encounter confirms your unique role in the center of the perfect world. In this case, being open and engaged helps you to lean into that which disrupts and alters your view. Taking the time to hear and consider the point of view of an irritating colleague who seems to always take issue with your proposals expands your reach. The key to being open and engaged is noting when you grip and tighten, or centralize whatever happens around a smaller reference point that is all about "me."

BOTH PATIENCE AND EXERTION

To employ shih requires a fundamental willingness to work with whatever outcomes arise. Trusting in the process of the interdependent world, you don't need to meddle and intervene at every point to bring about smaller goals, to make things come out your way. You know when to enter and when not to. Instead of fixing every broken thing, it may be more effective to hold your seat and see how the whole system responds to what is broken. Allow situations to ripen. Let the dough rise rather than yanking on the oven door.

Our usual word for this is *patience,* but *patience* can carry the sense of long-suffering forbearance. The kind of patience that allows you to employ shih is not about waiting until you get what you want. It is about suspending a limited, lower-level notion of getting what you want, so you are able to see victory arise in the moment. It's just being, not waiting. It's also called nonaggression, because you are not forcing things to conform to your plan or schedule.

This kind of patience takes a lot of hard work and disciplined attention to what is at hand, what we call exertion. Exertion does not necessarily mean busyness or doing a lot of things. Sometimes exertion may mean remaining attentively in place. In horseback riding, this is referred to as holding your seat. In his book *The Undisciplined Horse,* trainer Ulrik Schramm says, "A poor seat and unfeeling, uneducated handling of the reins will provoke a horse to misbehave as much as harsh punishment or excessive tolerance."[1] Holding one's seat through all the horse's movements takes tremendous exertion, but it is not about "doing something." In the same way, when dealing with someone in trauma who wants to communicate but is unable to do so, holding one's seat is critical. If you act too quickly and talk too much, it can confuse or overwhelm, and shut the person down. The appropriate moment has no chance to arise because you are taking up too much of the space.

Waiting in and of itself—just being—is very hard work, and there are so many temptations not to do it. Waiting for the right moment to act is not the same as avoiding conflict. When we give in to the seduction to fix things and to finalize results, we are clinging to partial solutions, and these only lead to further complications, especially since they often cloud what's really going on.

DON'T AVOID PAIN

The key to employing shih is in the ground between view and action. It resides in a gray zone, the uncertain moment between plan and action, between command and execution. Employing shih requires one to be comfortable with uncertainty, ambiguity, imperfection, and gestation. These are natural parts of the process of employing shih and cannot be avoided. The desire to resolve something is often a masked attempt to avoid pain. It is trying to achieve victory when there is no advantage and no victory ready to arise.

Many teachers and strategists strongly advise you to work with the difficult stuff, with uncertainty and discomfort, to lean into the edges, go where the discomfort is, to enter the space of not knowing. That's where innovation and discovery happen. And that is good advice, but the impulse to avoid pain is so strong a survival mechanism in human beings that even the best advice can become a haven to avoid pain. For example, if you proclaim leaning into the edges to the point that it becomes a rigid orthodoxy, you may avoid the sharp edges of critics who try to point that out to you. You are avoiding pain, just in a more subtle way. In the same way, your language might emphasize "not knowing" as your path, but it has become a bastion of certainty, another way to avoid pain.

Not avoiding pain is not masochism. You do not seek to inflict pain on yourself but rather are willing to live with the pain that arises. Doing so relies on a combination of feeling safe and being daring. Feeling safe isn't about warding off pain but developing a gentle strength and the confidence that you can withstand the challenges that arise in your life. Being daring isn't bold disregard for convention but a quiet willingness to go beyond using every experience to confirm what you already know. More than just thinking, it's about being "outside the envelope." You recognize this experience because it is an uncertain space, a step beyond your hopes and fears, and it hurts a little—and sometimes more than a little.

EVERY SMALL THING

Often when undertaking a campaign, we focus our attention on what seems to be the big, decisive moment, the important thing. Engaged in the foreground, we can lose track of all that takes place in the background. In the heat of battle, however, it is hard to know what will turn out to be the vital detail, the key moment, the pivotal point. Very often there is no single decisive moment that ensures victory in a campaign but rather a series of smaller moments. Some moments are indeed momentous, more important than others. That's the very essence of the node. But we don't know in advance which moments those will be. So we need to pay attention to the details and not let them slip from view in our obsession with the big deal.

In employing shih, each action is one step in a process that changes the ground, reorients the relationship among things, and creates different possibilities. Conflict is usually an expression of stuckness, and cultivating shih involves creating movement by rearranging elements. As soon as one step is taken, it is as important to look out to see new possibilities as it is to look back to see results. An action that seems final or critical can make the next action seem less important, but that next action is no less important from the perspective of taking whole.

Going about achieving our objective by taking one step at a time is something we are very familiar with in general. It is one of the essential elements in all methodology: breaking things down. It's how we deal with large projects. If we need to remove a stand of small trees, we pull each one out. If they're large trees, we cut the branches of each tree, then the trunk, then we pull out the roots. If we want to preserve a solid brick wall, we take it down brick by brick rather than demolishing it whole. Shih applies this simple understanding more broadly and to great effect.

Martin Gardner, *Scientific American*'s Mathematical Games columnist for many years, left a legacy to researchers, teachers, and entertainers, according to Edward Rothstein, writing in the *New York Times:* "Don't try to understand the whole world at once. Take only a small part of it." By examining small parts, you can make big discoveries. Origami, the Japanese art of folding single, uncut sheets of paper into beautiful figures, once offered only about one hundred designs. A mathematician inspired by Gardner's legacy points out that once mathematicians looked at the challenge more closely, they produced over thirty thousand designs. By studying the details, they unlocked worlds of possibility. Trying to make a figure of a tarantula from a single piece of paper could seem baffling or impossible, but by looking carefully at all the small elements, magically one can be made. "That magic," Rothstein wrote, "is produced when one begins to see a baffling puzzle from a different perspective: what once seemed impenetrable suddenly becomes transparent."[2] Creative solutions arise from many small steps and details that make the magical lightbulb moment possible.

Patience is critical in attending to small matters and details. Sometimes we feel so overwhelmed by the multiplicity of important moments, we are driven to simplify by sorting our reality according to what seems important and what seems irrelevant—even though we have no way of knowing in advance which will be which! This can often lead us to miss the critical moment when it arises. When you find yourself exhausted with the plethora of details, it is helpful to remember that you are only ever really dealing with one thing at a time.

You can see the forest *and* the trees. Big effects are made up of many tiny antecedents, each of which has contributed to the outcome, some in an obvious, discernible way and some by altering the shape of things. If you can keep these little things in play, then you are better able to capitalize on them if they grow to be significant and crucial. The ability to employ shih could be described as the ability to take advantage of the convergence of the smaller movements that make up the whole. This starts with recognizing the importance of every small thing.

ALWAYS THINK BIGGER, IN BOTH TIME AND SPACE

Always think bigger doesn't mean you can solve your problem by imagining you are bigger than you actually are. However, the stuckness you experience as obstacle and conflict is often the result of not seeing the larger environment around whatever is happening. Missing critical points, and sometimes obvious solutions, can be the result of having too narrow a focus. The antidote to that is to allow your mind to become bigger. A bigger mind leads to a bigger view, which gives rise to unusual solutions.

Thinking bigger takes place in the dimensions of both space and time. We commonly think bigger in time, as when we look at historical antecedents to better understand current events. Such perspective can give meaning to contemporary events that is otherwise dangerously absent. A narrow view of time can not only ignore history but also cause you to think you must take action sooner than need be. Panic, "running out of time," can propel you to make decisions and act when the situation is not yet ripe or advantage is not clearly available.

Thinking bigger in terms of space means literally looking above and beyond the immediate conflict or problem at all the elements of the larger environment—the ground, its conditions, all the people connected to it. Each element in a situation has its own ever-changing constellation of relationships, each is interconnected with the others, and all have some impact on your situation.

The encouragement to think bigger is not meant, though, to serve as an excuse for not respecting the integrity of whatever is at hand, as if it were empty of meaning or unimportant and the "bigger picture" were all that matters. Rather, thinking bigger means respecting every aspect of the situation while simultaneously looking at the larger environment within which it takes place. Like the lion who goes after the thrower of the rock rather than the rock, you get closer to the causes and conditions rather than chasing the surface manifestations.

BOTH LINEAR *AND* IN ALL DIRECTIONS SIMULTANEOUSLY

You can understand—through what you are told and through your observations—that the world is whole, interconnected, and interdependent; that one thing arises due to another; and that whatever happens affects all directions simultaneously. You might have the occasional experience that goes beyond the theoretical and gives you simple and direct insight into the multifaceted nature of reality. However, more often than not, you might fall prey to thinking that things occur in a linear fashion, as if you were trying to walk a straight line in a sobriety test.

Often, however, the way to shape a situation is not by linear progression from where you begin to where you hope to end up. Actions that shape the ground and bring about favorable conditions can be counterintuitive to the goal you envision at the outset. If, for example, you would like to enter into a long-term strategic partnership with someone, common sense might suggest that you wine and dine the person, to try to become friends, thinking that friendship is the best path to partnership. However, strong bonds can often be the result of a difficult experience. In the right setting, challenge and provocation may be a better way to test the mettle of the would-be partner and to find out how he or she might handle the difficult situations that will surely arise in a partnership. This approach may be less safe in the short term, but it encompasses many more possibilities and in the long run may be more powerful.

Nonlinear connections among things can sometimes reach what we could call the collaboration of extremes: the ends of seeming opposing groups or enemies are sustained by the same act or set of conditions. Some have argued that this was the case with the neoconservative end of the political spectrum in the United States and al Qaeda. Similarly, creative solutions can arise when collaboration occurs across completely unrelated disciplines or when distant analogies lead to new ideas, such as when a heart surgeon takes inspiration from an architect or a graphic designer, or when mathematical solutions for origami puzzles fuel research on the best solar panel designs for spacecraft for deep-space exploration.

Often the path to discovering a solution to a thorny problem does proceed in a linear way, with exertion reaching the level of struggle to find a breakthrough. Straight lines do serve a purpose, but often a breakthrough arises not on the next obvious linear step along the known path but when the exhaustion of the habitual mental processes produces a gap and new ground opens up.

NOT TOO LOOSE, NOT TOO TIGHT

A successful campaign begins with intense planning and preparation; the images of the naive expert and the idiot savant are charming, but they are hardly a proven model for success. Letting things hang completely loose awaiting a successful outcome is usually wishful thinking. Effective leadership requires forming a clear vision of your goal and holding it firmly while moving forward. But it is helpful to keep in mind that there are many ways to reach a goal and you may well see your objectives realized in a manner that you never could have prefigured. It may be counterintuitive and often difficult to learn, but gripping your plan too hard may result in a weaker hold.

When employing shih to accomplish an objective, you are required to loosen your grip on smaller objectives while at the same time opening up to a bigger view, which includes allowing even your most cherished and hard-won views to be open to change and disintegration. It is not as simple as abandoning the former in favor of the latter. Both must be held in mind, firmly yet loosely, like a baby's grip on your finger, the model for how to properly hold a golf club or samurai sword. This allows a creative tension, holding open the space between one's vision and the reality of a situation until a resolution arises from the ever-shifting ground. Curiously, this is strikingly similar to how quantum mechanics describes working with reality: shih is about plucking victories out of the realm of possible results in much the same way that quantum physics describes a scientist pulling particular results out of the matrix of possible outcomes.

IF YOU CAN'T GET DESTINATION, GO FOR DIRECTION

Leading involves proceeding *forward,* the name given to the direction in which you are naturally oriented, and when you lead, you are giving shape—in the form of a goal or an objective—to what lies ahead for those you are leading. It is as if you are setting the destination that your group is traveling to. At the outset, this destination is a summation of all your knowledge and best judgment, an expression of the final result of your efforts. It's where you want to get to, based on what you can see from your current location.

But with each step we take, our very movement changes our relationship to the destination. We are constantly challenged to learn new possibilities and pathways to our destination and, indeed, in some cases to adjust our destination. It is knowing—continually observing the changing landscape—that provides us with the means to adjust, to feel the new possibilities.

At times, then, when the destination may seem very elusive, distant, completely out of reach, or invisible, it may be best to simply work in a general direction, to maintain movement. Eastern European dissidents in the seventies and eighties who had seen crackdowns in Czechoslovakia, Hungary, and Poland could not fully imagine their final destination, but they decided to move forward in the general direction of behaving as *if* they were free and the regimes' hold on them did not matter. At such times, movement in a general direction changes the ground. As that occurs, we must be prepared to ask: what is the new pathway to the objective? Or even, has our objective changed?

If it's true that we live in a world that is whole and interdependent, then every action we take changes our relationship to everything else, or can change it. We are always entering new ground, which makes things possible that were not possible before. As accomplished negotiators and mediators know, when things are stuck, it's often simple movement rather than reaching a specific destination that provides the stepping-stone to effective action.

Dangers When Employing Shih

Employing shih to attain an objective is a powerful way of working with the world, but it's also not without its dangers. We may imagine that having a big view and high ideals entitles us to success. But when we carve off a section of the world to bring about advantage—which working with shih requires us to do—we open ourselves completely to the ways of the world, where success is never guaranteed. As we have pointed out, one corollary of seeing the world as whole, interconnected, and ever-changing is that it is also fundamentally uncontrollable and unpredictable. Thus, employing shih can, in fact, lead to greater chaos and conflict. Deeply considering the pitfalls of employing shih, being more aware of what is and is not likely to occur, can contribute to greater effectiveness.

Employing shih is not as simple as an easily repeatable trick or a habitual response. The Sun Tzu counsels us to cultivate the practice of employing shih in order to work with our world more effectively, and this will naturally result in familiar, repeated patterns of behavior. But employing these strategies in an effective and timely way always requires being attuned to a different, emerging scenario. As the text warns us, victories are not "known in advance." Each moment, each configuration of forces, is unique and requires a fresh response.

Thinking that cultivating the use of shih encourages a predictable, habitual response is one of the very traps the text warns against. Predictable patterns of behavior, no matter how profound, are limited in their ability to deal with changing ground. While our overall practice might form a recognizable pattern, employing shih does not rely on a particular repeatable act but is always in relation to the changing circumstances. So even the indirect approach—the way of employing shih that the text is most famous for—can emerge in a given moment as direct, forceful action.

It would be shortsighted to either dismiss shih or employ it solely as a means of controlling one's environment. The notion of "controlling" one's environment perpetuates a sense of separation and thus comes out of a very different worldview than that of the Sun Tzu. As we have presented, employing shih relies on the view that one is not separate from but rather a part of the interconnected whole. With the knowledge that outcomes aren't certain or controllable, employing shih in the attempt to control one's environment is sure to lead to frustration and likely will produce greater conflict and chaos.

Employing shih—indeed, the entire approach of the Sun Tzu— does not appeal to some people because it feels too much like manipulating from a self-centered reference point. While it may seem more comfortable to respond solely to what occurs naturally rather than through conscious effort and intent, in an interconnected world our actions always contribute to what's going on "out there," either passively or actively. We "manipulate" the moment we walk into a room. Assessing the whole of things need not be self-centered and self-conscious, but rather environmentally conscious—conscious of everything and our place within it. Acting on that assessment need not be ham-handed manipulation. And as we saw from the text, employing shih relies on becoming part of and responding to the nature of things on their own terms rather than changing them into something they are not.

It must be acknowledged, though, that carving off smaller chunks of the interconnected whole to bring advantage can work to accomplish small-minded objectives. Knowing patterns and capitalizing on them—seeing round rocks and rolling them downhill—works the same for narrow goals as it does for attaining genuine victory. All the levers and activators that the text presents to employ shih can be used to fulfill goals that are entirely self-centered, capitalizing on interrelatedness but with no appreciation for the bigger implications.

However, the by-product of this approach is resistance, a force that grows greater with every small victory, and the tension from that increasing resistance will surely perpetuate further conflict. Coal-fired power plants may reduce dependence on dwindling oil reserves but accelerate the negative impact of global warming. Gross domestic product (GDP) accounting may measure the economic activity of a society but doesn't include full natural resource accounting or assess a society's well-being and stability in the same way as something like the genuine progress indicator (GPI), which measures the actual effects economic activities have on quality of life. From the point of view of taking whole, using shih to achieve small-minded victories is short-term success and a pathway to continued conflict.

Mao Tse-tung, famously a student of Sun Tzu, won control of China and ruled it mightily for twenty-seven years through repeated artifice and misdirection of the Russians, his fellow communists, and his Nationalist adversaries. Yet he never came close to achieving his real objective—to become a ruler whose methods were repeated throughout the entire world—in a large part because his paranoiac style of rule at home gained him no lasting advantage abroad, once the fear of his various threats evaporated. At home, he amassed so many enemies by ruling through subjugating and starving the populace (seventy million Chinese died during his reign) and purging his political enemies that even before his death, the legacy of his rule was being erased. Twenty-seven years of short-term victories left a nation starved, in tatters, and heading in a direction that was decidedly un-Maoist.

Another common misconception is that you can successfully employ shih by imposing a strict logical cohesion between your view and the practices that follow from it. For example, if you hold the view that stealing is wrong, then one possible practice that could follow from that is that you should train your children to use handguns in order to shoot thieves who attempt to steal from you. But such strict logical cohesion is too narrow. Life doesn't fit into such neatly packaged intellectual solutions. Practices and actions artificially forced to coincide with a view can undermine the very heart of that view. Effectively employing shih comes from seeing and appreciating things as they are rather than forcing them into consistency.

Summary and Examples

The Sun Tzu presents a profound approach to working with conflict and chaos in all facets of human life, and the key to understanding the text's strategic practice is shih. Rich and complex in meaning, shih is the way that a particular configuration of forces in the world can focus power effectively and accomplish an objective. We can isolate a piece of this interconnected whole and work with it by making small alterations so that things come out a certain way. This is most effectively done by taking advantage of what is naturally occurring and can be as simple as one little thing over here affecting one little thing over there. It is a powerful way of working with the phenomenal world to bring about an environment conducive to victory.

If the presence of such a powerful way of working with the world has not been obvious to us before, it's because we were looking from the wrong perspective. Now, however, the view of the world as whole and interconnected is so widespread—proclaimed by former presidents, religious leaders, CEOs, as well as scientists and poets—it can allow us to see and understand the nature of things at a deeper level. This makes it possible to see shih, the configuration of power that is a natural part of interconnectedness, at play in the world. Seeing it, we can possibly employ it ourselves. Our use of shih begins with appreciating the ground of a situation and knowing the nature of things in themselves and how they will act under certain conditions in that situation. By not attempting to impose a particular outcome upon a given situation, we allow things to move and change in their own way. We do not see ourselves as an outside force seeking to control.

Our role as a leader in employing shih is as just one element in the whole, interconnected world. And as part of the whole, we are affected by the changing reality, and in turn, our gestures continue the process of change. We always look at the bigger environment, and so our actions are not limited by our focus on our objective. We are open to the creative options that arise in the midst of the situation, and so we can see how to encourage a new configuration of forces.

The great nature photographer Ansel Adams, famous for his stunning photographs of the terrain around California's Yosemite Valley, was once asked how he captured the magic and vividness of this place when his work often pictured such mundane elements as a hiker's boot washed up among the rocks in a dry riverbed. Adams explained that if you are walking along the riverbed with care and a keen eye and see a shoe lying there, you can capture the magical quality of that moment in a photo. If, on the other hand, you kick a shoe to place it among those same rocks, that photo will never turn out to have the same impact. Leading through control and manipulation is using a kicked shoe. Shih is the art of seeing and employing the found shoe.

Employing shih means keeping options open and making adjustments as the ground changes and new possibilities emerge. We may be willing to give up a specific goal in favor of moving things forward, because we are also thinking about how things might look two or three steps beyond our near-term objective. Our actions are determined not solely by what seems required to attain our goals but by the energies at play among things, how these energies can be activated to change the ground, and how that new arrangement can bring about movement toward our bigger objective—without conflict and engendering further obstacles. Employing shih is about seeing possibilities and trusting rather than seeing solutions and imposing.

In employing shih, the manner and style in which the goal is achieved sow the seeds for the next cycle. Often the most vulnerable point in the process is the moment when we have seemingly achieved our goal, and it is important to see what promises and dangers are inherent in that moment. The momentum of our current focused effort can be the opposite of what is required as the situation changes. The Cold War era, for example, shaped a bilateral fixation between the two great superpowers that propelled a certain view about the United States' role in the world. Then, at the moment when the USSR disintegrated as a world power—a time that seemed ripe with possibility—the United States' reliance on being the world's unrivaled superpower ill suited it to becoming a leader of grand coalitions. It was therefore unprepared to respond effectively to the new threats and challenges. Instead of breathing the air of victory and new possibility following the achievement of its long-sought aim, the country was perhaps more vulnerable than before.

Using our framework of view, practice, and action, let's review an example of how employing shih fits into an approach to effective action. In this example, we will draw a strong contrast between the common leadership style often referred to as command and control (C&C) and a style that more fully acknowledges employing shih.

While it would seem that we are criticizing the effectiveness of C&C to make our point here, clearly there are times when C&C is the most effective approach. An example is any situation that is not complex, has a predictable outcome, and where everyone agrees on what needs to be done, such as delivering supplies quickly into the middle of an area hit by a tsunami or hurricane. Leadership styles are not *good* or *bad* based on different worldviews, but they are *more* or *less effective* depending upon how they fit with the nature of the problems they seek to address. C&C is at times an important component of an overall response based upon employing shih.

The *view* of the command-and-control approach is that intelligence and decision making are centralized. Depending on the reference point, the intelligence resides in "me," "my brain," "my group," "headquarters," and so forth. The *practice* of command and control is based on managing change and assumes a reasonable degree of predictability and control. In this approach, while change may not be regarded as predictable, managing the response to it is. Therefore, the *action* of command and control is based on training, communication, and repeatable procedures. Effective action moves from the center out, or from the top down, through the system. In this approach, a leader measures success or failure by whether his or her initiative effectively addresses the problem as perceived and evaluated by the centralized intelligence.

In contrast, consider a style described as "disturb, not direct" (DND). In this approach, the view is that intelligence is distributed throughout the system. In a world that is whole, interrelated, and changing, there is intelligence in every situation that can be provoked and activated. Rather than directing a specific, repeatable procedure, practice in this model involves ways of disturbing the system. And action, then, gives the system's intelligence room to respond on the spot. In a complex, intelligent system in the midst of constant change, this response is more effective than whatever a centralized intelligence could impose. In this model, leaders capitalize on new ideas that arise from the fringes of the system that often exceed what those at the center could envision. It's not that training and procedure are overthrown; it's simply that practices and actions are not constrained by having to follow controlled, repeatable pathways. Training can be transcended, which is the end point of any real training.

In an excellent example of DND, we are familiar with a travel agency operating in multiple locations across a number of states that wins awards for the best-managed company. Declaring the familiar motto of "excellent customer service" as its top priority, the executive team of this company gives employees with direct customer contact the mandate to solve their client's problems in whatever way will continue to keep the customer satisfied. The executive team first established a situation that allows customer dissatisfaction to "disturb" its system and then turns its attention to figuring out how to fit the employees' creative solutions into the company's economic model.

In approaching customer service in this way, the leadership is trusting in the intelligence of the company's employees and the reasonability of the vast majority of its customers. Contrast this example with the typical telephone conversation with a customer service representative where the management-imposed hierarchy of responses to a complaint leaves the customers frustrated and the service reps feeling like pawns of their managers ("I'm sorry, sir. We are not allowed to do that").

A more sobering example comes to us from the latest developments in modern warfare. Military experts regard *The Art of War* as the world's central text on asymmetric warfare. Broadly speaking, asymmetric warfare refers to the indirect approach to battle normally associated with the Asian traditions as opposed to the force-on-force style of battle that characterizes warfare in the West. Because the practice of asymmetric warfare has become such a prominent and thorny issue in recent times, military theorists have put a lot of effort into coming up with a more quantifiable definition. Though the discussion is still in progress, one approach suggests that asymmetric warfare is characterized by two main features. The first feature is the inequality in size between the two sides, characterized by the "big actor" being at least five to ten times the size of the "small actor." The second feature is more technical, described as "the transformational use of familiar and unfamiliar capability clusters."

This second part of this definition seems at first glance a bit complicated, but it's the kind of thing you see all the time. When you're a smaller force, you need to find extraordinary ways to combat the material and manpower superiority of your larger enemy. You make do with the things you have and use whatever you can get hold of. Military weapons are employed in unusual ways (bombs used against civilian rather than military targets), and you use things that aren't normally considered military weapons at all (suicide bombers).

Here we have another reason why the Sun Tzu is so relevant for our times. Asymmetric warfare has become increasingly the norm in military and political conflict over the past fifty years. More and more, the world's large military powers use industrial-age hierarchies and massive force against much smaller, more loosely organized, and sometimes barely identifiable opponents who use unusual methods of combat. And, according to research spanning the last two centuries, evidence indicates that the "small actor" is winning these wars with greater and greater frequency.[3] Asymmetric warfare is a main feature of modern conflict all over the world, we don't seem to understand it very well, and the Sun Tzu is the bible on it.

But the relevance of asymmetric warfare isn't limited to military battle. Bonnie Bassler, associate professor of molecular biology at Princeton University, has been doing some very interesting research on communication in bacteria in recent years. For the longest time, bacteria had been regarded as the lowest form in the life chain—one whose only interest was in replicating itself. However, as the active force behind illnesses ranging from the bubonic plague to stomach cancer to Lyme disease, bacteria are also among our most fearsome enemies. Bassler's work with bacteria has turned up some excellent examples of shih in the natural world and perhaps some hints about how the lessons of the Sun Tzu apply more broadly than just the field of military conflict.

Bassler's research began with a type of squid that has the ability to change its color to protect itself from predators when feeding in dangerous waters. It turns out that this function is provided by a community of bacteria that live inside the squid! They work together to change the squid's color at just the right moment. A key to their effectiveness is that the bacteria seem to communicate well enough to know when they have reached a critical mass. The question for Bassler became, How do they know?

The answer she and her colleagues came up with was that bacteria aren't such stupid things. They have a language. They're social beings; they network. Who knew?

Bassler and her colleagues dubbed this communication "quorum sensing." It describes the ability of bacteria to await the moment when they've amassed effective power before they unleash their virulence, which makes them more effective, and more dangerous. Sound familiar? This is a perfect description of shih and node. It turns out that bacteria in our bodies seem to act much the same as the bacteria in the squid: when there are only a few of them, they lie low because they seem to know that our immune system will obliterate them. But they have the means to communicate with each other, to know when they've got the quorum to do the job, and to find the most effective moment to attack. As Bassler herself put it, "These guys [bacteria] know self and other, friend and foe, and have been doing biological warfare for over a million years."[4]

For the past hundred years, we've considered bacteria "stupid," and for the past fifty years, we've attacked them massively with a blunt instrument called antibiotics. After some notable successes, recent evidence shows that bacteria have used that time to learn how to protect themselves against this type of carpet bombing, and now our doctor has to be much more careful in the use of antibiotics when we take our sick child to the clinic.

Bassler's lesson has profound implications for the war against disease. To overcome the limitations of treating bacteria-borne diseases with antibiotics, she's learning how bacteria communicate in order to find a more effective method. The new direction in fighting bacteria may involve getting inside the communication system and messing up the messages the bacteria send to each another. This is a fine turn of events in "the transformational use of familiar and unfamiliar capability clusters."

Before we turn to our exploration of the central practices the Sun Tzu presents for employing shih, we have one more example about working with the world in this way. This story is about an administrator in an international NGO, a man we'll call Tom, who found *The Art of War*—especially the notion of shih—helpful in his work. In this instance, we couple his story with lines about shih from the text in order to help make the connection more directly. This pairing of lines and story follows the format we employ in chapter 6, where we use stories to convey how some have been inspired by the Sun Tzu to find effective action. These lines, which we saw earlier in our discussion of the qualities of shih, show that shih is not about whipping things into shape or inspiring heroism but about taking advantage of the natural power that exists in the situation to shape the ground and achieve our objective.

And so one skilled at battle
Seeks it in shih and does not demand it of people.
Thus one can dispense with people and employ shih.
[CHAPTER 5]

TOM AND "HIS TEAM"

Tom is the international program coordinator for a large nonprofit organization. His job involves managing a group of regional leaders stationed around the world, and his department operates within a tight budget. On good days, he views these challenges as requiring "creative solutions." On bad days, he just wants to give up completely. "I have a temper. I'm also very impatient. But I am motivated by a big vision that people seem inspired by, and I put a lot of energy behind it, which is why I suppose I was given this job."

Over time, several of the regional heads became friends with Tom, while others developed more prickly relationships with him. One person in particular was unerringly confrontational, constantly arguing with him and questioning his ideas. "A few times, I blew my stack," Tom says. "Our mission indirectly involves peace issues, so that approach got me into some trouble, and factions started to develop."

Some of Tom's "friends" in the organization began to shift their loyalties, and the situation became so uncomfortable that Tom started to hate his job. He considered quitting or getting some therapy to deal with his anger. In the end, he decided to turn to the Sun Tzu. "When I first read *The Art of War,* I was very excited by the ideas," he said, "but I had no real success in applying them. The notion of shih was pretty tough to understand, not to mention to use. I wanted to be told in simple terms what to do."

Nevertheless, he persisted in exploring the dynamics of shih in his organization. "Little by little, I began to see how power and energy were held by my group of regional leaders." Tom had been operating on the assumption that the regional leaders should function like members of a united "team." He expected them to embrace his ideas, rally together, and act like one big, happy family.

"Then it dawned on me: By continually trying to make this group into a team, I was, as it says in *The Art of War,* "demanding it of people" rather than looking at the configuration of the whole dynamic. I don't need to make this group into a team. My staff and I work as a team, but the regional heads are more like a council of tribal elders. Each of them is a leader in his own right and doesn't want to just be part of someone else's team. Like tribal elders, they each represent their people; they have a relationship with their own people that has to be respected. I can't just ask them all to drop that and become part of my team. Besides, their strength comes from their position within their own group."

When Tom began to view the situation in this way, his approach to working with conflict changed. "Strong disagreements, rather than being challenges to my power, became opportunities to see things in a bigger way." He says appreciating shih "made more energy available." Rather than struggling to create a team, he could now focus his energies on accomplishing his larger objectives.

"I stopped gravitating toward my pals and avoiding my adversaries. In some ways, I had less control but, strangely, more power.

I have much more to learn about working with shih, but just this first glimpse made a huge difference."

Shih, and how to employ it in your life, is a complex matter. It is not possible to easily define it, or to teach you to use it through logical argument. We have painted a picture of shih by talking about it from a number of different perspectives, which we hope has given you some idea of what it is, how it occurs in the world, and how you could employ it.

On the basis of this general notion of shih, we can now deepen and fill out our understanding of it by considering the strategic practices from the text that extend shih and give it practical meaning. Extraordinary and orthodox, forming and transforming, deception—these are chief among the powerful practices the Sun Tzu presents as the way to work with the world by employing shih, and this is where our exploration takes us next.

5

Strategic Practices
The Many Forms of Employing Shih

strat·e·gy n.   1.a. The science and art of using all the
forces of a nation to execute approved plans as effectively
as possible during peace or war. **b.** The science and art of
military command as applied to the overall planning and
conduct of large-scale combat operations. . . .
French *stratégie,* from Greek *stratēgiā,* office of a general,
from *stratēgos,* general. See stratagem.

—American Heritage Dictionary, *4th edition*

IF WE APPLY the Sun Tzu in all the spheres of life, we
can rewrite the definition of strategy. We could substitute *person*
for *nation, leadership* for *command,* and *campaigns in life* for
combat operations. Then, strategy becomes a concern for all of
us—during peace and war. We can all engage in "the science and
art of using all the forces" at our disposal.

As we have seen, "all the forces" can be summed up as "shih,"
the configuration of energy available to anyone who can tune into
it. Employing shih can take many forms and arise spontaneously
when we pay close attention to the configuration that surrounds us
and that we are part of. We see potential energies and notice how
we might interact with them and affect their flow to achieve our
objective.

If the story ended here, however, it would leave far too much to
chance. We could operate entirely intuitively and hope to employ
shih effectively on the spot as each encounter presents itself. That

kind of approach has its merits, but the Sun Tzu offers more. It offers an array of strategic practices—highly refined and honed from centuries of use—that help to ensure that our employment of shih suits the specific conditions in any given campaign.

Just as employing shih involves breaking the big interconnected world down into smaller parts, so does the Sun Tzu break shih down into specific strategic practices. In this chapter, we treat six of them, the three central practices in depth and three other important ones in summary form. There are more, but these six are some of the most important in the Sun Tzu. As we study them, we also begin to see patterns that are evident in all the strategic practices the text presents for working with shih.

As with all practices, the strategic practices of shih outlined here help train us to focus our energy in effective ways. Familiarizing ourselves with the extraordinary and the orthodox, deception, and forming and transforming gives us practical handles and means of working with the sometimes overwhelming power of shih. These are "strategic" practices, which involve methods and ways of being, rather than "tactical" practices, which are ways of ordering actions to fulfill strategy. One can take a tactical approach alone to working with chaos and conflict. "Never speak first in a negotiation," "Be the first to arrive," "Always consult before deciding"—these and thousands more are examples of tactical practices, actions that have worked in some situations in the past. They can be very helpful and one can keep a pocketful of them, or a briefcaseful of them, but tactics by their very nature are more limited than strategies. It's hard to keep track of them all, and hard to figure out which one applies when.

A strategic practice, by contrast, is the birthplace of many actions and many tactics, and since they arise from a deep understanding of method they don't need to be spelled out and written down. As we train ourselves in practices at the strategic level, we find a point where all of these practices agree. They all reinforce a way of being in the world that is resourceful and tirelessly inquisitive rather than complacent, satisfied with more limited forms of victory. The school superintendent, for example, had an abundance of tactics at his disposal, but most of them had exhausted their usefulness. What he wanted to learn was how to work at a deeper level with the tough challenges he faced, which only comes from applying strategic practices.

Extraordinary and Orthodox

The multitude of the three armies can be made to meet all
enemies without defeat.
It is the extraordinary and the orthodox.
[CHAPTER 5]

The intertwined pair of the orthodox and extraordinary is possibly the most profound of the strategic practices the Sun Tzu offers as a means to employ shih and attain victory. Introduced in the opening section of the chapter on shih in the text, it is presented as the way to be victorious in every battle. The other strategic practices the text presents for employing shih, such as forming and transforming, which we will talk about next, work in one way or another with the elements of the ground or environment. Employing the orthodox and extraordinary is working directly with other people's perception of the world. Here the message is clear: for victory, the battle is joined at the level of mind. And the instructions for doing this are direct and concise:

In sum, when in battle,
Use the orthodox to engage.
Use the extraordinary to attain victory.
[CHAPTER 5]

Throughout our discussion, we have touched upon the importance of intention and focus when employing shih: we separate out some part of the whole, interconnected world and work with it to effect change and accomplish our objective. Engaging is the critical point in this process—the encounter is joined, the commitment made. This moment is focused, not casual anymore. We are no longer at a remove, ignoring, observing, pondering, fretting, or speculating. We are in direct contact. In military terms, we are beginning to do battle. In everyday terms, this could be as simple as saying "Hello. How are you?" Whether we are hooked into conflict by emotions beyond our control or we consciously decide to effect change in order to attain our goal, engaging is the point when we have agreed to participate, to become fully enmeshed.

The Orthodox

At the critical and often messy stage of engaging, the text gives us a single tool to employ: the orthodox. It is, most simply, that which the other—the one you are engaging with—finds familiar, expected, and understandable, the commonplaces and the common ground that we share. Etymologically, *ortho-* means "straight" or "upright," and *dox* refers to thinking or belief; therefore, it has the sense of the agreed-upon or established faith. It is the common, or *ordinary* (as opposed to extraordinary), a word whose root originally described a row of threads in a loom, something in a proper pattern, orderly. The orthodox or the ordinary is always what the other expects, a routine or habitual gesture, a ritual or method faithfully followed, or the path most easily taken.

Using the orthodox to engage fulfills some important objectives that have to do with why and when we engage. Engagement may be forced upon us, as when all other options have been exhausted, or we may feel the need to engage to keep a situation from escalating. In any case, engaging is the point when we've decided to extend our intention into the world. We move forward with our objective, and we meet resistance, which ranges from inertia to outright opposition. The first effect of engaging with the orthodox is to cause the other to take a position, to organize around our gesture, and thus become fixed in space and time. Doing so reveals their strengths and weaknesses, their points of vulnerability and concentration. This allows us to know more about them, which is a critical step along the pathway to victory, as we know from our discussion of the view.

The benefits of engaging the opposition in order to fix their position is well illustrated in a story told about how writer and urban activist Jane Jacobs fought the massively powerful "urban renewer"

Robert Moses's plan to put expressways through Manhattan in the 1960s. Moses had succeeded in forcing through the Cross-Bronx expressway and several other roadways in the face of neighborhood opposition up to that point. While the strength that Jacobs brought in opposing Moses's remaking of New York City neighborhoods was her unique ability to articulate why human-scale space was what people wanted in a city, she was also savvy in her use of the media.

At one point, as the story is told, she and her colleagues learned of an expressway plan before the city was prepared to make it public and used the common tool of a press conference to accuse the city of planning to ruin some of the most beautiful and valuable property in the city. The ensuing public outrage forced the city to deny this plan, effectively killing any further consideration of this option. Engaging with the orthodox—the common tool of the press conference that Robert Moses himself would have used—forced the opposition to fix their position and limit their future options. Some say that Jacobs's efforts, particularly in stopping the Lower Manhattan Expressway through Greenwich Village, was the beginning of the end of Moses's reign.

Engaging with the orthodox also has the effect of creating a sense of comfort and predictability in the other, lulling them into relaxation by confirming their expectations. We can thus calm what is turbulent and clear the ground for further action. If we cannot engage the other, they may continue to elude us, allowing no ground for victorious action.

The Extraordinary

Inevitably, our goal is victory, the achievement of our objective, and the way to victory in the Sun Tzu is the extraordinary. Most simply, the extraordinary is whatever is outside of the expected order of things. Working with the enemy's perception of the world, we take a step that the other can't imagine, something outside or beyond what is usual. The extraordinary can sometimes emerge from expanding beyond the limitations of the routine or the ritual. You start out in Kansas, but suddenly you are not in Kansas anymore.

Because the extraordinary action is no longer connected to any prescribed, proscribed, or expected activity, it is free and creative. It also lies beyond the realm of safety and predictability. There is no single approach or answer to reside in. It is not a particular action; it is simply something that the enemy does not expect. The very fact that it is not a specific action drawn from a stock of ready-made responses is what makes it unexpected.

Using the extraordinary action to attain victory becomes possible when we think bigger, noticing what is outside the current frame of reference or just beneath the level of our current focus, as we discussed. Since such actions are not clearly tied to any concrete stratagem, they can seem like magic, yet they are not conjured. Like a shaft of sunlight suddenly emerging through the mist, such an act is striking but not artificial. In allowing the extraordinary to emerge, we let go of being the strategizer, puppeteer, and controller. Because we are not looking so hard for what we want to see, we see what others cannot. It often requires that we loosen the grip of the common reference points—hope and fear, gain and loss, praise and blame—that limit our options and govern the conventional notion of victory.

The extraordinary can seem like magic, except when magic is what everyone is looking for. The power of the extraordinary comes from what happens to our mind when it encounters that which is outside its expected range—not usual, normal, or customary. When things don't fit into the expected patterns, they perplex and arrest us. The extraordinary can also be thought of as the eccentric, that which is off center. If we always operate in terms of our central headquarters, fresh perceptions cannot emerge. The travel agents in our earlier example, free of the constrictions of specific procedures from the head office, turned customer service into a gateway to help their customers rather than a barrier to frustrate them, and thus built loyalty and repeat business. If we allow things to emerge away from the center, on the fringes, something new and striking and victorious can occur.

The extraordinary often emerges like the quality of a good sense of humor, with a feeling of discovery about the way something catches us by surprise, reveals something we didn't think of, and causes an irrepressible physical reaction. Seeing the humor of things in the midst of the tension and intensity of engagement allows our focus to be loose and relaxed, so extraordinary opportunities present themselves to us like the shock of ice-cold water hitting our face first thing in the morning.

This connection between humor and the extraordinary is illustrated in a story about a young father on summer vacation with his wife and two young children. He was about to cross from New Jersey into New York on the George Washington Bridge, which has upper and lower decks. He found himself in the lanes leading to the lower deck, but at the last minute, he decided he would rather be on the upper deck, which seemed to have a lot fewer cars, so he quickly crossed several lanes of traffic and began to head across a small berm into the lanes leading to the other deck.

At that point, a siren sounded, and he was pulled over by a New Jersey state policeman. The officer went through the usual drill at the window, looked around at the passengers in the car, and then in a somewhat unexpected move asked the driver to get out and summoned him to join him at the front of the car. The policeman, about five feet eight inches tall and very crisply attired, looked up into the eyes of the six-foot three-inch father dressed in a Hawaiian shirt and baggy shorts. He asked him, "Would you like the ticket or the ass chew?"

Nonplussed, the father suppressed laughter and replied sheepishly in an almost questioning tone, "I'll take the ass chew," whereupon the officer put his face right up under the driver's chin and began the most intense, military-style dressing-down imaginable, saying, "You disgust me. How can you call yourself a father when you would risk the lives of your family to pull a stunt like that? Do you see those trucks passing by? Look at them!"

The driver replied, "Yes, officer."

"Only scum like you would want to see your wife and children chewed up under the wheels of one of those trucks."

"Yes, officer."

"You are without a doubt the stupidest big man I have ever seen. Is there only shit filling up that big head of yours? Now, are you ever going to try something like that again?"

"No, officer."

The dressing-down continued in this vein for about five minutes until the officer said, "Now, get out of my sight before I have to be sick!"

Shaken, and ashamed of his thoughtlessness, the father returned to the car and the puzzled looks of his family, who had seen but not heard. Had he been given a ticket, he would have grumbled, paid it, and dismissed the incident as an inevitable brush with authority. As a result of the ass chew, he could never take such a thoughtless risk behind the wheel without recalling the drill sergeant–cum–police officer's warning of the dangers to himself and his family.

It was certainly not the officer's first ass chew and probably not his last. Its impact was not because the officer was aggressive, for that was merely for effect, a practiced deception. But it was not rote; it was spontaneously applied to this situation and this family. And the driver did not expect either the intensity or the humor surrounding the encounter. What began as a routine stop by a policeman turned into something extraordinary that changed his habit pattern.

Extraordinary and Orthodox Working Together

The Sun Tzu makes it very clear that if we want to attain victory, we must use the extraordinary. But the extraordinary can only come about in relation to the orthodox. No act is necessarily orthodox or extraordinary in and of itself. What is extraordinary is only extraordinary in relation to what is orthodox in the particular set of circumstances we face, and vice versa. It is the nature of the orthodox and extraordinary to be intertwined, and their power arises from how they work together.

It is the interplay, then, between the orthodox and extraordinary that provides the pathway through conflict and chaos to victory. The text first describes this interplay by using the elements and the natural world to convey to us its special qualities—boundless, inexhaustible, unending, and cyclic:

> *And so one skilled at giving rise to the extraordinary—*
> *As boundless as heaven and earth,*
> *As inexhaustible as the Yellow River and the ocean.*

Ending and beginning again,
It is the sun and the moon.

Dying and then being born,
It is the four seasons.
[CHAPTER 5]

Here once again the text evokes powerful images from the way the world around us works and how we experience it in order to suggest how we ourselves can take effective action. In this case, each image conveys that the starting and ending points are inseparable, that each can take place anywhere along a continuum, and how one can easily become the other. And just as nature surprises with extraordinary events that emerge from within its predictable patterns, so can we.

Like the waxing and waning moon and the cycle of the seasons, the acts that come to be described as orthodox and extraordinary are not two things that oppose or contrast with each other; the extraordinary is not the antidote to the orthodox. Rather, they are, like the Möbius strip or an M. C. Escher painting, a curious continuity that requires us to stretch our normal range of perception to experience it. When the extraordinary arises to achieve victory, it soon becomes incorporated and understood, and thus turns into the orthodox. The most common and orthodox of acts can totally surprise, if the other is awaiting a wild and extreme gesture. At times, Miles Davis walked off the stage, with his horn slung over his shoulder, before a set had finished, while the other players continued playing. Rather than waiting for the usual rapturous ovation and applause, he just vanished. It was a simple move, but extraordinary.

The vast, interconnected, and ever-changing world is complex, and while each situation and configuration we encounter is new, there are patterns that emerge. These patterns are the consistency of what we see, the familiar way things hang together, the characteristics of style and method in phenomena. Each father driving his family recklessly into harm's way is unique, and yet all have features in common that enable a police officer to effectively engage each family and make an impact. The patterns that make up the way we see are the orthodox and thus set the stage for discovering the extraordinary.

In employing the orthodox and extraordinary to work effectively with the world, seeing the deep patterning reduces the complexity to something we can get a handle on. In *Patterns of Home,* a follow-up to the landmark text on the fundamentals of design *A Pattern Language,* the authors talk about the power of patterns as "tools that we count on to help us through a new experience, and they can become so familiar and natural that we use them intuitively, no longer having to think before we act."[1] We can write volumes without repeating a single sentence, and yet each sentence contains a subject and a predicate. Ancient rhetoricians developed the notion of *topoi* (from places—by extension, places to find things), recognizing that in constructing a presentation out of the vast possibilities, building a work around familiar topics makes it easier for the writer and reader to share a common ground of understanding.

As the text goes on to elaborate on the interplay between the orthodox and extraordinary, it shows how working with patterns as the orthodox is not just about making the world small but about how to discover the infinite options for action through working closely with the limited number of things:

> *Musical pitches do not exceed five,*
> *Yet all their variations cannot be heard.*
>
> *Colors do not exceed five,*
> *Yet all their variations cannot be seen.*
>
> *Tastes do not exceed five,*
> *Yet all their variations cannot be tasted.*
>
> *The* shih *of battle do not exceed the extraordinary*
>   *and the orthodox,*
> *Yet all their variations cannot be exhausted.*
> [CHAPTER 5]

Here the Sun Tzu treats the vast and complex world as workable without diminishing its vastness and power. The multiplicity of the world—its manyness, as it were—is accessible through the limited number of options available to us in every engagement. This both makes the complex world manageable in the midst of the seemingly overwhelming confusion and chaos we often experience, and gives us the powerful tools we need to take effective action and attain victory.

Orthodox and extraordinary are only two, but just as in the analogy of the tastes, colors, and pitches, the number of their manifestations is inexhaustible. We do not need to keep an enormous storehouse of tricks on hand in order to "respond from the inexhaustible" but only see how one effective action to engage turns into another effective action to attain victory. And we have experience of how they change into each other—how what is extraordinary at one time (instantaneous electronic communications in the late seventies, for example) becomes orthodox (the age of ubiquitous e-mail and instant messaging that began in the late nineties). If every police stop ended in an ass chew, the ass chew would transform into the orthodox, and the extraordinary would need to emerge from another direction. When we go beyond applying a particular learned response, we can give rise to the action that brings victory in the unique formation of the moment.

> *The extraordinary and the orthodox circle and*
> *give birth to each other,*
> *As a circle has no beginning.*
> *Who is able to exhaust it?*
> [CHAPTER 5]

Finding the Extraordinary

We can all identify the orthodox, that which is the ordinary, the expected, the patterns that we see. But finding and using the extraordinary is elusive and somewhat mysterious. It isn't about mere unpredictability, acting randomly for randomness' sake, or guesswork, taking wild stabs and seeing what happens. We've all experienced how those approaches are hit-or-miss at best and more often than not create greater chaos and confusion, leaving us further from our goal. What is it, then, that helps us find the extraordinary action that makes victory attainable?

If we want to find something outside of the ordinary pattern of things, we've got to look in a new way or look in places we don't usually look, often both. Another story from the mystic-fool Nasruddin illustrates a frequent stumbling block in searching for the extraordinary:

A group of people came upon Nasruddin one night crawling around on his hands and knees under a lamppost.

"What are you looking for?" they asked him.

"I've lost the key to my house," he replied.

They all got down to help him look, but after a fruitless time of searching, someone thought to ask him where he had lost the key in the first place.

"In that dark alley over there," Nasruddin answered.

"Then why are you looking under the lamppost?" he is asked.

"Because there is more light here," Nasruddin replied.

So often we search for the key to unlock effective action in the places familiar to us, the "well-lit" areas where the looking is easiest. But we understand from our earlier discussion that the extraordinary arises from the eccentric. In fact, an alternative English word for the Chinese character we translated as "extraordinary" is "the strange." This points us in the direction of the foreign, the unfamiliar, to the uncertainty of the unknown.

We aren't easily attracted to the strange; in fact, we deeply resist going into it, which makes cultivating and employing it difficult. Yet the rewards for doing so are becoming evident in some interesting places. As we noted in chapter 3, research in medicine and science has long focused on the larger data sets, the "normal" things that happen most often. Many researchers, however, are now receiving funding for studying the occurrences on the fringes, the aberrations, the things that don't fit in, because many now believe that that's where the important clues are hiding. In his bestselling book, *The Black Swan: The Impact of the Highly Improbable,* Nassim Nicholas Taleb celebrates the strange by pointing out that we so often err in our planning and strategy by focusing so heavily on the predictable and by underestimating the power of the outlier, the sudden odd occurrence. No matter how many swans we have seen, we still cannot say that "all swans are white." Appreciating the strange means being willing to stray and wander into what Taleb calls "the unread books in the library."[2]

The last century opened with a worldview in the West marked by confidence in objective knowledge and the promise of scientific certainty based on Newtonian physics. Then came Einstein's general theory of relativity, Heisenberg's uncertainty principle, and quantum theory. When researchers set up experiments to see if light was made of particles, the answer came back yes. When they set up experiments to see if light was wavelike, the answer also came back yes. Strange. Complexity and chaos theory began to show just how big and how connected things were, and still we couldn't predict exactly how something would turn out. And recently researchers announced evidence that, in fact, contrary to what our mothers said, some things can actually be in two places at the same time. Very strange.

It is hard to find and use the strange and be comfortable with the uncertain. When we encounter something different that challenges our current perception, we tend to reprocess it until it fits in. A classic description of this reprocessing comes to us from those in the Buddhist tradition studying the nature of mind. They report that our view colors our perception to such a large degree that it dictates our thoughts so that they support our view, and we get caught in a vicious cycle of confirming what we already know. This insight is echoed by the neuroscientists we discussed previously, whose research shows how persistent top-down processing is, how intensively the brain imposes meaning on the external image coming into the brain as light upon our retinas. It's just very hard for us to take in new information, to see and apprehend the strange, we might say. Even when we focus our minds, we miss something that's right in front of us.

Even worse is how we tend to distort perception through groupthink—whereby no one is willing to share with the group anything he or she sees that lies outside what the group holds to be true—and with calamitous consequences. NASA went through several tragic disasters as a result of this phenomenon. Some military and government leaders have pointed out a pernicious form of groupthink they call "incestuous amplification." It occurs when a group of people share a view so deeply that they believe something more strongly in the group than any of the individuals would believe on their own.

Former senator Bob Graham pointed out the dangers of this in a Senate speech on the topic of intelligence reform in the United States: "The only people who were at the table are people who have the same point of view. Their views are then vetted through people who again share the same beliefs. As a result, the original conclusion is not only validated, it is amplified. After the attacks of September 11, the intelligence community was accused of failing to connect the dots. Incestuous amplification is unlikely to either connect the dots or expand the number of dots which are visible."[3]

If we are going to do a better job of connecting the dots in our lives, we need to see more dots. We have to find a way to see more clearly, beyond the limitations of how our minds habitually distort our perception of things. In fact, this sort of clarity is familiar to us as part of being human. It's the more open quality of mind that occurs in an experience of extreme danger or profound relaxation, speeding down a steep ski slope or watching as the sun sets lazily into the ocean amid a blazing red sky.

We talked about this ordinary state of mind in our discussion of knowing in chapter 2 as the contemplative approach, which helps us to suspend the habitual frameworks we tend to impose on our experience. Here contemplation doesn't mean controlling your mind with an iron will or performing mental gymnastics. Rather, it's about how discipline and exertion can produce a certain combination of openness and focus apparent in the skillful gestures of the potter, the martial artist, the jet fighter pilot, or the musician. The space provided by the contemplative approach is where the "eureka!" moment comes from. It allows us to access a deeper well of intelligence and creativity and to make deep connections between things.

This openness of mind breaks the pattern of self-confirming thoughts and allows us to see. In fact, many prominent educators are saying this is how we need to teach children to prepare them for the kind of very challenging and uncertain world we live in. Educator Tobin Hart refers to the contemplative as "a third way of knowing that complements the rational and the sensory." Quantum physicist Arthur Zajonc, who promotes a form of contemplative learning drawn from the work of Goethe, says that "knowledge, from the point of view of any contemplative tradition, is not primarily object-oriented. It is epiphany- or insight-oriented. It's not good enough to know *about* reality; you need to change how you see reality."[4]

The contemplative approach has the effect of interrupting the orthodox chain of thought, allowing us to see the strange, the phenomenon or the occurrence we have not been led to suspect. Again, it comes about from not holding on too tight, like the soft but commanding grip on a tennis racket or golf club. Consider what happens if you use a flashlight while walking on a pathway at night in the country: it brings illumination to the path, but it heightens the contrast and therefore makes it much harder to see what might be lurking in the woods. In attaining victory, both the focus and what is outside the focus are included. The orthodox is the shining light; the extraordinary, the eccentric, the strange, the source of victory, is discovered at the edges.

We do not find victory by looking in the expected places or by attempting to repeat the victories of the past. In applying the Sun Tzu, victory cannot be *made*, but it can be *found*. And we can find it by cultivating what lurks outside our accustomed frame of reference: the strange.

Forming and Transforming

Forming and transforming is a vital pair of strategic practices in the Sun Tzu, and each is a powerful practice in and of itself. In learning to practice them, we cultivate an important means of employing shih. Forming is the particular shape we give to ourselves and our world. Transforming is the way that shape changes in relation to the conditions in the world, and most particularly in relation to our objective and the obstacles that might lie in our path. In the final battle in the 1991 war in Iraq, U.S. troops amassed for a final assault along the border, then sent a rapid flanking movement to avoid the enemy's entrenched position and avoid casualties from direct confrontation. Seasoned negotiators may take a hard line initially in order to soften and become more "friendly" and workable as discussions go on. Forming and transforming is another way of creating the orthodox and discovering the extraordinary.

Forming and transforming is a natural extension of the view of the text: if we are a part of this whole, interdependent, and constantly changing world, then how we take our place in it will affect the larger world. We are, in fact, forming and transforming things all the time; these strategic practices don't start with manipulating something "out there." Our basic being, how we are and how we interact with everything around us, is the basis of working with our world in this way. The text makes clear that we start the process of forming and transforming by working with ourselves, creating the victorious conditions first in ourselves in order to foster victory in our campaign:

> *Of old the skilled first made themselves invincible to await the enemy's vincibility.*
>
> *Invincibility lies in oneself.*
> *Vincibility lies in the enemy.*
>
> *Thus the skilled can make themselves invincible.*
> *They cannot cause the enemy's vincibility.*
>
> *Thus it is said, "Victory can be known. It cannot be made."*
> [CHAPTER 4]

The text's emphasis on starting with oneself is also a doorway into understanding its passages on the importance of taking a strong defensive position ("invincibility lies in oneself"). But the strategic practices of forming and transforming are not about creating invincibility by building a solidified invulnerable fortress. They are a powerful way of shaping any situation so that the very nature of our engagement with "the enemy"—which we usually think about in limiting terms such as when, where, or whether to do battle—can be transformed into a victorious ground, where achieving our goal no longer requires battle at all.

Forming

The simplest elements of our existence give rise to the skill of forming. How we conduct ourselves and interact with others communicates so much to the world around us. We can feel how a person's view or state of mind pervades the atmosphere. That's why the text presents knowing oneself as the first step and why we emphasize the importance of character, as in the quote from General Schwarzkopf we discussed earlier.

Another dimension of one's own form, of "character," is conveyed by the word *presence,* the quality of being fully present and connected to the world in a way that brings effectiveness and confidence. Presence can have a significant impact in ordinary times, but it brings even greater benefit in the midst of the more extreme conditions that the practices from the Sun Tzu are most helpful for. Like a military commander in battle or a teacher in a chaotic classroom, anyone able to hold her composure and perspective in the middle of chaos—to absorb the energy, integrate, and hold it while others might be freaking out—communicates confidence and strength to those around her.

Extending to the world, then, becomes a natural gesture of interdependence:

> *One skilled at moving the enemy*
> *Forms and the enemy must follow,*
> *Offers and the enemy must take.*
> [CHAPTER 5]

From here, forming is any gesture of extending into space, starting with the simple arrangement of things in your world. How you set up your work space, what chair you sit in for a meeting, what food and drinks you serve, the air and the lighting, how you begin a meeting, the moment you choose to shift the course of a discussion—all these have impact. On a slightly larger level, the position you take on a critical issue will shape the decision-making options for your colleagues and coworkers. These kinds of strategic actions can contribute to creating victorious environments.

In shaping the ground, big ideas and grand pronouncements are often less important than seemingly insignificant gestures. Think of a speed bump placed in a quiet neighborhood to slow down cars trying to circumvent rush-hour traffic. The form and structure of a situation shape the energy around it. They organize the ground of any situation while allowing the content of that situation to manifest in various ways. Freeway interchanges direct speeding commuters headed to different destinations through a series of lane mergers, on- and off-ramps, bypasses, and overheads with remarkable safety. Forming the ground can sort out all that takes place within, providing a balance between accommodation and boundary.

Forming is most effective when it includes the perspective of the whole, paying attention to all the factors likely to affect a situation. A farmer pays attention to the details of climate, terrain, soil, seed, labor force, and market affecting his operation. If you are working with growing things, then with the right mix of air, heat, water, and earth, the seed can take root and flourish. If those aren't balanced properly, it may not matter what else you do.

Since forming is a way of working with shih, it emerges from the same basic view and expresses the same qualities. For example, a powerful quality of forming is how it can project a message that is indirect and environmental rather than direct and confrontational, which has several advantages. An indirect and environmental message invites others to read and understand the ground of the situation for themselves, which can provoke a learning experience, resulting in a more likely pathway to lasting change. Arthur Zajonc, the physicist and educator mentioned earlier, says that to expose students to what is most profound, he "can't just give it to [them] at the beginning. I can't just put it on the board." Rather, he invites them to observe and inquire, and as they "move from one observation to the next, they develop the capacity to see more and more deeply." And how others respond to what you show them can also reveal much about their view, furthering your ability to know the other. This approach is a hallmark of the path of "disturb, not direct."

Another important element in forming, and one consistent with the approach of employing shih, is how effective it can be when you need to express your view of the "truth" or reality about a situation, which we sometimes call "giving feedback." When you need to make such a statement, it is often more powerful to do so by implication rather than proclamation. When the "reality" of a situation is expressed in the environment, it becomes a more powerful message and gets beyond the battleground of my truth versus your truth. Declaring what is "right" or "true" serves primarily nowadays to mark battle lines, as evidenced by most media reporting and political debates. Asking a gently probing question or simply allowing space in a conversation can bring about an insight, or even a mutual discovery, that slips past fortified defenses. While declaring our view of reality effectively is a challenge, we are required to do it much of the time. The text's teaching on forming once again leads us to a way of doing it more consciously and skillfully.

An example of forming came to us in a story about a scenario occurring in many towns across North America. It's a story about a city councilor whose neighborhood became a battleground that pitted students, landlords, the university, and local homeowners against one another. The university's enrollment and housing policies resulted in an increase in the number of students seeking off-campus housing in what had been family neighborhoods around the university. A "perfect storm" unfolded whereby the rental housing owners used loopholes in the city's zoning policies to create rooming houses, the students were forced to pay rapidly rising rents for increasingly subpar housing, and the resident homeowners were finding that the noise and garbage levels were seriously diminishing the quality of life in neighborhoods they had spent lots of money to live in. While the easy responses to counteract this trend included increasing police patrols and fining the students, these did not deter the landlords from setting up more substandard rooming houses. It was not possible to affect the landlords' behavior simply by punishing the students.

The councilor took the unusual and politically dangerous step of pushing through a bylaw that assessed fines on the landlords for infractions committed by their tenants. This immediately brought the wrath of the landlords upon the councilor's office and jeopardized her reelection. However, it also had the effect of getting their attention, of bringing them to the table to take part in the discussions, something they had previously refused to do. She then was able to show them that their responsible behavior would strengthen rather than threaten their rental business; as a result, subsequent fall move-in seasons have been successively more quiet. She formed the ground by an action outside of the habitual self-interested approach of protecting her political future. Her act of forming brought the others to meaningful discussion and achieved a result no one would have imagined possible at the outset.

The notion of "reform" can be an act of forming things in a new way, just as the name implies, rather than directly attacking the preexisting rules and norms. Vermont, like many states with aging populations, realized that its nursing homes were "an outdated model," in the words of Patrick Flood, commissioner of the state's Department of Disabilities, Aging and Independent Living, at the time when Vermont began to rethink care for the elderly. "We are never going to build another nursing home," he said. Instead, Vermont began offering to pay family members to care for indigent aged in their homes as an alternative to a nursing home. Not only did this fulfill Vermonters' desires to keep their families together, but the state calculated that home-care costs were over 30 percent less. Vermont's example inspired the federal government to begin offering grants to states to develop Vermont-like programs.[5]

We have many such examples in our lives and in the world around us, experiences of forming that we might otherwise call "thinking outside the box" or "nonlinear solutions." The profound practices of the Sun Tzu are based on human faculties and skills that are not foreign to us. Studying the text helps put those skills into a coherent framework—in this case, ways of employing shih—that supports consistently effective action.

THE CONTAINER PRINCIPLE

One powerful way of describing the practice of forming self and other is the metaphor of the container, or what we've come to call "the container principle."[6] A container serves to hold something, either something of value we want to protect or something we want to limit the spread of. The container, as we define it, forms the environment for that thing by establishing boundaries and points of entry and exit, which we call gateways. (Container is another way of talking about the mandala principle we discussed earlier.) The boundary—most often the walls or the sides of the container—provides the obstacle, the resistance, the hard part, the "no." And the gateways have the quality of openness and vulnerability, the soft part, the "yes." An effective container is made up of the right relationship of boundary and gateway. The boundary or barrier is definite, but the gateway makes the container permeable.

Our lives are filled with examples of the container principle. Our houses or apartments are containers, not only for people and goods but also for the energy and activity that go on there. It's a commonplace that how a person's home is set up says a lot about him or her and says a lot about how we will feel when we are there. In some homes, we walk on eggs. In others, we feel we ought to just plop down anywhere. And in still others, we would like to leave as soon as possible. Temples, cathedrals, legislative chambers, museums, and myriad other public spaces are all intended to inspire a particular frame of mind and sense of reverence—and egress and ingress are carefully guarded. Offices, cubicles, and work spaces of all kinds heavily influence the activity that occurs within, as can be seen by looking at pictures of office spaces from different eras. As we move from the physical, the container principle can also be seen at work in societal norms, government laws, treaties, and rules of engagement, which shape our behavior in the same way that mountain slopes shape the flow of water forming streams and rivers.

In experiences that are all too common, such as facing a critical meeting at work or having to deliver a difficult message to a teenage child, we are so focused on the impending conflict that we don't think about how the container or meeting environment can aid us in our task. Yet we can feel the difference between a formal meeting across the boss's desk and coffee at the local café. We're familiar with the limits of screaming about homework over the chaos and noise called family mealtime. Events and their environment—the container and its contents—are intimately interconnected, and missing how the environment affects the outcome loses a definite advantage of employing shih.

The container principle, or forming generally, isn't just about creating boundaries to ward off or keep undesirable elements out but to provide structured and controlled access for that which is to enter. Therefore, the relationship of boundary to opening, of wall to gateway, is critical. Together they create a pattern that allows for energy to flow from the inside to the outside and back in again.

By providing boundary and gateway, the container shapes the contents and establishes an orientation. For our purposes, the "contents" would be the people and environment in any situation we are faced with. The container serves to project our view or message into the environment and extends toward our objective. For example, imagine the effect of one of the earth's great places—say, looking down from the rim of the Grand Canyon—as contrasted to walking into a modern fast-food restaurant. In the case of the Grand Canyon, the container evokes the experience of something magical and wondrous and opens our mind to possibilities. Entering the fast-food palace conveys something else.

The impact of forming in this way can be either to accommodate or to intensify experience, both of which can help to sort out chaos and clarify the ground. Accommodation in this case doesn't necessarily mean comfort and ease, as sometimes an open ground can bring confusion and claustrophobia. An effective container can function like a pressure cooker, which employs a harsh environment to produce a gentle, processed outcome. Basic training in the military, medical school, and other kinds of environments for training people to serve in dangerous, chaotic situations provide this kind of intensified container. An apprenticeship for an art or a trade can be a container that balances intensification and accommodation, since it is intended to not only train in technique but also foster discovery and creativity.

Transforming

If forming is a natural extension of the reality of our world's being whole and interdependent, then transforming is a natural extension of the reality of change.

> *Now the form of the military is like water.*
> *Water in its movement avoids the high and hastens to*
>   *the low.*
> *The military in its victory avoids the solid and strikes*
>   *the empty.*
> *Thus water determines its movement in accordance with*
>   *the earth.*
> *The military determines victory in accordance with the*
>   *enemy.*
> *The military is without fixed shih and without lasting form.*
>
> *To be able to transform with the enemy is what is meant*
>   *by "spiritlike."*
> [CHAPTER 6]

The whole interdependent and changing world continues to change, and to attain our objective we must continue to change and transform ourselves in relation to it. We can't allow ourselves to get stuck in the ground we've shaped. Transforming relies on the nature of things rather than on changing them, which is again one of the basic qualities of shih that we learned about in chapter 4. Water seeks the low; the military strikes the empty. And how we transform is always determined in relationship to the goal we seek and the obstacles to achieving it. There is no lasting form: no matter what worked in the past, another way of forming may be called for now. Even the specific means of employing shih that were effective last time will not necessarily work for us now.

While transforming, we always maintain an orientation toward our objective. In terms of the Sun Tzu, this begins with a definite aim or direction, but perhaps not necessarily a solidified, specific objective. Of the astronomical number of nursing homes in America, not all will have their problems solved by the "Vermont solution." Solving the Vermont nursing home crisis is about satisfying the needs of the elderly and their families in Vermont, with its unique combination of social, political, and economic realities. California will surely be different. So victory is about finding a solution, not about installing any particular solution no matter how successful it has been elsewhere. No matter how fantastically brilliant or successful the plan that got you where you are, holding on to it can become a liability if it doesn't continue to reflect reality as the ground continues to change.

Loosening the grip on a specific, known solution allows space for transforming. Then, multiple options or solutions can arise, for both ourselves and others. And the text tells us that transforming renders you "spiritlike"—untouchable, not graspable or solid, and thus not able to be attacked. By holding firmly yet loosely to the aim, we give the chaos and uncertainty the space to sort themselves out, and insights beyond what we might expect—like the strange we talked about in our discussion of orthodox and extraordinary—can arise more readily.

A Case Study of Forming and Transforming

One example of forming and transforming comes to us from recent trends in the software application industry. This is a story about salesforce.com, the company we discussed in general terms in our example of how view, practice, and action work together. Its product is the on-demand, or Web-based, access to business software applications, an approach that we contrasted to the enterprise, or software-sold-in-a-box, approach, which requires version control, platform uniformity, IT departments, and upgrading.

Salesforce.com started in business by trying to convince both big and small companies to use its Web-based customer relationship database software for a monthly user fee rather than purchasing it from their regular vendor as proprietary software from disks or download and installing it on their own computers. Marketing on-demand solutions was not an entirely new idea. Others had tried it before and failed, but salesforce.com thought itself uniquely positioned and well prepared to make this business a success.

In the early phases of its launch, salesforce.com's efforts were met with the usual resistance in the marketplace as it tried to establish a new business proposition. As the company began to demonstrate the value of its on-demand solutions, the marketplace's initial reaction of skepticism to outright criticism softened and turned into interest and modest acceptance. Throughout this entire phase, the multibillion-dollar companies leading the field of enterprise software criticized both the business model of on-demand solutions and salesforce.com's ability to carry it out successfully. The Web was far too unreliable and insecure, these big companies argued, for any company to trust putting its valuable data somewhere other than on its own servers, which is what the on-demand solution requires. And, they added, salesforce.com was too small to provide the complete and reliable business solutions that their own enterprise software had long provided to this market that they controlled.

Salesforce.com began to grow rapidly. A major break came after just a few years, when it earned first the respect and then the business of a number of large, influential financial institutions. Not only were these important clients in themselves, but they also represented an important economic sector notable for not wanting to have their data on outside systems. Still, the large enterprise companies continued to criticize the on-demand approach, responding to salesforce .com's proclamations of business success and increased market share by going on record in public forums and magazine articles to argue that on-demand was simply not a good choice and repeating all the reasons that their enterprise software was better. Meanwhile, the business press was confirming salesforce.com as the pioneer in this emerging and promising new field, and the business world was confirming salesforce.com as a company to contend with, noting its rapid sales growth and increasing stock value.

Then, around the time salesforce.com's sales approached $500 million and were projected to reach $1 billion within a few years, the big competitors flinched. They decided that this market was important to them, and so they changed direction and publicly announced that they would be aggressively entering the on-demand market-place. They announced that they would be offering their customers a choice of either the Web-access or enterprise software option. This announcement put them in an awkward position. The business model had been proved by a smaller competitor, and they became late entrants to a market that they had spent the previous six years telling everyone was neither reliable nor a good business choice.

Salesforce.com successfully formed the ground. It entered into a relatively uncontested market—what the Sun Tzu calls "unpeopled ground"—with a new model and business proposition. The company grew rapidly, solidified its position among industry experts as the market leader, and proved both the value of the market for on-demand access to software and its ability to exploit that market. All the while, it played the role of upstart and provocateur, publicly proclaiming its victories and market advances against competitors fifty times its size, and in so doing provoked those companies into making very public statements criticizing the wisdom and viability of on-demand. Then, when these much larger players were compelled to enter this valuable new market, they had the disadvantage of having to promote themselves against the momentum of their own negative statements about the product they were now trying to sell. In addition, the on-demand and enterprise software markets require different sales approaches and internal systems. This means that the bigger competitors' decision to offer both options split their efforts, creating an additional competitive disadvantage as they tried to play catch-up in the on-demand sector.

Now, since these enterprise companies were at the time still fifteen to twenty times the size of salesforce.com, they had the resources and expertise to enter this market and quickly threaten or even overcome salesforce.com's predominance in this field. This scenario has played out many times in the dot-com industries. A young upstart company grows quickly and establishes early business success while being ignored by the big boys, only to later be bought out or eclipsed by them. Anyone remember when a Web browser by the name of Netscape was all the rage?

At this stage of development, the challenge for salesforce.com becomes how to transform itself in order to maintain its competitive advantage. While it gained success by playing the role of pioneer and irreverent upstart, and grew rapidly by moving through an open ground, the focused competition from the industry giants seriously changes the ground. Salesforce.com can now transform itself from upstart outsider to consolidate its hard-won position as industry leader. The effect of such a move would be to strengthen customer confidence and once again shape the ground so that its competitors would have to continue to respond to salesforce.com rather than shaping the field for themselves. If salesforce.com clings to the same upstart mentality that served it so well during the earlier phase, the market's perception of the company as the industry leader might very well be undermined and its options for future success diminished.

We use this example not as an argument in support of any particular approach to software or business solutions; we are not privy to the inside story, nor are we experts in this field. But it is an excellent example of forming and transforming, something that we experience in our lives all the time. For example, we might employ a particular approach intended to shape the ground for our teenage son—say, attempting to encourage a sense of responsibility by requiring that he complete his household chores before taking the family car. But then, once he displays the ability to take responsibility for his world, continuing to apply these initial ground rules might seem punitive and undermine the dynamic of trust and mutual respect that has been achieved. The ground has changed, and a new approach is called for.

A simple, everyday example of transforming comes from the world of the grade school classroom. To make the chaos of a third-grade classroom workable, a good teacher has to consistently create and maintain a container for learning, to form the maelstrom of energies flying around the room into a learning environment. Naturally, this involves a relatively high degree of control, but as educator Richard Brown points out, this control can become an obstacle in class discussion. "As teachers, we can hold on too tightly to our idea of having a successful classroom, and in asking students to share their thoughts, we can subtly try to control them." Brown teaches a "three-second wait" technique that asks teachers to wait three seconds before calling on someone. Inevitably, more hands go up. After calling on someone and hearing his or her response, they are asked to wait an additional three seconds before commenting. In that short period of time, Brown says, teachers can transform into listeners, or learners.[7]

Forming the ground starts with the intention for and exertion toward success, but when we push something and then it moves and changes, we've got to adjust our exertion to respond to the changed ground. First we form, but then we must transform. We cannot remain fixed, nor can we expect to permanently fix others or the environment. Continuing to push in the same direction that got us to where we are can be counterproductive. Employing shih is never a onetime fix and then we're done. We have to be aware of the delicate balance of the interconnectedness in relation to the objective we strive for, and transform accordingly.

Beyond Form

The key to the practice of forming and transforming, as the text so clearly tells us, is being without form:

> And so the skilled general forms others yet is without form.
> [CHAPTER 6]

Here we are going beyond the step of not getting stuck in the particular form we are currently employing to the much larger leap of not solidifying or fixating on form itself. Being "without form" means regarding the form of any situation not as the ultimate reality but rather as an ever-changing manifestation. This has simple yet profound advantages:

> The ultimate in giving form to the military is to arrive at formlessness.
> When one is formless, deep spies cannot catch a glimpse and the wise cannot strategize.
> [CHAPTER 6]

Formlessness means shaping the ground, taking a firm and definite position, yet not fixating on it as the only solution. This does not mean we don't really care or believe in the position we've taken. It is maintaining an allegiance to a bigger solution, one that serves the larger whole more than it serves one particular plan. Being formless isn't abstaining from engagement; indeed, it is engaging deeply and entering the play of forming and transforming. It simply means not grasping onto any particular form, which allows the forming and transforming to be powerful and effective.

The martial art of aikido offers a fine example. The founder of aikido, O'Sensei Morihei Ueshiba, was acknowledged as a great adept in many of the traditional martial arts in Japan during his early life. After he mastered these disciplines, it dawned on him that no matter how strong he might become, there could always be someone stronger, and he would therefore ultimately find himself in a battle he could not muster the strength to win. Out of this realization he took parts of all the existing disciplines and created this new form of martial art. It was based not on solidity and strength but rather on not offering a fixed form or position for his opponent to direct his or her attack against. Thus aikido is a practice of forming and transforming, using the opponent's own energy of attack to bring about a victorious resolution, by becoming formless. In a counterintuitive move, his insight was that not taking a fortified position—not being "there" in a solid and fixed way—was the strongest position of all. It is the combination of forming and formlessness that gives this particular practice of shih its power and effectiveness.

As with shih in general, the ability to respond to form is not about how many clever plans we can devise but about how we can embody the view, be in touch with whatever arises, and capitalize on the emergent solutions:

> *Do not repeat the means of victory,*
> *But respond to form from the inexhaustible.*
> [CHAPTER 6]

Formlessness can serve as the basis of effective action because it is based on beginning from victorious ground:

One skilled at battle takes a stand in the ground of no defeat
And so does not lose the enemy's defeat.
Therefore, the victorious military is first victorious and
    after that does battle.
The defeated military first does battle and after that seeks
    victory.
[CHAPTER 4]

Once again, it is important to keep in mind that standing in the ground of no defeat does not mean keeping a distant smugness or false sense of invulnerability. You cannot feign victory. Being victorious first means rising above the mentality of the battleground in your own heart and mind in order to take full part in the battle. It's about being beyond reach while still being open and connected. There must be some openness and contact but nothing to grab on to, which leads us to our next practice in employing shih, what the text calls deception.

Deception

For many people, deception is the hardest piece of *The Art of War*. In part, that's because convention holds that deception—most commonly anything that involves the deliberate misrepresentation of the truth—is a bad thing. Of course, there are numerous examples of humans employing deception for biological, evolutionary, or realpolitik reasons. In fact, everybody does it, though mostly we don't want to acknowledge that we do. Then, there are those of us who just want to know how to do it better, not the mundane version but the really skillful deception that allows us to attain victory without being hurtful. So, though deception is an ordinary part of our everyday lives, it is complex ground.

Deception is complex in part because it isn't just one thing, like "breakfast" isn't just one thing, since it can describe everything from a piece of toast to a smorgasbord. "Deception" is a single label that covers a complex range of meanings that share a common nub of separating us from the way things really are. Deception can be characterized by acts of omission or commission, acts that are benign (sometimes it is nobler to lie when other's feelings are at stake) or malicious (people can get a certain satisfaction from keeping someone in the dark). It can apply with equal effect to another person or to ourselves, in the form of delusion, or self-deception. Deception is celebrated, delighted in, and rewarded at the poker table. We experience deception as wonderment in the performing arts of prestidigitation, magic, card tricks, drama, movies, humor, and anywhere that artists project assumptions upon us and then prey upon those assumptions. As the illusionist might say, "The obscure we see eventually; the obvious seems to take longer."

While the *Iliad* celebrates power and strength, the *Odyssey*—a seminal text in Western literature by anyone's reckoning—places Odysseus's cunning, guile, deception, and shape-shifting in the forefront. Odysseus, "who plies all manner of wiles," rarely can achieve his aims through head-on, straightforward contesting. In the climactic story of the epic, when he returns from his decades of wandering to find Penelope surrounded by young suitors, he sees he is outnumbered. Taking them on one by one or all at once—à la many a martial arts fantasy movie—will not work. Only duplicity will help him achieve his aim. He does not reveal who he is, because the suitors would immediately slay him. Then, gradually, in a series of steps, he arranges for the suitors to end up in a room where he is the only one with arms. While contests of strength may be won by the young, Homer seems to suggest, living to a peaceful old age requires employing circuitous routes.

Deception is possible because we live in a complex world, where things aren't always what they seem—a notion familiar to us from our earlier discussion about how our view of the world shapes our perceptions and our actions. It's not very easy in such a world to sort out deception and truth. We have everyday experiences of the validity of different stages of meaning for different people. What is "true" for a child may not be true for an adult. What is "true" for a Masai tribesman may not be true for a resident of Manhattan. What's true from one perspective is not necessarily so from another. Postmodern relativism paves the way for truthiness rather than rock-solid truth. Is Pluto a planet? Fuzzy logic reigns supreme.

Social scientists will tell us that as societies become more complex, deception plays a larger role. In order to deceive, we need to be able to think strategically, to think about future implications of our actions, about others' needs as well as our own, and to manage our own emotions. Deception that is considered acceptable in intrapersonal, interpersonal, and group settings can be deemed criminal activity in commerce or the courts. And, inevitably, there are the times when we feel that a deception has left us betrayed, violated, insulted, and angry, and we regard the deceiver as having done something really bad.

It is not our purpose here to write a treatise on deception, to establish moral or ethical justifications for it, to convince you that it's good or bad, to provide a rationale for duping and duplicity. But, clearly, deception is a central theme in the profound practices of the Sun Tzu, a key component in employing shih. So it is important to look into the role of deception in employing shih, how it works with the subtleties of extraordinary and orthodox, with forming and transforming, and thus how to employ shih as a way of attaining victory. And that discussion starts with the observation that, good or bad, deception is something we all do, and sometimes there are very good reasons for that.

Importance of Deception in the Text

If attaining victory without battle is based upon knowing in the Sun Tzu, then deception is critical, because it's all about preventing the other from knowing. *Deception* comes from the Latin for "ensnaring" or "seizing," and it carries with it the sense of "stealing the opportunity to know" from the other. In our discussion of the view of the text, knowing is the basis for effective action and victory in the world. Thus, preventing others from knowing renders their actions hit-or-miss at best, and most likely ineffective. Deception is all about attaining victory without battle by working at the level of mind and strategy, by shaping others' perceptions, and thus limiting their knowing:

And so the superior military cuts down strategy.
Its inferior cuts down alliances.

Its inferior cuts down the military.
The worst attacks walled cities.
[CHAPTER 3]

The successful action that uses deception can make one totally un-graspable—beyond the reach of the enemy's intelligence, strategy, and effective action.

Deception follows from the text's view of the inevitability of change in the same way that conflict follows from the text's view of the interconnectedness of the world. In the ever-changing and ultimately uncontrollable world, there is no solid preexisting an-swer waiting for us. There is a field of possibilities and potentiali-ties. Uncertainty and ambiguity reflect our experience of life as full of color, multiplicity, and many possibilities rather than as black and white, a monoculture, one-dimensional. For deception to be possi-ble, our basic perceptions must first be called into question, which then opens the mind to the multiple possibilities. Ambiguity and uncertainty are the roots of deception, actively loosening the grip of certainty and thus creating greater possibilities of what will arise in the next configuration of things.

The Sun Tzu is widely acknowledged as the world's preeminent manual of indirect warfare, which is about focusing energy on the undefended and unexpected rather than about direct confrontation. As such, the text upholds deception as a core value, implicit in all its practices for bringing about effective action. Indirect action isn't synonymous with deception, and certainly not in its pejorative or smaller-minded meanings, or in its manifestation of fooling our-selves—self-deception. Successful indirect action uses deception to open up gaps in the most solidified of defenses and thus paves the way for effective actions where none could be seen before. During a corporate retreat at a mountain cabin, one of the leaders spent a lot of time working inside the cabin. As she looked out the win-dows, she would frequently find people looking at their reflections in the windows and preening themselves. The way the light hit the windows, it was very hard for them to see in and very easy for her to see out, forming a kind of two-way mirror. This enabled her to be near to people yet "manifest as far," in the words of the text. She was tempted to tell people about it (and eventually she did), but she was fascinated by how she could see people so clearly when they thought they weren't being watched, and in fact thought that they were watching themselves. This small "deception" revealed volumes.

How to Employ Deception

In extraordinary and orthodox, deception can be both an aid in establishing the orthodox and a pathway to discover the extraordinary. As we discussed earlier, using the orthodox to join battle involves keeping our actions within the realm of what is expected and acceptable to others. Employing deception can be as simple as allowing others' projections and assumptions to be as they are without offering any resistance. We expend no energy disabusing them of their false notions. This has the effect of relaxing their initiative and allows time for the situation to change and for the extraordinary to arise.

One of the common synonyms of *deception* is *deviousness*. Being devious is generally considered a bad thing. But the metaphor frozen within the word reveals something: originally, *devious* simply meant taking a path other than the main road. In the Sun Tzu, employing deception is about not following the accepted, conventional route to attain victory. In terms of using the extraordinary, deception has the effect of unsettling the solid ground of conflict so that the *strange,* the word we discussed earlier as one translation of the *extraordinary,* can arise.

In the practice of forming and transforming, we are shaping the appearance and the patterns of things in order to shape the perceptions and thus the actions of those around us. In this practice, we form ourselves or the ground to capitalize on the projections and desires of others, not as an expression of our own deeply held convictions. Forming and transforming uses deception as it preys on others' wishful thinking and counts on cognitive dissonance in order to attain objectives.

The skillful use of deception in forming and transforming starts with the ground of some acceptable commonplace, some shared reality, so that how we shape the ground can't be rejected out of hand. Most think it is simply about pretending to be something we aren't, but deception has to be plausible to be effective. It's not so easy to do. If we think of a poor public relations campaign or marketing pitch, we recognize how transparent it is. We see through it when it is so obviously at odds with what common intelligence tells us.

The ability to employ deception effectively comes from deeply internalizing the view of the text. To begin with, fully experiencing the world as whole, interconnected, and constantly changing makes it very difficult to solidify or fixate on any particular form or manifestation. If you are not attached to a position, then there is no solid point for the other to grasp on to. On the other hand, if you don't solidify or fixate, it is possible to embody any position or form required to bring about victory. Not being a particular thing frees you to be whatever you need to be.

Though we may talk about the view of the text with a clear understanding, practically speaking it's not so easy to hold that perspective when working with the chaotic and demanding day-to-day level of things in our world. We all have assumptions, attachments, desires, and aspirations, all of which affect our view and all of which are hard to let go of. The view of the changing world is inspiring as long as it doesn't threaten our sense of being. We feel compelled to stake our claim to firm ground, even when we are uncertain and even when it is evident that this holding on is the source of further difficulty.

In the morning session of one of our seminars, which took place as part of a bigger conference, we split our participants into two groups and gave everyone the task of telling the other conference attendees about our seminar when they spoke to them at mealtimes and in casual conversation throughout the day. But we directed the two groups to convey different messages: one had to describe the seminar as exciting and stimulating while the other was told to describe it as boring and disappointing. We let the participants each create their own explanation so they could share their "opinion" with a personal flare and passion. The exercise was designed to help the participants create the experience of deception in themselves, to see what feedback it brought from others, to observe how the two messages moved throughout the larger assembly, shaped the ground, and to what effect.

A most interesting discussion erupted during our review following the first meal break. Clearly, this assignment was very troubling for those who had to convey a message they didn't believe in. One participant in particular was horrified to find herself in the position of strongly criticizing a seminar she was enjoying, particularly when she discovered that one of her breakfast table companions was a senior member of the conference organizing committee she was quite friendly with. The stronger the participants' image of themselves as "honest," no matter which message they were asked to impart, the more difficult it was for them to fully engage in the task they were given as part of this exercise. There is an element of play to the practice of deception that is very hard to do. It takes us out on a limb, without question. But the text does not equivocate about it:

> *The military is a Tao of deception—*
> > *Thus when able, manifest inability.*
> > *When active, manifest inactivity.*
> > *When near, manifest as far.*
> > *When far, manifest as near.*
> > . . . .
>
> > *Attack where he is unprepared.*
> > *Emerge where he does not expect it.*
> [CHAPTER 1]

Our habitual grasping on to and solidifying things is out of sync with the text's view of the world as constantly in flux, and it impedes our ability to make use of deception to employ shih. This grasping arises as a regular occurrence in our own minds, and so it is here that we first have to work with the impulse to fixate and solidify. Generally, we solidify because we have the mistaken notion that we must do so in order to attain strength and be effective. But in fact, the strength we seek comes not from solidifying further but from relaxing further.

As a wonderful proverb from the Zen tradition goes, if you want to control your bull, give him a large pasture. This proverb is used as a lesson to the Zen student about the practice of meditation and how it gives space to the mind, and the dynamic it describes applies to how we could work with the grasping and fixation that get in the way of employing shih. In difficult situations, trying to control by force only increases the resistance. Boundaries are important, but as we discussed in "Forming and Transforming," the best approach is not too loose, not too tight. The more you relax, the more things will be controlled—or contained, in the language of the container principle.

Good deception is always based on the truth, which is the most powerful basis of deception. When deception is based on something totally contrived, or if it dismisses others' intelligence altogether, it usually doesn't work so well. People are smart; they recognize petty thievery or cheap deception. Marketing professionals know that the strongest means of getting out a message is the genuine sharing that takes place among networks of people talking to one another about something they care deeply about. When that communication goes viral or hits the tipping point, a message or product is adopted far beyond anyone's attempt to promote it. However, efforts to duplicate that natural occurrence, sending actors into bars to order new liquors to simulate actual consumer appreciation or paying bloggers to promote products as if for real, have proved to be weak substitutes for finding the actual points of passion and helping that momentum along.

By contrast, skillful deception can exploit the momentum the other brings to an encounter. A new police officer, for example, feared that she would have difficulty serving warrants on unruly men. Then she found that tough guys were often inclined to flirt with her when she approached them. She learned to play along with this and thereby lull them into easy compliance. Going against them, she said, only "agitates them needlessly," while going along "calms them down."

It is possible, though, "to make something out of nothing," to employ sleight of hand on a large scale. This kind of feint, ruse, or grand magical display expresses the beauty of deception. It is very similar to what an artist does in creating a reality out of artifice that is so compelling that we take it as real. The skillful sage commander can create a compelling new reality to replace the one to which the enemy holds. On a clear night in the country, many stars shine brightly in the sky. Yet when the sun rises, it is as if they no longer exist. The sage commander can shine a light on one part of the scene to focus the enemy's attention there, leaving other parts fully imperceptible. What isn't there appears to be there, and what is there is obscured. When the magician directs our eye to what's in his right hand, what he is doing in his left hand goes utterly unnoticed.

Challenges in Using Deception

Deception is the most difficult aspect of the Sun Tzu for many people, partly because employing deception seems to accentuate the feeling of separation or duality that gives rise to conflict in the first place. In the military context from which the text arises, and in other contexts with the same level of urgency, conflict can be more easily cast as doing battle with the enemy, as "us" versus "them." In the more mundane parts of our lives, even where conflict is rampant and extreme, it has become clear that victory is in jeopardy as soon as we solidify others in this way.

One challenge in employing deception is in understanding how to work skillfully with duality and separation. When we regard duality as the foreground against the background of wholeness and interconnectedness, deception becomes a valuable tool. We can employ deception, or steal knowing from the other, and not perpetuate conflict. It goes back to view, about how to regard the other as a part of the interconnected world—but a part that nonetheless needs to be separated out and related to in order to address a source of conflict. After all, that's the very principle of employing shih that we started with: knowing that the world is whole but separating out one part of that world to accomplish an objective. Employing deception can work to attain victory when it is employed from the point of view of the whole.

The key to using deception in this way, as part of transformative action, is in employing it to bring about the larger sense of victory, to bring others around to a larger view rather than merely bringing someone around to your narrow and solid viewpoint. Deception is a problem when it is the means to centralize everything back to yourself, to diminish others into your smaller framework. When it does not acknowledge the whole, it perpetuates conflict. Deception works when actions are based on trust in the big picture.

When President Nixon went to China, an event that is celebrated as perhaps the one monumental breakthrough in a disastrous presidency (it even became the text for grand opera), the president and Henry Kissinger had no intention of giving Mao the momentous level of legitimacy he sought. Yet the gambit served to break an East-West logjam and instantly changed how people everywhere viewed the boundaries of the world. No longer was it possible to treat China as an alien black box. Ironically, it helped to pave the way for the destruction of the Maoist legacy, even as it appeared to legitimize it. Now that the world was beginning to peer into China, the wall of secrecy Mao required to carry out his vision eroded further. Deception in the service of bringing others around is hailed as brilliance, skill, and audaciousness. Brute honesty and guilelessness in such situations can mean no movement and can lead to disaster and, in extreme cases, death.

More Ways of Employing Shih

Shih manifests in many different ways, and the text offers a number of specific practices for working with it. We've discussed the central and most powerful of these practices at some length. Each is rich and multifaceted in and of itself; no amount of discussion could exhaust the pool of valid and helpful insights about them. We certainly do not presume to do so here. Rather, our approach has been to explore the underlying logic of the practices and offer examples of them to spark your own intelligence. Our goal is to encourage your own discoveries of the power of these forms of employing shih and thus enable you to apply them in the appropriate circumstances in your life.

Among the additional important practices of shih that we have not yet discussed, three stand out: circuitous and direct, empty and solid, and employing spies. It will be helpful for us to explore these further. But our goal in doing so here is to establish the ground for you to continue the exploration on your own, so we will only touch upon them briefly. It is our experience that once an understanding of the basic pattern of shih emerges, looking into the additional practices of the Sun Tzu becomes a rich learning experience. While each is distinct in itself, they all repeat a motif of subtle knowing of the interplay of energies—of shih—that begins to become apparent. And once you understand these practices as variations on the theme, your own exploration of them will yield more lasting insights. In this way, the new practices can become your own and at the same time deepen your overall understanding of shih.

The Circuitous and the Direct

> The difficulty for a contending army
> Is to make the circuitous direct
> And to make the adverse advantageous.
>
> Thus make their road circuitous
> And lure them with advantage.
> Setting out later than others and arriving sooner
> Is knowing the appraisals of circuitous and direct.
> [CHAPTER 7]

Skillful action is all about accomplishing our goal, about changing things, about moving from here to there. As we've been told, the shortest distance between any two points is a straight line. And as we know from our experience, the obstacles and challenges that arise—things that force us to go around them—make our journey longer and more arduous. So in all things, direct means the shortest, simplest course, while circuitous is the longer, roundabout path. Direct is the easy and effortless, while circuitous requires the greater effort and expenditure of resources. This experience of the circuitous and direct is present in all campaigns, from those we undertake in our ordinary lives to those that occur on the battlefield in warfare.

Employing shih in the way the text tells us—in this case, transforming the circuitous and direct—starts with working more skillfully with those circuitous moments we encounter in our campaigns. Making the circuitous direct—turning obstacles into advantage and moving through them with seeming speed and ease—confounds others' expectations, disrupts their fixed strategies, and gains the element of surprise. When we see our enemy do things quickly that should take a long time, we wonder about other ways they might not be subject to the usual laws that govern action. But still, the circuitous path is not desirable, for the text counsels the sage commander to seduce the enemy onto a path that will be more circuitous for them by offering them advantage.

Employing the circuitous and direct is a way of working with shih because it relates to the subtleties of how energies and positions transform and invert, how the adverse can be made into the advantageous, how the circuitous turns into the direct. Like the extraordinary and the orthodox—and the solid and empty, which we will look at next—the power comes from the interplay and exchange of the pair rather than the fixed position of either one.

In the first chapter, we told the story of a midlevel employee at an engineering firm who took the initiative to work up a proposal to redesign the company's overcrowded offices only to find his efforts rewarded with complaints and rumors about his motives. He was discouraged and hurt, and his efforts were seemingly shunted to the sidelines as everyone else in the office got involved in the project. Then, however, while the rest of the office had spare evenings and weekends consumed with meetings that deteriorated into continual disagreements, he had the time to take his original design to the next level and surprise management with an exciting alternative just when everyone was ready to give up on finding a suitable plan.

Circuitous and direct is about how to move through time and space in a way that makes possible a victory that didn't seem to be possible.

One who knows in advance the Tao of the circuitous and
direct is victorious.
[CHAPTER 7]

The Empty and the Solid

How a military comes to prevail, like throwing a grindstone
against an egg.
It is the empty and the solid.
[CHAPTER 5]

These lines reflect a fundamental element of the view of the text, one that leads to the Sun Tzu's overall strategic approach of not attacking a stronghold while maintaining a well-fortified defensive position that cannot easily be attacked. The solid describes all that is whole, focused, unbroken, strong, unanimous; the empty describes that which is vacant and unoccupied, containing nothing, void, lacking defense. As we discussed in our review of the qualities of shih, the skillful action finds victory through preponderance. So employing the solid and the empty is about how to gather and organize your strength and focus it at the enemy's weak point. This way of skillful action has a sense of ease and an economy of effort, conveyed by the image of how easily the grindstone crushes an egg or how a lazy cow napping in the meadow under the midday sun rolls over and unknowingly flattens the farm cat that was seeking shelter in her shade. Bringing the solid to prevail against the empty is amassing strength so that a simple gesture can bring about the moment of victory.

Here again, the empty and the solid are not absolute reference points but transform and have meaning in relation to each other and the bigger situation:

Now the form of the military is like water.
Water in its movement avoids the high and hastens to
the low.
The military in its victory avoids the solid and strikes
the empty.
Thus water determines its movement in accordance with
the earth.
The military determines victory in accordance with
the enemy.

The military is without fixed shih and without lasting form.
[CHAPTER 6]

Employing the solid to strike the empty is not about maintaining a fixed strategy or purely amassing power. It is the ability to transform and refocus yourself according to the situation and not get caught in predictable routines or habitual responses. Victory is finding and focusing whatever power you have at the open and undefended spot. And this can be done despite the actual relative size of the opposing forces. You can be a smaller force, focus your efforts at the opponent's empty space, and be victorious. The Sun Tzu talks about this in the chapter on the solid and the empty as "using one-tenth to strike one." Our story of salesforce.com's rapid growth in the on-demand software market against its giant competitors is an example of using the solid to strike the empty. Taking action at the right moment to bring about victory is about relationship, seeing how things change and how advantage can be gathered and focused, and then taking action in the moment of preponderance.

In her story of caring for her elderly parents, Jane could not successfully persuade her father to move out of his house and sell his car, even though living alone and driving were very dangerous for him. These were important symbols of his independence, and he fought fiercely against losing them. Only at the moment when he thought he was dying and needed surgery, when his defenses became "empty" and vacant, was Jane able to bring about change in both areas, and then it happened swiftly and without resistance or serious repercussions.

Employing Spies

As we are well aware by now, knowing is all-important for the sage commander. It is the basis for effective action. And superior knowledge will assure victory—"know the other and know oneself, then victory is not in danger." Since conflict of any kind can be costly and destructive, it is the leader's duty, then, to obtain such knowledge as will assure the victory of taking whole. This next set of lines from the chapter on employing spies describes the consequences

when the sage commander is not willing to do all that is necessary
to know the enemy:

> *On guard against them for years to contend for a single*
>   *day's victory, yet by begrudging rank and the reward*
>   *of a hundred gold pieces, he does not know the nature*
>   *of the enemy.*
> *He is utterly inhumane.*
> *He is not the general of the people.*
> *He is not the assistant of the ruler.*
> *He is not the ruler of victory.*
> [CHAPTER 13]

In this passage, the general's reluctance to employ spies through
the conventional system of rewards and acknowledgments pro-
longs the destruction of human life and fails to attain victory. Spying is an important means of gaining knowledge because it's about
observing closely and knowing from the inside, from where plans
originate and decisions are made. Thus the knowledge available
from spying is of a different order and of elevated importance:

> *And so the means by which an enlightened sovereign and*
>   *a wise general act, and so are victorious over others*
>   *and achieve merit superior to the multitude's—*
> *This is foreknowledge.*
> [CHAPTER 13]

Foreknowledge—knowing in advance what others intend to do—is
especially valuable and especially difficult to obtain. Projection, the
logic of inference, and extrapolation each have their place, but at best
they are just more sophisticated versions of guesswork. To be sure
about important things, the sage commander looks for knowledge
that is firsthand, immediate, concrete, and detailed. Its best source
is direct perception, and sometimes that means employing spies.

Foreknowledge cannot be grasped from ghosts and spirits,
Cannot be inferred from events,
Cannot be projected from calculation.
It must be grasped from people's knowledge.
[CHAPTER 13]

Employing spies is among the most provocative injunctions in the Sun Tzu. It speaks to the importance of gaining intimate knowledge—not second-, third-, or fourthhand but from sources right on the ground, in the middle of the fray, with a stake in the action. The importance given to foreknowledge and the employing of spies confirms that, in the end, knowing is not abstract, conceptual, academic, or ideological. It comes down to employing the human faculties we use every day to survive in order to gain accurate information, not projection or logic. The knowing of simple facts—who is going to do what where, when, and how—provides the powerful elements that allow us to employ shih.

While employing spies has always been accepted in warfare, statecraft, and to a lesser extent in business, it has a mixed reputation in other spheres. Though spying is about close observation, it is about doing so in secret and with hostile intent. It conveys the notion of stealing knowledge that the other does not want to give up. It requires us to assume a duplicitous role, where disinformation rules, things can quickly go wrong, and trust is broken. Questions related to spying are not easy ones to answer: Should a mother read her teenager's diary just because she suspects serious health consequences from her child's behavior? Should employers spy on workers where delicate trade secrets may be exposed? Does a democratic society spy on its citizens when threats of terrorist attacks are present?

Though we may question the activity of employing spies, we do not question the benefit: obtaining reliable foreknowledge. When we gain a moment of certainty, of knowing that goes beyond speculation, we can be confident that our action is based upon a sound foundation and therefore stands a greater chance of effectiveness. And the more extreme the conditions, the more helpful it can be.

Our friend Jane was having a terrible time keeping her parents in their first assisted-living home through the date of their anniversary party. But the valuable information she was able to get from private calls in confidence to staff members she had cultivated allowed her to speak with greater authority when arguing with the owner to allow them to remain for a few weeks more. Likewise, in the earlier scenario when her parents were barely safe in their own home, reports from the home-care staff that her father hired and tried to control enabled her to base her care decisions on the real facts on the ground, despite her father's attempt to paint the rosy picture that everything was going well. When the leader's goal is to take whole, the deception of employing spies can be a part of genuineness.

In most cases in our campaigns, the activity of obtaining foreknowledge and employing spies arises long before the questions of duplicity and trust become obstacles. In even the most entrenched and fortified of oppositions, there are opportunities to gain some access, directly or indirectly, to someone inside the other camp, someone well placed who knows what's happening and can tell you. Sometimes this is even institutionalized, such as back-channel communications in diplomatic relationships, where both sides gain more direct information from the other than is commonly known.

Summary of Practice

The Sun Tzu is about "military methods," profound strategic practices that have been proved effective in the world over the past several thousand years or so. Our discussion here has been focused on how we can practice these methods today, how we can employ them in all aspects of our own world—from the home front to the battlefront.

To aid in this process, we have looked at the practice of the Sun Tzu as part of the fabric of the larger view of the text. This helps us to see how the practices and methods of the Sun Tzu are born from the view, extend the view, and express the view in particular actions in the world. In exactly the same manner, a classical pianist will undertake a particular set of practices best suited to express the vision that Beethoven had when he wrote his sonatas. Understanding practice in this larger context leads to effective, intuitive decision making rather than a tedious application of habitual, piecemeal gestures. In the intense situations the Sun Tzu addresses, practice must be a deep part of our character and being. Action can then arise with spontaneity, freshness, and accuracy.

Practice is the transition from view to action, and the pattern of behavior for working with the world. In the Sun Tzu, practice is all about shih, the powerful way the text describes of shaping and responding to the changing world to bring about favorable circumstances and achieve an objective without perpetuating further chaos and conflict. The practice of shih, both in general and in the strategic practices that extend it, is about riding the energy and "going with," about when to move and when to hold, and about seeing the rhythms and levers of the world clearly enough to know how to act in the critical moment to bring success.

Practice is the way of being, the pattern of behavior, that makes our broad view manifest in the day-to-day world. So this naturally brings us to an exploration of action, the particular gesture specific to the unique circumstances that challenge us. Here, we will hear the stories of people whose actions illustrate how the sage advice of the Sun Tzu can make us more effective and successful, and lead to a discovery of a different way of acting. In turning to our study of action and reading these stories, we reach the final stage in our exploration of how to apply the wisdom of the Sun Tzu to the challenges in our lives.

6 _____

Action

Stories of Applying the Sun Tzu
in the World

The power of the narrative approach is that . . . it offers
a radical shift in our usual epistemology—our ways of
knowing—and that is what makes it so transformative.
—*Paul Costello*

Being human is a story.
—*Michael Ignatieff*

OUR STUDY of the Sun Tzu's effectiveness and skillful
action now turns to the thorny question of what happens in the
world when, as an old saying puts it, "rock meets bone." In the end,
it all comes down to one of the most often asked questions: what do
I do now? This question arises whenever we're faced with a challenge and confounded about how to proceed. There's precious little
time to review our chosen practices and reflect on our view. And it's
often spoken with a sense of frustration, because we so want to take
an action that is effective, that leads forward to a successful campaign that achieves our objective without more resistance and aggression. The very need to act effectively is what brings the Sun Tzu
into being and makes it so relevant for us.

Responses to the question "What do I do now?" are plentiful,
all around us. Do this, follow this philosophy, attend this leadership training, pay for this exclusive seminar. Many people are ready

with an answer about the right technique, the right training. We agree that this is the right question and we respect the frustration, but this question must be answered very carefully. We just don't think that generic answers and ready-made solutions serve us best when we are faced with the question of what action to take in a unique situation.

Our entire approach to making the wisdom of the Sun Tzu more accessible has been to open up the view of the text, so that its modern-day students and would-be practitioners can see how closely it fits the world we live in now, and then to suggest how the text's profound strategic practices can be applied to the widest range of challenges. If indeed the Sun Tzu is not foreign, ancient, or restricted to use only in military settings but rather based on universal human faculties, it is then a wisdom available to all. Thus modern-day readers can internalize these views, make a genuine connection with the text's practices, and find victory in tough places. Those who make this wisdom their own stand a better chance of having a strategy that "survives contact with the enemy," as the old military adage goes. And as you shall see reading through the stories in the coming pages, the notion of "enemy" from the text can include a broad range of people: those who would do us grievous harm, those who merely oppose us, and those who are friends and adversaries both.

While we cannot rely on simplistic prescriptions, we do have helpful signposts in the form of examples of people whose effective action in the midst of campaigns and challenges in their lives clearly demonstrates the principles of the Sun Tzu. We think that a little guidance can go a long way to spark your own insights and give rise to creative solutions. And so rather than presuming to provide you with the definitive "answer" about what a particular line means or how a specific strategy manifests in each situation, we present groups of lines from the text and couple each with a story of how someone has found a way to act that went beyond his or her own expectations for success.

First, we'll briefly refresh our understanding of action in the context of view, practice, and action.

What Is Action?

In its simplest meaning, action is doing something. It is what we do when we focus energy and project it into the world, signaling that we are no longer on the sidelines, no longer in the realm of vision, ideals, hopes, or dreams. Actions are the natural extension of view and practice, and are meant to effect change, to fulfill an objective. In the Sun Tzu, that objective is described very simply:

> *If it accords with advantage, then act.*
> *If it does not accord with advantage, then stop.*
> [CHAPTER 11]

> *If it is not advantageous, do not act.*
> *If it is not attainable, do not employ troops.*
> *If it is not in danger, do not do battle.*
> [CHAPTER 12]

Action, then, is what you do in order to gain advantage, and advantage is whatever is required to achieve your objective. But as we've learned, the Sun Tzu measures advantage within the larger objective of taking whole, for that is what defines victory for the sage commander. For example, the so-called three strikes laws that some believe have lowered crime rates by mandating long prison sentences for repeat offenders have also resulted in costly, overcrowded prisons, which in turn produce a hardened criminal population and intensified cycles of violence. Achieving your immediate goals may not bring advantage if it is done in a way that compromises your bigger campaign.

Actions, judged successful or not, always have an effect and bring a result. They arise from conditions established as a result of previous actions, and they set up the ground that will condition future options for action, which we talked about in the guideline in chapter 4 about going for direction if you can't achieve destination. When acting to effect change and bring about a result, we apply force, the exertion of energy and exercise of strength that is common to all human gestures. Force, in this sense, is an aspect of any action.

However, actions, or force, can be applied directly or indirectly and through natural as well as human-made means. The practice of employing shih is a human gesture that triggers other actions. It sets events in motion, and we benefit from the advantage brought about by the ensuing changes. Forming, one of the practices we explored in the previous chapter, is often an indirect action. For example, in health promotion, some people are starting to do what they are loosely calling "environmental diagnostics." Rather than looking mainly at people's unhealthy habits and trying to change their "bad" behavior directly, they look at the environment the people are in and what forces are "training" them to behave the way they do. Having diagnosed the environment, they then look to making environmental changes that will effect personal changes as a result.

Action takes place in the whole, interconnected, and ever-changing world. Consequently, there is no promise of success or even a particular result, and no ability to control the outcome. When our actions bring feedback, we can learn more about the world, and about the accuracy of our view and our practices. If things aren't working, we have the opportunity to think deeply about our view and our practices to bring about more effective action. If we don't learn from the effects of our actions, we can wind up more deeply mired in chaos and confusion, as so often happens when we repeat ineffective actions. Jane was frustrated by her failure to get the medical, insurance, and elder-care services to respond in the way she wanted in order to end the chaos in her life created by the difficulty in her parents' lives. However, when she realized that her campaign was in fact to ease her parents' end-of-life transition, she stopped battling these agencies and received the advantage of their considerable skills and services, and the negative impact on her own life subsided as a by-product.

The Power of Stories

No one can tell us exactly how to act in a particular situation; the "right" action in the unique configuration of a future scenario can never be fully known. Not only is the Sun Tzu very clear on this point, but we all have our own experience of failed attempts when trying to apply the same old tools one more time in an emergent situation in the present. But we know that it is possible to learn how to put the text's profound practices into action, as we've seen many examples and heard many stories from people we have worked with over the past twenty years who have been inspired to turn to the Sun Tzu. Hearing these stories can help us to do the same.

In order to aid in this learning, we'd like to share a few of the stories that have come to our attention. Some of these stories come from people who have been working deeply with the Sun Tzu for many years, some come from people who have worked with it for a few years, and some come from people only recently introduced to it. A few of the stories are from people who had exposure to a few key principles from the text, yet soon connected an action in their lives to the text's strategies.

Each story is presented with a short excerpt from the text that it connects to, but the relationship between the lines and the stories varies. In some cases, specific lines inspired a specific action or series of actions. In other cases, the storyteller acted from tapping into a deeper understanding or a spontaneous insight, and the lines illustrate and reinforce that understanding or insight. Rather than explaining away the meaning of an excerpt, the best kind of story enlarges the lines and makes them live. It unlocks and unfolds the meaning rather than spelling it out. Lines in the text are not an answer to a question. They are a gateway to a bigger view, a new story waiting to happen.

As we know, narrative is a profound and effective way to communicate. Interestingly, the root of the word *narrative* is cognate with "knowing," one of the main qualities of the sage commander, the paragon of effective practice in the text. Stories communicate beyond the limitation of merely making an argument by piling up individual points and building their correlation. Stories—and indeed, all art forms—present a whole cloth that conveys how things are woven together and include important elements that never make it into the argument. Thus stories may be the best way for readers to "know" what the text is all about.

In addition, telling stories creates a relationship. Everything exists in relationships, and telling a story is a way to experience and acknowledge the connection. In our case, the use of stories to communicate the profundity in the Sun Tzu connects us with the oral tradition of the text itself and the wisdom lineage that gave rise to it. The text has always been studied and learned about by the fresh insight of its practitioners at the time, and in telling our stories, we are joining in this long tradition.

We don't presume that these stories illustrate or cover all the important parts of the Sun Tzu; the text is too vast for that. Likewise, the headings we've provided are simple labels, not a list of key topics. For every story we include, a dozen others could have been put forth to illustrate a different and equally insightful aspect of the same lines. The stories are meant to provoke sufficient insight to show how you can make the connection to the lines, thereby creating a pathway to make the whole text more accessible. The particulars of a story may not apply to your life, or even appear relevant, but if the story opens your understanding of the lines and the text, it can then lead to skillful application of the text's principles in your own realm. The stories are not to define your understanding but to inspire creativity in further study and application.

These stories aren't anything mystical or miraculous; rather, they are practical and immediate. They are about people like us and situations we could be involved with. They display the extraordinary power of ordinary things that people already do, and can do more often and more intently by applying some study and exertion to this wisdom text. They demonstrate how the things we do are often examples of the kind of skilled action the text talks about and how our actions can be further empowered by connecting to a bigger strategic view. As well, these stories show the relevance of the strategies in this military text to the battle and conflict we all experience on a daily basis.

On the face of it, some of these stories might seem obvious or simple. The strategic advantages may appear at times to emerge from coincidence or serendipity, but in the context of the Sun Tzu, coincidence is a natural part of employing shih: by not working so hard to make things happen all by ourselves, by tuning into minute turns of events, we bump into opportunities to employ shih more often. We can command coincidence. In most cases, the stories form a narrative with only a few variables, which makes them easier to use as examples. We trust that, although simple, they may provoke insight into stories from your own life, full, as they no doubt are, of myriad variables known and unknown, all complexly interwoven.

Reading and Reflecting on the Stories

Each story of action is coupled with specific lines from the Sun Tzu, which we've identified by chapter so that you can easily find them in the translation of the text that appears at the end of this book. It might be helpful for you to take a few minutes to read the lines in the context of the chapter before reading the story that follows them.

Immediately following the lines from the Sun Tzu is our commentary, excerpted and adapted from commentary we wrote for our original translation. We provide it here because we know that the text can be tough to understand at times, since it is rich with imagery and implications, and difficult to penetrate on first or second reading. Readers throughout history have needed such help, which came mostly in the form of commentary by Chinese army generals of the time. Here we offer commentary of our own.

Following the commentary, we present a story that is connected to that set of lines, introduced with only a brief description of the person and his or her situation. We expect that initially you may read through the entire chapter, engaging with each text excerpt, commentary, and story in succession. In doing so, you may find that certain stories spark your insight more than others. Taking in the entire group of stories provides a window into the rich variation in approaches to understanding and applying the text.

The line-and-story combinations can also be read selectively, at a slower pace, taking time to consider the connection and meaning more deeply. Over time, perhaps you will return to certain stories that you find particularly helpful or particularly difficult. People have found this practice useful when stymied about which action to take in a difficult campaign of their own.

Sometimes the meaning of the lines or the connection between the lines and the story may not be immediately clear. If so, don't press yourself to come up with the meaning. Just let the uncertainty rumble around in the back of your brain for a while and see what insights or connections arise at odd times and places.

One additional suggestion that you might find helpful: keep in mind the text's instructions to the general about evaluating situations by finding how the heaven, earth, and general principles are manifesting. You can ask yourself: What is the view of the person telling this story, the way he sees his world and the goal of his campaign? What are the challenges, obstacles and elements the person is working with—the earth principle—and what methods is she employing in those conditions to achieve her objectives? And how are the person's actions working for him or her, and what might work better?

Reading and considering these stories can be helpful when you seek to connect some of the insights of the Sun Tzu to a difficult situation you are working with. Remember, these are examples of how to apply the view and put the practice into effect in real-life situations. The underlying meaning of the text is unveiled in that very process, and the skillful action of the Sun Tzu becomes apparent.

Fourteen Stories of Effective Action

1. Taking Whole

Taking a company whole is superior.
Destroying it is inferior to this.
[CHAPTER 3]

■ *Commentary*
The skillful general conquers the enemy without destroying them. "Taking whole" leaves them intact, transforms them. It builds upon itself. By contrast, "one hundred victories" places battle at the center, ignoring the fact that conflict may lead to further conflict. This principle extends from the smallest to the greatest.

This is not an argument against the use of force. Instead, it sees battle in the context of victory.

■ *From a psychology and neuroscience researcher in a lab attached to a prestigious midwestern university*

We're an environment that prides itself on the judicious combination of tradition and innovation. Our boss gives us considerable autonomy in how we design our work, and she expects the highest standards of us. These challenges suit me perfectly: I'm never stuck in the same-old, and I can use the natural restlessness of my mind to the benefit of the lab. Yet there are always limits to how much an institution can stretch and grow. And size matters—if I feel cramped and crimped in my work, then the very basis of my engagement is undermined.

All this came to a sharp point last month. As is normal, my boss and I met to discuss some projects we had under way. Right off, though, I noticed a subtle tension in our conversation. As we were getting tea, I made a small joke, which she sidestepped, as if to avoid the intimacy of meeting my humor. And gradually, as we spoke more substantively about the projects, her anxieties took concrete form. She described how I always "pushed the boundaries," using a phrase that could mean that I was either innovative and progressive or dangerous and destructive—someone who might be a great asset or a grave embarrassment. Though her outer tone remained considerate, kindly, and always reasonable, I could sense her increasing discomfort. It was clear that something large was in the process of emerging, and that I might even be fighting to keep my job.

I made a mental list. As each incident was put on the table, I noted how I could counter her attack with an equally equipoised and rational justification, an explanation of how my work not only fit within but actually enhanced our institutional culture. But her list of charges continued, and her discomfort grew. Finally, she got to the pièce de résistance. She described a situation that I myself recognized as extreme. I could offer detailed explanations for it: I was taking chances with a very unconventional line of research, but taking chances was the point. Nevertheless, I knew that no rationality would overcome the fearfulness of her response nor persuade her of the reasonableness of my course of action.

She was nearly apologetic in making her charges—she is an exceptionally good boss. And when she had completed her litany, she offered me a chance to defend myself. I felt my list of justifications melt away. The biggest thing in the room at that moment was her distress, and so I found myself speaking to that. "What can I do so that we don't have this problem?" I asked.

She was taken aback. Expecting a spirited defense, she met instead someone who was appreciating her point of view. She offered an innocuous suggestion or two, nothing pointed, and we chatted in relief and with even a bit of humor. Two things were obvious to us: first, that I could not continue with my approach to the research, and second, that her biggest fear had not been the research plan (which, in any case, she had the power to block) but rather my variance from her sensibilities. As I was leaving her room a bit later, she returned to what I had said. "I don't know anyone else who would have responded that way," she said appreciatively.

And so we parted with the warmest respect for each other. And I began thinking about another job, where my vision would be a better fit. There was no hurry about it, though. She and I had opened sufficient ground right here where I could thrive a bit longer.

2. Shaping the Ground

One skilled at moving the enemy
  Forms and the enemy must follow,
  Offers and the enemy must take.
  [CHAPTER 5]

■ *Commentary*

Do not fight the enemy head-on. Instead, shape their ground. This narrows the enemy's course of action, leading them where you want. They have no alternative. If your offer is made from the perspective of victory, they choose it as if it were their own idea. This is skill.

■ *From a woman who started a bakery-café*

After a number of years as a foodie, I finally decided to open my first business, a bakery-café in a hip town known to have many excellent cafés and espresso bars. I found an ideal space in the perfect neighborhood. During our construction phase, I noticed that there weren't many power outlets along the wall where the customer tables were to go, but I didn't assume that we'd need any more and I didn't want to spend more money than I had to, so I didn't ask the electrician to put in additional outlets.

I was so happy when we became popular right from the start. Everyone liked the decor and the baked goods especially, which was great because I was the baker and that was the way we were trying to make our café different from all the others. As the place got busier, we noticed that customers with laptops were settling in at the tables with the few available outlets. People were plugged-in, which was great, but these tables were always full, and often the tables were used by only one person working on a computer. It became a problem, one that all the other cafés had, too, I soon learned. I didn't know how to deal with it, and I didn't want to waste valuable staff time trying to keep track of how long people were on their computers or ask customers to respect a time limit as some other places did. It got to be a real battleground, creating friction between staff and our patrons, and ruining the ambience of the place. I had to find a solution, but one that didn't make things worse.

During this same time I was also struggling with what to do about part of the kitchen that had never really worked in the way I'd planned. No one wanted to use it and I didn't know what to do with it. Then I realized I could convert this uncontested space into a solution for my problem with the laptops users. Even though it was an expense I hadn't budgeted for, I brought in the carpenters to remodel this area into a twenty-foot section of bar seating. Then I had the electricians install lots of extra electrical outlets along that bar, sort of like the Xanadu of electrical outlets. So now I had tons of plugs available to customers with laptops but they were all concentrated in one area, which was a bar where each laptop user would only take up one stool, not an entire table.

After the work was done, when customers asked if there was a place for them to plug in their laptops, we showed them to the back bar area, and they felt as if there was a special place created for them. They told all their laptop-using friends, and they were happy and we were happy. Every once in a while, the laptop users overflow to the tables, but it's nothing like the problem it used to be. The increased turnover in the main seating area made the remodel expense a good investment. And we did it all without having to say anything to our customers about "the problem" with the laptop users.

3. CULTIVATING TAO

And so one who is skilled cultivates Tao and preserves method.
Thus one can be the measure of victory and defeat.
[CHAPTER 4]

■ *Commentary*

Tao is the way things are, the way things go of their own accord, the natural momentum. Method is ordering human actions in ways that are in accord with Tao. The general assumes this power when he is tuned in to the larger perspective, thus becoming the governor of victory and defeat.

■ *From a young lawyer who represents whistle-blowers in cases against the government and other employers*

A few years ago, my supervising attorney assigned me to present oral arguments before a federal appeals court in a case that had nationwide implications for employees who became whistle-blowers owing to perceived harmful acts of their employers. The assignment was a shock, since I had only been practicing law for over a year, and the case was to be heard before one of the most powerful, and conservative, courts in the country.

The case revolved around a group of whistle-blowers employed at the only nuclear warhead dismantlement program in the country. The whistle-blowers had pointed out several critical safety flaws in the procedures. Their concerns, though vindicated, led to hostility and harassment from management because revising the procedures compromised the schedule and lowered profits. As the administrative review court noted, the level of hostility and harassment suffered by these people, including death threats, was among the most severe it had ever reviewed. This severe harassment occurred under the pressure of physically dismantling numerous decaying nuclear warheads on a daily basis.

Nevertheless, the appellate court found against the whistle-blowers. The judges argued that a strict test recently set forth by the United States Supreme Court for employer-liability standards did not apply in cases of discrimination against whistle-blowers. Instead, the court relied upon an older—and much more employer-friendly—test. Under the lenient, older test, the court found that the employer "had done everything" it needed to do to insulate the whistle-blowers from harassment, and hence, the whistle-blowers were not entitled to recover damages. Superficial actions and lip service were deemed sufficient.

Unfortunately, the decision provided a model for savvy employers to act as if they supported whistle-blowers while doing nothing in fact to support them. The decision established a national precedent. The judges set a very high hurdle that threatened whistle-blowers across the country.

It was my job to argue before a very employer-friendly appeals court that the decision was wrong, in that the court had applied the improper test to whistle-blowers, and under the correct test, my clients deserved to win. I prepared the briefings, reviewed the judges' histories, and traveled to the court site the night before the argument.

In the hotel, I spent several hours on the phone with one of my client whistle-blowers, who detailed the harassment and terrible stress he suffered. My parents, who lived not far from the appellate court location, decided to join me for my big moment. As we walked together into the immense and majestic courtroom, I became aware of a monstrous dichotomy between my clients' representation and the opposition's representation. I was the sole attorney representing the whistle-blowers; the United States government and the multinational employer had at least four representatives. Their counsel table had boxes of documents stacked all around it. At my table, I had my laptop and the Denma translation of *The Art of War*. After greeting the other, more experienced attorneys, I had a moment to breathe and open a page from *The Art of War*.

I read the passage "And so one who is skilled cultivates Tao and preserves method. Thus one can be the measure of victory and defeat," and then I read the commentary.

In contrast to how wrapped up in the moment I was—that this was such a critical case and how inadequate I felt to present arguments before the judges—the passage highlighted the immensity and natural flow of phenomena. The awareness calmed me and swept away my focus on me and my big, scary moment. What would unfold became an open question.

The judges entered. I introduced myself and asked if I could bring my laptop up to the podium. One of the judges allowed for that but wanted to know if the laptop could help me explain why my whistle-blowers even had the right to take the employer to court! Suddenly, I faced what it really means to be in a courtroom stacked clearly against you. My legal explanations fell on very critical ears. I had a total of only fifteen minutes to argue, so I kept trying to persuade the judges to move on to what I presumed was the real battlefield, but they were focused on ambushing me before I could start marching. Somehow I remained calm amid this nightmare. After ten minutes, I broke off the argument to save five minutes for rebuttal after the other attorneys had their say.

Interestingly, the government attorney supported some of my assertions when he spoke. In contrast to their numerous, biting questions to me, the judges just allowed the other attorneys to argue their positions. The employers' counsel, of course, gleefully accepted the judges' lead.

When my five final minutes of rebuttal came, I knew I had to open up to the moment. Instead of arguing with the judges over the legal hurdles concerning whether my clients should even have had the opportunity to get into court, I focused on the conversation with my client the night before. I highlighted the harassment he suffered on a daily basis. The recounting allowed the judges to put themselves in the shoes of my clients, who had simply tried to honor safety principles while dismantling nuclear warheads. I could tell I had their attention. With my last minute, I focused on the horrific stresses suffered by my clients and asked the judges how these conscientious workers could be denied the opportunity to seek redress. Further, I said, if the employer really did support the whistle-blowers as they and the government argued, then why did the harassment worsen after they kept having to blow the whistle? The judges smiled.

In closing, I argued that if they did not overturn the decision of the lower court, employers would continue to harass whistle-blowers such as my clients with impunity. As my time ran out, two judges congratulated me on a "fine argument."

Two months later, we got the decision. The court ruled against my clients but overruled the older employer-friendly standard adopted by the lower court. My supervising attorney considers the decision one of the greatest wins on behalf of whistle-blowers.

4. THE EXTRAORDINARY

In sum, when in battle,
Use the orthodox to engage.
Use the extraordinary to attain victory.
[CHAPTER 5]

■ *Commentary*

Engage people with what they expect. It is what they are able to discern and confirms their projections. It settles them into predictable patterns of response, occupying their minds while you wait for the extraordinary moment—that which they cannot anticipate.

The orthodox prepares the ground for the possibility of the extraordinary. Only through complete training in the conventions of your craft are you able to recognize subtle variations in your enemy's practice of it and respond immediately to them.

The extraordinary is unanticipated, but the orthodox is not fixed either. It changes as people's perceptions grow and shift. Use of these two thus requires constant awareness of the enemy's developing state of mind. It is a contemplative exercise, not a repeatable trick.

■ *From a student looking for an apartment*

When I first moved to the city, I found an apartment through a friend of mine. It was too expensive for me to afford on my own, but I needed a place, so I took it. It had two bedrooms, and I was willing to share the living room with another person. Tuition was high, my parents couldn't help that much, and I was on loans. I didn't have much money, so I needed to find someone right away.

I put up flyers all over the neighborhood advertising that I needed a roommate. A week went by and I didn't find anyone. I began to get very anxious that I was going to lose the apartment, and with the chaos of having to find another place, I would also fall behind in school.

I went into the computer lab at school and started to design a bigger and better flyer and to put announcements up on a number of Web sites. Then, I looked up from the computer screen, glanced around, and realized there were fifty people in the room about my age. So I just stood up and called out, "Is anyone here looking for an apartment?" A girl just two computers away from me said, "Yeah, I'm just writing a flyer asking if anyone has room in an apartment." We met and talked. She was great. She moved in the next week.

5. IN ACCORD WITH ADVANTAGE

If it accords with advantage, then act.
If it does not accord with advantage, then stop.
[CHAPTER 11]

- *Commentary*
Advantage is anything that brings victory. Victory comes about by taking whole, which leaves the enemy intact or transforms them. For the sage commander, there is no other motivation to action.

- *From an arts administrator and museum director*
For quite a number of years, the museum I worked with had been on the decline. At its lowest point, it turned into a two-person operation, with both people working very hard just to keep their heads above water. During this period, I was reduced to part-time, worked as a consultant, and didn't keep regular office hours. I was engaged in a lot of other projects to make up for the time I lost.

Given the circumstances, it was a very tough time to accomplish anything around the museum. There were plenty of projects, but it was all routine work that was getting done very slowly and without much enthusiasm. There was almost a feeling of drudgery. The staff and volunteers were always looking to me to step in, not only to provide the supervision but also to do most of the work. If we had a museum consultant in town, I'd have to pick her up, buy the pastries, arrange the lunch, and clean up afterward.

I found it very frustrating that I couldn't figure out how to get anything moving. I thought if I jumped in and did everything, it would set an example and others would follow suit. But it didn't happen, and sometimes my attempts to motivate people left me feeling that I was being harsh. I was feeling terribly burdened by having to do everything myself, but I felt I couldn't step back because the whole thing would fall apart.

The museum had lots of enthusiastic supporters, and people were always approaching me to get involved and start this reclamation project or that touring exhibition. Most of the time, these people didn't have much experience, and so I would spend most of the time educating them about the realities of the museum and conservation world. Even though the ideas were often very good, I knew they couldn't be accomplished without lots of support and supervision, and that wasn't going to happen the way the museum was currently functioning. It would just mean more demands on my time and probably more resistance from the staff.

Finally, when I was at my wits' end about how to get things moving, I decided I had nothing to lose, so I plunged ahead with one big initiative that I really cared about: recovering a series of works that would require painstaking and tedious effort to save them from fast-approaching demise. A couple of museum supporters were hot on this idea and put up the seed money to hire a new person to help me get this project under way. The staff was wary and not that cooperative. The new hire was enthusiastic and his energy was infectious, and shortly after that, we got another donation to add a technical person to the new project. The new work started up at a faster pace than even I had hoped, and the place began to hum with fresh energy.

It was coming up to the critical time of year for us to apply for federal funding to hire art students to work on projects for the summer. We had refrained from making government funding applications for several years, even though we desperately needed help with important projects we couldn't afford to hire people to do. I was worried that even if I could find time to complete the application, I couldn't imagine who would supervise the work. And if we handled a government grant project poorly, it could seriously threaten any future funding opportunities. Somewhat encouraged by the success of the new project, I decided to go ahead and submit the application, and we actually got the funding.

My big fear, of course, was that none of the regular staff would step forward to hire and supervise the student, and then fill out all the project reports the government required. I could feel the age-old patterns of jumping in to save the day emerging. But I decided I was going to try not to do that this time. This was it; I would stop stepping in to cover every base and tie up every loose end.

In fact, what happened was very positive. The staff actually did step forward in the end, pretty much everybody worked on it but me, and the project went really well. New and old staff joined in and started working together and pooling their strengths. Everybody liked the fresh energy, and they created a work culture that hadn't existed in the museum before.

I knew the energy had been blocked, but I thought that I had to be the one to keep it moving. Instead, when I stopped trying to do that by running myself ragged or pushing the existing staff, but rather added fresh energy with the new project, the energy started to flow on its own and people stepped forward. My guess is that next year I won't have to be involved in the grant applications at all.

6. Offering Advantage

How one can make the enemy arrive of their own accord—
offer them advantage.
[CHAPTER 6]

■ *Commentary*

You shape the conflict, bringing the enemy to the battlefield of your choice. Offer real or imagined advantage to move them, threaten real or imagined harm to restrict them.

■ *From a secondary school history teacher near Brighton, England*

I had been working for a number of years with a major cultural institution to bring Holocaust survivors into the school to tell their life stories to the children. I struck up quite a good relationship with the people in the cultural center who deal with Holocaust survivors and education. So, on the sixtieth anniversary of the Warsaw Ghetto Uprising, I received an invitation to attend a one-day conference in London about the uprising.

I was very pleased and touched to be asked to attend, and I felt it would help my teaching about this difficult topic. But when I went to see my head teacher and showed him the letter and told him how much I wanted to go, he thought about it for a while but finally said, "No, we're too short-staffed." I was very upset. I knew the head teacher to be a good and a fair man, but like many beleaguered school administrators, if you questioned his decisions, he would tend to dig his heels in.

I called my friend at the cultural center, and I was explaining to her that I couldn't go. Really just suddenly, an image came to me about not attacking a strong fortification head-on but rather finding its vulnerable spots and being able to use feint and deception. Then, an idea popped into my head. I asked my friend if she wouldn't mind sending a fax to my head as if I'd never spoken to her. In the faxed letter, she should express her appreciation to the head for having the foresight and the vision to allow a member of his staff to go to this conference, saying how well it reflected on him as a leader of the school and how not many heads would have had that kind of vision to rise above the day-to-day demands to do something dynamic.

The next day, in my pigeonhole at work, there was a little note from the head teacher saying that he had reconsidered his opinion and he thought maybe it would be a good idea if I did go to the conference after all.

7. Summoning Others

Thus one skilled at battle summons others and is not
summoned by them.
[CHAPTER 6]

■ *Commentary*

Arrive first at the place of battle, gain the initiative, and wait. Because you appear unexpectedly at a vital point, the enemy must rush to meet you. Hurried, they labor. Laboring, they are insufficient. These are mental as much as physical conditions. They divert the enemy's attention and cloud their sight.

■ *From a woman who lost her mother and had to care for her schizophrenic brother*

A few years ago, my mother called from a convalescent home and asked me to come across the country and help her get back to her house. My brother had had a psychotic break, and after trashing their house, he ran off in their car to parts unknown. He and my mother had lived together almost all his fifty-seven years. Doctors had diagnosed him variously as a paranoid schizophrenic or manic-depressive; she had fractured her pelvis and at eighty-seven was getting quite frail. Each seemed to feel that without the other their survival was at stake, and my relationship with each of them had become distant. I didn't know it then, but I was about to go into battle.

I arrived late at night, after an eighteen-hour flight on progressively smaller planes. When I reached my mother, her face was swollen and covered with hives. She looked barely alive. I touched her arm, and she said, "My daughter's coming; my daughter's coming." I said, "I'm here." She hardly recognized me.

I spent the next day with her, then drove the twenty miles to her house, arriving after dark. Crossing over glass shards from a broken window, I went in through her bedroom door. The house smelled dreadful and was in a horrible state. Every day, for three weeks, I cleaned for two hours in the morning, visited with my mom for the day, came back in the evening, and cleaned again. I fixed the bent front doorknob, changed the locks, fixed the broken window, cleaned, washed, and laundered everything that could be. After the house was clean and made accessible, my mother came back.

Then, I focused on my brother and finally tracked him down. Toward the end of one of his running-away episodes, he would usually wind up in the hospital, initially checking himself in for physical ailments but in a few days ending up in the psych ward. This time, he landed in San Francisco, and they wanted him to go back to Oregon.

My mother asked if I'd mind if he came back before I left. I'd talked this over with protective services workers and my brother's case manager—and we all knew that no matter what he did, my mother would take him back: "But he's my son. What would you do?" I insisted on the condition that I didn't want any alcohol in the house while I was there because alcohol didn't go well with my brother's medications. My mother agreed.

They drove my brother back home about three days before I was due to leave. It only took about a day and a half before my mother gave him money to buy food, but more than he needed, with which he bought a very large bottle of wine—to celebrate all my hard work and departure, of course. That night, they got quite drunk and mocked me as being a "party pooper." "Why don't you just relax?" I nearly missed the plane the next day, because my brother insisted on taking a "longcut" to the airport.

Six months later, things had worsened considerably. My brother's behavior was so erratic and aggressive—he also had a gun—that my mother signed a restraining order against him, and now he had once again wandered off. My mother was soon in the hospital with stomach cancer. By year's end, the nurses called to say that I had better come. My mother had little time to live.

After another eighteen-hour journey on various planes, I walked into her room. All she had were her glasses and her teeth. No pictures, no books, no flowers, no clothes, no Christmas cards. I gave her a soft, fleecy shawl I'd brought with me. She petted it and said, "It's so soft," and smiled. She didn't complain of being cold again. My mother died a few days later.

Because of the restraining order, I had no idea where my brother was, though with her death, the restraining order expired. I was scared of my brother and didn't know what to do. I turned the water and electricity off at the house and moved back to the motel. When, once again, I found my brother, he had signed himself into a halfway house about twenty miles from his home. I spoke to his case manager and the crisis worker, who agreed to tell my brother the next morning that our mother had died. He called me on my cell phone immediately afterward, and I spoke to him for the first time since the spring, when I had left promising I'd return and telling him that I had promised my mother three times I would not desert him.

When I got back to the motel in Oregon, I had a long talk with Dolores, a caregiver at the halfway house. She told me my brother was one of their best patients. He always took his medication; he was very quiet and helpful, and very smart. Thus began a phase where I, with the help of many allies—principally my brother's caregivers and a lawyer—worked to keep him safe and, with any luck, give him a boost on the road to sanity, without "rescuing" him. My brother kept talking about wanting to move back into the house or maybe selling it and living in the Eagle Hotel—a very seedy, run-down place in the Tenderloin District in San Francisco. Either of these actions would be the death of him, sooner rather than later. There was very little way for me to have influence, but I realized that with my mother gone, my brother needed me. But if there was to be any hope of his leading any kind of worthwhile life, I could not simply replace her and let him dictate the terms of the relationship. It would be a long campaign.

In a few months, I came back. I decided to stay at a motel near the halfway house and drive my brother to the family house each morning, returning him to the halfway house in the evening (since I had to return to my motel each evening, I avoided creating a situation where it would "seem easier" if we both just stayed in the house). Every morning I'd pick him up, then pick up some breakfast and lunch and a pack of cigarettes for him, take him to the house, where we'd discuss the plan for the day and eat—he in my mother's old chair and me in his. I told him I would never lie to him

and conducted any family business in his presence. I never talked
to him about the past except in almost offhand factual and nonjudgmental terms.

Gradually through the month I was there, he started sitting up
straighter, finally shaving his scruffy beard off, then progressed to getting his hair cut, to wearing one of his tweed caps, and finally to smil-
ing and walking lively to the car when I picked him up in the morning.

One day he said that he felt he'd "blown it" over the past year,
that he didn't like how he was when he was not on his meds. He
didn't want to live in the house anymore; it was too much of a burden. Then he said maybe he wouldn't move down to the Eagle Hotel
in San Francisco. It would just be repeating old patterns. I didn't
really say much. I just listened.

The day before I left, we went to a forest reserve and spread my
mother's ashes around a redwood tree as she'd wished. My brother
looked up at the trunk and saw that it split into three trunks from
one base. I'd discovered a brother.

8. IN THE GROUND OF NO DEFEAT

One skilled at battle takes a stand in the ground of no defeat
And so does not lose the enemy's defeat.
Therefore, the victorious military is first victorious and after
*   that does battle.*
The defeated military first does battle and after that seeks
*   victory.*
[CHAPTER 4]

■ *Commentary*
For the skilled general, victory is attained before the battle is
joined. Abiding in his invincibility, he awaits the moment at which
he can seize the enemy's vincibility. A military that rushes to the fight,
hoping for victory, assumes the ground of defeat.

■ *From a policeman in London, England*
I had been a patrol cop for about ten years, and it wasn't clear
that I was ever going to advance much past that. I was assigned to
patrolling a council estate [public housing project] in North London

where there was a quite large group of tough young people, aged from about fourteen to seventeen. They regularly harassed and taunted me. Whenever I would start my patrol, they would make a point of looking me over and making fun of me, with nasty comments in vile language. They would even go so far as doing some damage to my van or throwing something, like a bicycle, at my dog. This assignment coincided with a very difficult time in my life, and I started to feel quite defeated. I found the harassment hard to deal with. I was timid, and I let them have free rein in the estate, despite what most residents desired. I didn't know where to begin to change the situation, because any move I made was exactly the kind of response they were looking for, and it just made things worse. I kept sinking lower. I was not very happy. I was scared, and I thought a lot about quitting my job.

One evening, I was reading through *The Art of War* and spent some time considering that section on the notion of the ground of no defeat. It sort of got under my skin, as it were. The next morning, I got up earlier. Before leaving to patrol the estate, I sat quietly for a while, and then I went out running. I washed and ironed my uniform. I polished my boots, washed my van, groomed my dog, and went to work. I felt completely different about what I was doing, and the situation began to change that day. The next day, I came down hard on the young toughs, but only when they really stepped out of line. At the same time, I gave them all the respect they deserved, which was a lot more than they usually got from others. The next day, a few of them came up to me and apologized for the shit they had been putting me through.

9. LET IT SUBSIDE

When it has rained upstream, the stream's flow intensifies.
Stop fording. Wait for it to calm.
[CHAPTER 9]

■ *Commentary*
Some conditions take time to run their course before they are favorable to your movement. If you face a surge of enemy force, it may be best to let it subside before acting.

- *From the mother of a college student*

My daughter Emily was midway through her third year at a very tough college. She had adapted quite well, both socially and academically, to being far from home and thrown in with students who had all been at the top of their high school classes. I began to sense, though, that there were very serious problems brewing. Emily had always been the first person to accommodate her friends. Whatever they wanted to do, she went along with it, not placing much value on her own instincts. The roommate she shared her apartment with was turning out to be a serious party girl. The life of every party, she was also inviting an unending string of rowdy young people into an increasingly trashed apartment. Meanwhile, Emily was changing, valuing quiet time much more, turned off by the party scene, which seemed to be based more on desperation than celebration. Yet she refused to confront her roommate, who had been her closest friend since the first day in the dorm.

In phone call after phone call with her, I felt exasperated and powerless. I knew exactly what Emily was going through, but the little speeches that had worked back in high school just didn't seem to fit now. If Emily cried over the phone, which often happened, I spent a sleepless night. All I could do was listen and blather on about my own college days and my struggles not to be defined by what others expected of me. It was OK to go out on your own for a while. She never seemed to believe it.

Things got worse at the apartment, and then, cowed by her roommate, Emily signed a lease for another year without our knowing about it. I felt things were bad enough already; if she lived there another year, it could make it difficult for her to graduate and might even jeopardize her health. There were signs of extreme stress. She was losing a lot of sleep and sick all the time. Exasperated, my husband called the landlord to inquire whether the lease could be broken, to no avail. My husband and I wanted to fly up and fix things, but just before we were about to drop everything and buy tickets, we realized if we stepped in and took over at this critical juncture, Emily's confidence in her ability to assert herself and be in charge of her life would drop even lower. We didn't know what to do, but we knew we couldn't send in the cavalry. We decided to do nothing other than be there for our daughter. It hurt a lot.

Then one day, something happened. Emily called and said her landlord had helped her find a nice little place where she could live by herself, which she was very happy about. The landlord had been through enough and decided to ask them to leave. Emily's roommate wanted them to find a place together, but Emily let the roommate know that it was time for her to go out on her own. The roommate did not react well. Their relationship was tense, but now much more honest than before. Emily had a completely new outlook. She said, "Thanks, Mom, for all your help."

10. TAKE THEM BY THE HAND

And so one skilled at employing the military takes them by
    the hand as if leading a single person.
They cannot hold back.
[CHAPTER 11]

■ *Commentary*
Your command is so intimate, the troops hear you as if you were speaking singly to each of them. United in this kinship, they cannot but follow you.

■ *From a naval commander*
To lead large groups of people and to be able to count on them in a crisis, I learned over time to focus a lot of my effort on empowering the middle-level and junior people on the ship by paying attention to what they do, asking them about their work, and generally showing appreciation for their efforts. There is a risk that such attention might be seen as violating the chain of command, so I had to be very careful not to give orders or criticize what each person's boss may have told him or her. If such intervention appears necessary, it has to be taken up within the chain of command.

It's acceptable to offer personal experience to junior people in such a situation to educate or advise, but again, there's a fine line there. I found if I practiced this "management by walking around" with a light touch, having influence in small ways, everyone felt empowered rather than diminished by my coming around. It is also important, I found, to pay a lot of attention to the environment and how that influences the way people perform: having a clean place to live, good food, being paid on time, all the aspects that make up a sailor's daily life. A commander can have a lot of influence in those kinds of indirect ways, more than just going around telling people what to do.

When I took command of my first ship, it was in dry dock for overhaul. As the overhaul neared completion, we knew that there were going to be a lot of loose ends and potential glitches and machinery problems and that we'd be tempted to try to extend our time in port so the shipyard could work out all the kinks. I could see that if we let the crew wait around while somebody else took care of the ship, it would change their perception of the ship and of the importance of time. I told the crew that as soon as we could get the basics checked out—steam up, engines and steering working, lights on—we would steam out of port and over the horizon. And that's what we did. The whole purpose was to let the crew know that the ship was ours to use and make work, and not the responsibility of the shipyard. Because I had cultivated the trust and respect of the crew, they were willing to give up the leisure time in port and make the remaining repairs at sea.

11. Do Not Engage

> *If it is not advantageous, do not act.*
> *If it is not attainable, do not employ troops.*
> *If it is not in danger, do not do battle.*
> [CHAPTER 12]

- *Commentary*
Victory is the general's goal. Do not engage in military activity if no benefit will accrue from it.

- *From an executive in a large media conglomerate*
I worked for many years as an executive in a worldwide media company. It had always run its operations such that each country

was a separate legal entity with its own financial statements, even though each had many divisions in common with other countries. At a certain point, upper management realized that if it put the same divisions—say, for example, the publishing divisions of each country—into one multinational company, it would benefit from having one of the world's largest publishing companies rather than seventeen smaller divisions in seventeen different companies. I was chosen to be part of the management team given the task of unifying these seventeen different national divisions into one corporation.

Our team spent months preparing the structure and logic of how we'd go about it, then went from country to country to speak with the management in each country's publishing division. We'd talk to the execs running the division to establish that they now reported directly to the new multinational, and we'd get the financials from the national CFO to build our new financial profile.

Then, in one of the larger European countries, we hit a snag. We encountered vehement resistance from the top financial manager and his staff. He didn't want to see us break up his company by taking one of his divisions out because all his financial projections and bonuses were based on the numbers it contributed. He started out just trying to dissuade us from moving forward, then hinted at refusing to give us the information we needed. We couldn't get our job done if he wouldn't give us the numbers and information we needed in order to integrate his numbers into our plan. It was looking as if this could turn into a huge international fight within the corporation that would slow down and maybe stop what we were trying to do. Our performance and the reputations of our team members were starting to be called into question.

Our team held long strategy sessions to try to figure out how we could talk this guy out of his irrational objections and move forward with our plan. He was pretty powerful and very impassioned and emotional, and none of us wanted to take that head-on. Then I realized we didn't have to do that. It made no sense for us to be sidetracked by this guy. I suggested that we not focus on his anger and resistance but find a way around it. We wound up suggesting that he could continue to include the publishing division's numbers in his financial statements; that wasn't our concern or under our authority. All we needed was for him to give the numbers to us and let us incorporate them into our plan so we could include the information in our report. We figured we'd let international headquarters tell the CFO that the numbers no longer belonged to his company.

Our team succeeded in completing our report without fighting our colleague head-on. In fact, our solution left him pretty much intact and still able to fulfill goals that were important to him. Our insight was based on taking the approach that the publishing divisions worked for us already, not that we were going to have to convince anybody that they did. We went in, took a head count, evaluated the licenses, got the revenue numbers, and added those numbers to the international books. We didn't ask if we could move the country's publishing numbers over to the international division, because the answer would have been no. Once we took that approach—that the information we were seeking was already ours—and supervised people from that point of view, things moved much more quickly.

12 LOOK TO THE ENEMY

Thus the wise general looks to the enemy for food.
One bushel of enemy food equals twenty bushels of mine.
One bale of fodder equals twenty bales of mine.
[CHAPTER 2]

■ *Commentary*
The impoverishment of battle reaches to every part of the economy. It not only affects material goods but also frays the social fabric. The general does not burden the state because he obtains his food and supplies from the enemy.

■ *From a conflict resolution trainer*
Several years ago, I started doing seminars on a certain method of conflict resolution. I had lots of teaching experience, but this was the first time I'd entered the training and workshop "industry," and so I was new to many of the tricks of the trade and expectations of the people attending.

In one of the very first seminars I did, I ran into a little problem. I was halfway through the first session of the second day when, during a ten-minute break, two of the participants approached me and asked if they could speak to me outside. I was aware that both of them were not connecting to the material or the seminar very well. One of them had very clearly expected more of the "softer" skills training, like movement and music. The other one had been the head of his company's coaching and skills-training division for many years and used his extensive experience to place my presentation in relation to the other methodologies that he was an expert on. I knew I hadn't found a way to reach either of them. So I agreed to speak with them, but I walked to the door with them with some trepidation.

It was very important to them for us to be safely out of earshot of the other participants when they delivered their message: they very gently told me that they wanted to "renegotiate the learning contract." I wasn't familiar with the terminology they were using, but I got the idea that they didn't think the workshop was very good. I had been trying to outline the basic framework for our inquiry, the essential principles, and they clearly desired more group interaction and opportunities to talk and move. They were feeling claustrophobic, and they wanted things to change.

I found myself standing in the hallway listening to these two, trying to get past my irritation and the knee-jerk response of defending myself. Then I realized that the energy they were presenting was exactly what the seminar was lacking: an immediate, experiential example of conflict. So rather than just work out some fixes by talking with them, I suggested we bring their request into the center of our seminar discussion to see if the principles we were supposed to be studying could in fact help.

When the session resumed, I asked them to present to the group their point about renegotiating the learning contract of the seminar. Then we went around the room so that everyone else could respond. To my surprise, most of the people used the material from our seminar to evaluate the validity of the observations and suggestions for change. In the process, the participants showed respect for the complaint and agreed to some changes, while also pointing out that they didn't see a big problem. In fact, some remarked that the irritation displayed by these two had been a cause for concern. During this whole time, I didn't say a word. I could never have planned a better learning example.

13. Spiritlike

Now the form of the military is like water.
Water in its movement avoids the high and hastens to
the low.
The military in its victory avoids the solid and strikes
the empty.
Thus water determines its movement in accordance with
the earth.
The military determines victory in accordance with the
enemy.
The military is without fixed shih and without lasting form.

To be able to transform with the enemy is what is meant
by "spiritlike."
[CHAPTER 6]

■ *Commentary*
The essential quality of the all-victorious military is that it has no fixed form. This is its power, that it manifests in whatever way is required to attain victory, spiritlike, transforming without obstacle, without hesitation. It takes shape in response to what is given—the enemy, their disposition, the terrain, any aspect of battle.

■ *From a father, on growing up with his teenage daughter*
We decided late in life to have children. Both my wife and I had demanding professional careers we were committed to and enjoyed, and we didn't seem to have time for domestic stuff. Then, just before my wife turned forty, we decided to try, and luckily we got pregnant and had a beautiful baby girl. She quickly became the central reference point in our lives. We weren't the most experienced or skillful

of parents, but we loved Ashleigh so much that we rearranged our work lives to be around as she was growing up.

As Ashleigh got older, the biggest challenge for me was to keep up with how quickly she changed from ages ten to eleven to twelve to thirteen. These were just one-year increments, but in her life they represented huge shifts of who she was and who she was becoming. When I tried to continue the approach that had worked when she was eleven, I quickly learned that it failed because she was very different at twelve. Some days it seemed like she was changing on an hourly basis. Some days I was totally lost.

The toughest time was, as you might well expect, when she turned thirteen. She wasn't what you'd call a "problem teenager." She never went through the pattern of alienation and resentment, of rejecting and acting out that I heard about from other parents. But she was definitely going to do things her own way. Since she felt a lot of pride about doing things well and she was a good student, I didn't want to complain about the little things too much.

When she started getting a lot of homework, Ashleigh would stay up late in order to complete it to her own high standards. But she really needed her sleep, and when she didn't get enough, she was very cranky and unpleasant, and I worried that eventually her work would suffer, too. Her staying up late became a huge issue between us. I set bedtime curfews for her so she'd be more decent at school and home. The weird thing was that I wasn't dealing with drugs or sex or rock and roll; Ashleigh was staying up late to do her homework! She was developing a remarkable work ethic and sense of responsibility for such a young person.

Ashleigh increasingly resisted my efforts to set bedtime standards, and things got worse and worse. She started to express her anger at me in all kinds of areas, like not doing her chores around the house and not being as good about calling home when she wasn't going to be where she was supposed to be. When her schoolwork started to suffer, I got really worried.

Then, sometime in the middle of the most difficult period, I realized that I was actually creating a bigger problem than I was trying to solve. Ashleigh was growing up to be an adult, separating from her parents, needing to make some important decisions for herself, and taking control over her life. But I told myself and her that I wanted to make sure that she got enough sleep so she would do better at school and around the house. This had worked well a year or two earlier, but now that she was in junior high school, it was undermining her growing sense of taking responsibility for her own life. So I gave up the curfew demand and let her make her own bedtime decisions, which included dealing with the aftereffects of being cranky and sleepy at school. I realized that I was trying to make sure that she wasn't cranky so I wouldn't have to be subjected to it, but it was more important for me to trust her growing sense of responsibility, even if it meant I had to deal with the unpleasantness of her being cranky around the house.

14. Seek It in Shih

And so one skilled at battle
Seeks it in shih and does not demand it of people.
Thus one can dispense with people and employ shih.

One who uses shih sets people to battle as if rolling trees
*   and rocks.*
As for the nature of trees and rocks—
*   When still, they are at rest.*
*   When agitated, they move.*
*   When square, they stop.*
*   When round, they go.*
Thus the shih of one skilled at setting people to battle is
*   like rolling round rocks from a mountain one thousand*
*   jen high.*

This is shih.
[CHAPTER 5]

■ *Commentary*
Victory does not come from accumulating troop strength or being heroic. Rather, bring about advantageous shih to shape the field of

battle. In the defile, one person stands off one hundred. In winter, the enemy's impassable river becomes your road of ice.

Relying on shih, the battle of army against army need not occur. This is the highest skill. It is victory.

Victory is not based solely on the quality of your people or their strength of will. Thus there is no need to remake or alter them. If you know their nature, you can position them so that they become natural weapons. Thus you take advantage of the way power arises in the world.

- *From the CEO of a small medical products company*

Our company had a staff of seven or eight people when I took over, and we've grown to nearly forty-five people now. Since I joined the firm, my major initiative has been to develop a customer-centered approach to replace the product-centered approach that I inherited: instead of treating customers as objects to be sold to, we treat them as partners in the process. The first thing we did was to say to our customers, "Tell us what works and doesn't work for you. Tell us what you don't like about our products and other companies' products. Tell us how we can make our products, our services, and our processes work better for you." This kind of open conversation transcended the boundary between producer and user, sales team and customers.

Our relationships with our customers grew closer, and so we decided to include them in the product development stage, turning the marketing process on its head. As we went through the prototyping process for a new product, we treated our customers as our colleagues, essentially saying, "If this product makes sense to you, we'll make it and then you can buy it from us." Selling to them after that became kind of a no-brainer. Since the customers had been involved in the development, they were asking us when it would be ready!

As a small company surrounded by large competitors, we wanted to find something unique that stood out from the crowd and that we'd be recognized for. We also wanted something that the other players in our industry—all of whom were much bigger than we were—would not regard as competing. This would allow us to continue to benefit from collegial relationships with them—which are common in our industry—rather than be pushed out by them.

So we came up with a product concept that would benefit both customers and competitors and worked on it for about four or five years. We received a lot of encouragement from opinion leaders in our industry, who thought we had developed a really interesting product with very big potential, particularly for such a small firm. We were ready to take our product to the Food and Drug Administration for approval, feeling very encouraged. We thought we had convincing data, and our collaborators and the opinion leaders seemed to concur on the soundness of what we had. However, the FDA expressed a lot of concern about the fact that what we were doing had not been done before. That was the point, we countered, but despite our entreaties, they asked for more studies. We kicked and screamed and lined up an impressive array of allies, but to no avail. The FDA was adamant.

This whole process had involved a lot of time, energy, and money. We hesitated to continue down this path and decided to look back and try to understand the landscape. We concluded that our market was very conservative, and with good reason. The FDA, which dictates what products can be sold, has two elements in its mandate: safety and efficacy. Products have to be proved safe and effective. If safety cannot be proved, you have no product. We thought we had a great plan supported by the skillful consultation with our customers (which was what we used to grow our company) and our competitors, but it failed because we did not take into account the power of the regulatory environment. We needed a new strategy.

We decided we would have to find product ideas that would be completely noncontroversial from a regulatory standpoint and yet look different enough to end users to make them want our product. However, it became very clear that such a strategy would also shift our relationship to our competitors, because rather than flying under their radar with our totally new and different product, we would be the little guy going directly up against them with a similar product.

We had to do it, though. We decided we couldn't be unique in the sense of offering a product new to the world, but we could be *uniquely better*. At that point, the strong relationships we had developed with our customers, our careful listening and trust building, paid off. While our new products were not as radical as we had striven for under our previous strategy, they were indeed uniquely better, because we learned exactly what our customers wanted and gave it to them. And were the years we spent in developing a unique product a complete mistake? Not really. We learned an awful lot, and we also got a lot of recognition for trying something really interesting and revolutionary. Yet again, we gained the respect of our customers.

7

How to Enter This Wisdom Lineage

Go to the pine if you want to learn about the pine, or to the bamboo if you want to learn about the bamboo. And in doing so, you must leave your subjective preoccupation with yourself. Otherwise you impose yourself on the object and do not learn.

—*Matsuo Basho*

Stagger onward, rejoicing.

—*W. H. Auden*

IN OUR STORIES OF ACTION, we got a glimpse of how some people have made a connection to the Sun Tzu and employed its practices to achieve something unusually skillful in their lives. These lessons apply to the whole range of mundane and extraordinary goals—launching a new business product, reviewing a teenager's study habits, improving an NGO's negotiating position with a variety of government interests, or moving troops to take a strategic position. Previously we described these instances as ordinary magic. They are ordinary because the skillfulness to bring about victorious circumstances arises through working with the common, known elements in the world that are readily available to us through our human faculties. But they are magic because the causes of our actions are not always transparent to us or those around us, and the effects of our actions do not leave a mess behind. *The Art of War* tells us that this is possible if we connect to and work with reality at a deeper, more intuitive level and respond to conflict in a subtler manner. Beyond being simply a hit-or-miss occurrence, this skillfulness can be cultivated as a way of being and acting in the world. What do we have to do, then, to cultivate it?

The Art of War text doesn't provide a summary chapter that neatly orders all of its lessons and profound skills; just so, we aren't going to offer one now. The wisdom of this lineage is about a living process, about a way of being that changes to remain in step with a changing world, so our lessons can't be easily summarized and our study is never done. We are not presenting a new "system" to deal with conflict but rather a way of viewing the world that can be integrated into everything you do. Learning to use the Sun Tzu is not about perfecting the accomplishments and becoming "the master" but about living more skillfully as a human being in the world. So, in this final chapter, we are more interested in presenting some possible ways forward for you to consider rather than tying everything up neatly.

Any uncertainty about how to proceed should not be treated as an obstacle to learning what this wisdom lineage has to teach us. If we can maintain open inquisitiveness in the face of the discomfort that things are not perfectly tied up and resist grasping for "the final answer," we will be better prepared to enter this tradition. This transition phase is integral to any genuine learning process. Between the time of absorbing something new and executing it well, there is always a period of awkwardness and uncertainty, a kind of gestation period when a deeper change is taking place. Learning *The Art of War* is very much like that, since the answers from the text aren't crisp and clear. For a dancer, a gardener, a jet fighter pilot, a golfer, or anyone learning a discipline, the experience of frustration and futility serves to break down the old habits—the process of "unlearning"—and open the ground for new ones to take root. It takes exertion and commitment to move through this difficult phase in any learning process, no less so for the study of this text. As the saying goes, if it were easy, everyone would be doing it.

In the tradition *The Art of War* comes from, even great skill and accomplishment does not promise to save you from experiencing difficulty. We can't arm you with a new set of skills that ensures that you will conquer all enemies and win all battles. Just as conflict is an inevitable part of human life, so are hardship, loss, and disadvantage. You will at times draw the short straw. Nothing we say about this text will help you avoid that experience in life.

In fact, employing the profound methods of the text and taking whole means you will get your hands dirty, because it is in the dirt and grit of conflictual situations that the text's skillful actions are found. Many approaches to learning nowadays promise that "things are messed up, but if you learn this system, it will make them all better." We can't promise that because we don't know, and wishful thinking won't make it so. Maybe things will get better and maybe they won't, but the skillfulness learned from this wisdom tradition will be helpful to you in either case.

As we presented here, one of the reasons the Sun Tzu is so popular is that it acknowledges what we experience to be true every day: conflict is a fact of life. With that as ground—the earth principle—the text goes on to describe its profound practices in the language of warfare, of enemies and battle. This can seem to reinforce the experience of separation and duality that perpetuates conflict. But as we presented in our discussion of deception, awareness of duality is the foreground that stands against the background of wholeness and interconnectedness. We share the same world with our neighbors even after we've fought with them about our differing visions for our common border. The notion of enemy in the Sun Tzu is the personification of the resistance and obstacle that we experience when trying to get something done, be it from friend, colleague, family member, or foe.

We aren't about to eliminate the experience of duality, enemy, and conflict. However, working with the world at a deep level in the way the text teaches us means suspending our limiting habitual patterns in dealing with them. This opens up a large field of play for fresh, creative action when working with these challenges. When viewed as the text views them, conflict and chaos give rise to new opportunities for effective action whenever we are trying to accomplish a task or carry out a long campaign.

A Way of Knowing

From this point of view, then, what practical guidance can we provide about how to proceed, and how to cultivate the way of being that the text presents? In general, the most meaningful pathway to ongoing study of the Sun Tzu is one that leads to getting to know the text and its tradition from the inside out, which we have talked about as joining the lineage. This means continuing the study in a way that combines openness and attention, a way that fosters a direct experience of things rather than relying on theory alone.

We start where the text tells us to start:

Knowing the other and knowing oneself,
In one hundred battles no danger.
[CHAPTER 3]

Knowing the other and knowing oneself is not based on supernormal powers but rather on the common ways we come to know things. Our senses and sense perceptions—our ability to feel things in our world—are the gateway to knowing. So learning about how the text works starts with sharpening these faculties. As we might suspect, this is not a simple task. In our discussion of knowing and shih, we talked about the obstacles to perceiving accurately what's around us, the strong habitual patterns of mind tending to reinterpret our perceptions in terms of our existing internal framework. In *How Doctors Think,* Dr. Groopman indicates that it takes more than just knowing about cognitive errors to avoid them. He warns doctors that they need to be wary of diagnoses that appear instantly obvious, that it's important for them to doubt their thinking and ask questions—What else could this be? What am I missing?—to provoke a broader view. Any methodology, no matter how powerful, needs this extra step to avoid cognitive errors fulfilling one's own projections. If we want to know our world more fully, we have to go beyond seeing only what we want or expect to see.

So the place to start is with any discipline that helps with knowing, with clearing up obstacles to perception, whether they are physical, emotional, mental, or spiritual. There are many approaches and disciplines to work with the habitual patterns of mind. We've seen a variety of successful approaches, so we will mention a number of disciplines, but we aren't suggesting any one approach in particular. But the effective disciplines seem to be those that can be sustained over time rather than those that promise easy, dramatic results. The approaches that work respect and engage one's inherent intelligence rather than rely solely on doctrine. They also require an accomplished instructor but they don't always defer to external experts. And they all include ways of working with the undercurrent of fear and hesitation, and the confusion brought about by holding on to mistaken beliefs about how things really work.

The importance of finding a more effective way of knowing is what leads us to a contemplative reading of the text, using our ability to maintain an openness that allows us to see things clearly. In this contemplative approach, the "noise" of our mind that often obscures perception of what is right in front of us is temporarily suspended.

Acknowledging that we've all had this direct experience of things is the starting point, because it helps us to realize that clear perception isn't something foreign, or beyond our reach. But the pathway to ongoing study, to a deeper understanding of the Sun Tzu, lies in finding a way to cultivate this experience as an ongoing orientation to the world through some type of discipline or practice. It could be anything that combines concentration and openness, that brings us to the edge of habitual thinking and face-to-face with fear—and that encourages us to step beyond. There are so many disciplines that we could use for this work: from the arts (such as dance, pottery, calligraphy, or flower arrangement), from the martial arts, or from the contemplative traditions that seek to deepen mindfulness and expand awareness. It is helpful if the discipline involves working with the body as well as the mind. And it's not about perfecting a discipline but just engaging the world in this way, through all the stages of exertion, awkwardness, openness, and daring, and occasional accomplishment. Ideally, it will be something that goes beyond the habitual centralizing on ourselves that is the root of fear. Whatever it is, it's not always just about us but about a gateway to a bigger world.

Again, we are talking about ordinary things. The discipline could include things like mountain biking, working out in a gym, learning ballroom dancing, knitting, or home repair. Everyday activities can be the basis of a meaningful discipline, if we do them differently. And, on the other hand, consider the drill practice of a soldier, an ancient military method. In a sense, it is nothing more than walking, and yet it can foster a sense of attention and rhythm that are vital for the work of a solider. Indeed, being in tune with his or her body and the surrounding world is the first duty of every soldier. If we can find a discipline to practice, it can open us to the world around us rather than close us off and solidify our world. Making ourselves and the world solid perpetuates the sense of separation, takes a lot of energy to maintain, and creates obstacles to an accurate view and effective action.

Developing our faculty of knowing ourselves and our world is the important first step. It can be worked on in so many ways, using things quite close at hand. It works with anything that helps loosen the grip of the internal narrative, the endless process of "butchering reality" that shields us from seeing what is. The experience of a gap in our fictional reality fosters a direct perception of the world as interconnected, interdependent, and constantly in flux. This allows us to connect to the worldview inherent in the Sun Tzu and to develop the faculties required to work with the world in this way.

Mixing Your Mind with the Sun Tzu

Now we turn our attention to how to undertake a closer study of the text itself. *Study,* in the way we use it here, refers to the whole range of ways people relate to learning *The Art of War,* including something as simple as taking the text off the shelf from time to time and spending a few minutes with it. As we discussed in the very first chapter, we have found that an excellent way to study the text is what we have come to call "reading practice." In reading practice, we carefully read and reread short sections of the text aloud in a contemplative environment. It differs from what we commonly call study, because it isn't solely about acquiring knowledge from outside us but rather about mixing our mind with the world in a way that also provokes the wisdom inherent in us.

Whether you are studying the text in a group or on your own, reading practice can be approached in a similar manner. First of all, choose a short segment to focus on. It can be a single line, a couplet, or a short section that presents a theme of special interest to you. It could be a theme that seems especially relevant to the events in your life or one that seems especially dense and difficult. As long as there is some interest in or connection to the lines you have chosen, your choice doesn't really matter. Next, find or set up an appropriate place to read aloud—a container of the kind we discussed when we talked about forming and transforming. This can be any space—your office, den, or favorite quiet outdoor spot—that is open and conducive to learning, one that reinforces your study.

To begin the reading itself, take the point of view that you are a member of this wisdom lineage, at once both ancient and up to date. Read the chosen passage aloud, with careful diction and an awareness of the space around the words, but still in a relaxed and normal reading voice for you. This is not a theatrical performance. Allow a brief gap, less than half a minute, to consider and contemplate what you have read. Read the lines aloud again. If you are studying in a group, the reader can then begin the discussion by sharing what the lines mean to him or her or what questions arose. If you are studying alone, consider how these lines connect to the specific situation in your life you are focusing upon. In both cases, retain the sense of open space and inquiry throughout.

As we have noted, reading the Sun Tzu is challenging, because the text is pithy, at times opaque, repetitive yet inconsistent. It doesn't surrender its lessons easily. But this is also a key to its power. The Sun Tzu text began as wisdom passed on through an oral lineage for hundreds of years before it was written down. It was composed to be recited aloud and remembered, so it is rich with imagery and poetic language. Its rhythmic cadence helps penetrate beneath superficial discursive thinking.

Since it was based on memorization, the text relied on a poetic structure—sound and feel, tone and pace—to carry its message forward intact. Reading tunes us in to the sound-based nature of the Sun Tzu, helps us to "hear" the deeper meaning of the text, and thereby make a more genuine connection to it.

Reading aloud involves both speaking the text and listening to it. Interestingly enough, the communication and learning happen in the listening part rather than the speaking part. Listening is a way to connect to your sense organs and perceptions, and through them to your world. When we talk about a contemplative approach, it's just another way of saying "simply listen."

We often do listening exercises in our *Art of War* seminars, and you can do a simplified version of them on your own. It can be woven into your study of the text. When your study becomes too discursive or disconnected, take a break and do this listening exercise.

It starts with just being quiet, either in the middle of a room or outdoors. First, bring your attention to whatever you hear. Suspend the impulse to judge or name sounds; just let them be. Notice where sounds come from, when they arise and when they disappear. Begin to notice the details you are missing. Notice what you are doing when you aren't listening. You can do this on a regular basis or from time to time. You can do this anywhere, or you could go to someplace special to do it. It is helpful at first to do this listening practice in less busy places so you can more easily discriminate sounds. After a while, you can move on to places where the sounds form a symphony.

Through a discipline like listening practice, you begin to discover that there are rhythmic, harmonic beginnings and endings going on all the time in our world. Chaos and order are turning into each other repeatedly. The energies and activities that make up our experience, those elements we touch when we employ shih, are always at play in this ever-changing world. It is possible to notice and even tune in to them. One of our colleagues, a professional musician and teacher who developed the listening exercises,[1] tells us that when you play jazz, for instance, you don't think up or decide what to play or react on first impulse. Rather, you *hear* what to play. A problem arises in playing music if when you're not playing, you're waiting to play. In the same way, problems arise in communication if when you're not talking, you're waiting to talk. As with playing music, skillful action is self-evident in the situation, if you're listening.

Reading practice helps in our ongoing study of the text because it is based on and strengthens our natural inquisitiveness. It fosters a greater openness to exploring the experiences in our lives. This is equally true for practices that work in this same way with our other senses. In fact, we also include in our workshops a practice involving nonjudgmental observation of what is in our field of vision in a given environment. Learning, whether *The Art of War* or anything else, is the act—or the art—of "knowing" as we understand it in the Sun Tzu. It's not a matter of collecting information but rather absorbing what's going on around us. We are learning not so we can use things at a later point but because we have an appetite for discovery and exploration of our world.

With ongoing study of the text through reading practice and the listening exercise—or other contemplative techniques—the profound strategic practices contained in the text's lines begin to seep more deeply into your system. Then, in situations of conflict and challenge, the text's pith instructions begin to shape the way you think and act. Rather than applying a "learned" technique, you allow a new way of viewing the world to emerge. Knowing more clearly the elements of your present situation gives rise to the kinds of skillful action that lead to taking whole.

Transforming Chaos and Conflict

Any pathway for ongoing study of *The Art of War* would be incomplete if it didn't include mixing our understanding of the text's lessons with the challenging situations in our lives. We touched upon this in the reading practice. Now it becomes a more central feature of our study. We started by working on the ways we know about the world, the common human faculties and the disciplines that can strengthen them. We've contemplated the text in detail through reading practice and now may have some insight into the view and principal strategies. Next we consider how all this might apply to our own life experiences.

The key to mixing our study with our life experiences is to maintain our orientation of knowing—marked by an openness and a brief moment of reflection—at the point of engaging conflict and chaos. This allows the new ways of working with the world that we have learned from the text to emerge. It takes a disciplined effort to bring our understanding of the text to the point of engagement in this way, because this is when the urge to wrestle, force, or bully the obstacles in front of us is strongest. It is when the heat of battle typically diminishes our intelligence and narrows the options, most commonly referred to in the military as the "fog of war." But maintaining that bigger perspective enables us to take a fresh view, to see creative options in the immediate environment—the "strange," as we called it in our discussion of extraordinary and orthodox— which lead to effective action.

Bringing the lessons from our study of the text to the field of our interaction with the phenomenal world can be embarrassing. It can be embarrassing because mixing our learning from the text with these "battle" scenarios typically uncovers the limitations of our deep habitual patterns and how often we repeat unsuccessful strategies. We are aware of our aspiration to do things differently, and we are just as aware of how often we fail to do so.

But when we begin to respond to the energy of chaos and obstacle as the inspiration rather than the enemy, many things become possible. The eight ways of relating to the world that we presented as reminders when employing shih—such as not avoiding pain, always thinking bigger, and not too loose, not too tight—arise as surprisingly natural gestures. Working with mixing our experience and the text in this way is continuing an active dialogue with this wisdom tradition, the basic ground of becoming a member of this lineage as so many others have done before.

We can see how reshaping the moment of engaging with conflict can work in the story of Richard, a consultant called in to help a company that he had previously worked with for many years. He knew the people, the company, their promise and their problems. The company had hired another consultant who was an old friend and former colleague of Richard's—we'll call her Nancy—to revamp its IT systems. But after a long time, the project got bogged down, and management was losing confidence in Nancy and doubted that they wanted to continue. The managers knew it wasn't Nancy's failure solely, that they themselves had been unclear about their goals (their view), which is a deadly start in such a large and expensive undertaking. But still, the momentum began to build to blame Nancy for the project's impending failure. Richard analyzed the project to date and concluded that indeed it would not be completed to the company's satisfaction and advised the executives that they had better move on to another scenario beyond their contract with Nancy.

In a surprising turn of events, the company asked Richard to inform Nancy that things were not working out and that her tenure would most likely soon end. He was in a quandary about how to do that, since they all knew one another so well and future working relationships had to be protected all around. Looking from the bigger perspective of "just getting the job done," Richard saw that the habitual and "easiest" path for him would be to lay blame on Nancy when talking to the company and to lay blame on the company when talking to Nancy. This would be the usual method. It would play on everyone's assumptions and projections, and would all be done with a wink and a "You know how messed up they are" kind of rationale. Richard imagined that this "solution" would allow him to avoid the immediate impact of negativity and ill will. Yet he was nagged by the likely by-product of this course of action: hurt feelings and self-justifying rationales that would certainly arise as a problem in the future.

Seeking advice from the text for an option of taking whole, Richard suspended the momentum to push ahead in a habitual fashion and looked at the bigger questions and feelings arising. As he did so, a more complete picture of the conflict arose more clearly in his mind. He realized that the obstacle—or "enemy"—was his own fear and hesitation to experience the pain of hurt feelings and potential difficulty. He didn't want to be the bad guy. When he realized that he had the ability to experience that pain, a different approach dawned on him about how he could create the ground for everyone to walk away with their dignity and with future possibilities left open.

He took Nancy out of the embattled office atmosphere to a familiar restaurant for a nice lunch and assured her that he understood that the company had not set the project parameters out fully and didn't know what it wanted, and praised her for how she had fared in that difficult work environment. After hearing Nancy's relief at his candor, but before she had a chance to lapse into denigrating the company, he let her know that she, too, hadn't communicated very well when things became difficult and that she shared in creating the difficult relationships with all the staff.

When he returned to the office and met with the company executives, Richard reported on the direct feedback he had given Nancy and assured them that she was ready to leave the project gracefully and without rancor. But before they had the chance to conclude that the problem was all about Nancy's well-known limitations, Richard added that their confused view of the project hadn't really given Nancy a fair chance to be successful, and so firing her wasn't going to magically solve their internal problems. Both Nancy and the company were relieved to be parting on good terms. It was also acknowledged that some of the benefits of Nancy's long efforts could contribute to the next attempt at an IT overhaul, and no effort was wasted on managing the fallout from the project's failure. Richard was relieved to be able to work with a client without resorting to low-level manipulations that would just have confirmed the client's narrow assumptions. He was left with the awkward feeling that often accompanies doing things in a "different way" but also had a sense that integrating the insights from the text might be easier the next time.

Letting Go

The result of working closely with the text in this way, of getting inside this lineage, is noticing that it has truly seeped into your way of thinking and being. Something will arise, some experience of conflict and chaos, and all the standard linear ways of reacting to it will arise with it—I didn't get what I want, this is bad news, I have to find out who is at fault, I have to fix something. And in the end, impatiently, you may react in that linear way. But at the very least, there is the strong hint of seeing the larger perspective that surrounds this scenario and, with it, the possibility of something new and creative emerging from that space—a space you don't have to create, manipulate, manage, or fight against.

One of the wonderful qualities of ordinary magic is that it is also magic to us. When an extraordinary moment of exceptional skill and taking whole arises in our action, it can be as much a wonderment to us as to others. How did that happen? This is not an aberration but rather a condition of employing the text's profound practices.

Yet the workings of the Sun Tzu are not so very mysterious after all. You've done all the hard work and study, but then, as with mastering any worthwhile discipline, you just have to let go. It's no longer about apprehending something external, or even about your great realizations, but just about being in the world in a simple and straightforward way. You are free of the burden of carrying around a bundle of external wisdom that will make you more effective. You don't go back to the lesson plan yet again before you teach the class. It's like eating a meal and then digesting your food so that the proteins and carbohydrates contribute to making your muscles stronger. When you can lift a weight that before seemed too heavy for you, at that point it's no longer about the nutrients.

The elements of the world and your life become real and immediate. Round rocks will roll and square rocks will stop, and you don't have to crank things up to make it all work. The experience that used to feel like pushing boulders uphill all the time feels more like riding a wind of energy that is provided by the experiences in your life. The conventional boundaries of hope for success and fear of failure don't pen you in and limit your options for action. Overcoming conflict is no longer a project made leaden by motivation or planning. Everything in the world doesn't have to be fixed: "the victorious military is first victorious and after that does battle."

A natural state of relaxation develops, and everything becomes so ordinary that it becomes extraordinary. And yet, that's no big deal.

The extraordinary and the orthodox circle and give birth to each other,

As a circle has no beginning.
Who is able to exhaust it?
[CHAPTER 5]

The promise of making the connection to this wisdom lineage turns into just dealing directly with whatever arises. The world becomes a place to be rather an enemy to fight. Challenges continue to arise in the normal course of events and, with them, the energy to respond. Skillful actions arise and bring possibilities of taking whole, and you act accordingly.

The Art of War
The Denma Translation

Passages that rhyme in Chinese are indicated by a ∿ placed at the end of a line. We have used the mark § to indicate where we believe section breaks occur in the text, but the original Chinese contains neither punctuation nor paragraphing.

I
Appraisals

Sun Tzu said:

The military is a great matter of the state.
It is the ground of death and life,
The Tao of survival or extinction.
One cannot but examine it.

§

And so base it in the five.
Compare by means of the appraisals.
Thus seek out its nature.

The first is Tao, the second is heaven, the third is earth, the fourth
is the general, the fifth is method.

Tao is what causes the people to have the same purpose as
their superior.
Thus they can die with him, live with him and not deceive him.

Heaven is *yin* and *yang,* cold and hot, the order of the seasons.
Going with it, going against it—this is military victory.

Earth is high and low, broad and narrow, far and near, steep and level, death and life.

The general is knowledge, trustworthiness, courage and strictness.

Method is ordering divisions, the Tao of ranking and principal supply.

As for all these five—
No general has not heard of them.
Knowing them, one is victorious.
Not knowing them, one is not victorious.

§

And so compare by means of the appraisals.
Thus seek out its nature.
Ask—
Which ruler has Tao?
Which general has ability?
Which attains heaven and earth?
Which implements method and orders?
Whose military and multitudes are strong?
Whose officers and soldiers are trained?
Whose rewards and punishments are clear?
By these I know victory and defeat!

The general heeds my appraisals. Employ him and he is certainly victorious. Retain him.
The general does not heed my appraisals. Employ him and he is certainly defeated. Remove him.

§

Having appraised the advantages, heed them.
Then make them into *shih* to aid with the external.
Shih is governing the balance according to the advantages.

§

The military is a Tao of deception—

Thus when able, manifest inability.
When active, manifest inactivity.
When near, manifest as far.
When far, manifest as near.
Thus when he seeks advantage, lure him. ∼
When he is in chaos, take him. ∼
When he is substantial, prepare against him. ∼
When he is strong, avoid him. ∼
When he is wrathful, harass him.
Attack where he is unprepared.
Emerge where he does not expect it.

These are the victories of the military lineage.
They cannot be transmitted in advance.

§

Now, in the rod-counting at court before battle, one is victorious
      who gets many counting rods.
In the rod-counting at court before battle, one is not victorious
      who gets few counting rods.
Many counting rods is victorious over few counting rods,
How much more so over no counting rods.
By these means I observe them.
Victory and defeat are apparent.

2

Doing Battle

Sun Tzu said:

In sum, the method of employing the military—

With one thousand fast chariots, one thousand leather-covered
      chariots and one hundred thousand armored troops to
      be provisioned over one thousand *li*—
then expenses of outer and inner, stipends of foreign advisers,
      materials for glue and lacquer, and contributions for
      chariots and armor are one thousand gold pieces a day.
Only after this are one hundred thousand soldiers raised.

§

When one employs battle—
　　If victory takes long, it blunts the military and grinds down
　　　　its sharpness.
　　Attacking walled cities, one's strength is diminished.
　　If soldiers are long in the field, the state's resources are
　　　　insufficient.
Now if one blunts the military, grinds down its sharpness,
Diminishes its strength and exhausts its goods,
Then the feudal lords ride one's distress and rise up.
Even one who is wise cannot make good the aftermath!

Thus in the military one has heard of foolish speed but has not
　　　observed skillful prolonging.
And there has never been a military prolonging that has brought
　　　advantage to the state.

§

And so one who does not thoroughly know the harm from
　　　employing the military ⌇
Cannot thoroughly know the advantage from employing the
　　　military. ⌇

§

One skilled at employing the military
Does not have a second registering of conscripts nor a third
　　　loading of grain.
One takes equipment from the state and relies on grain from
　　　the enemy.
Thus the army's food can be made sufficient.

§

A state's impoverishment from its soldiers—
　　When they are distant, there is distant transport.
　　When they are distant and there is distant transport, the
　　　　hundred clans are impoverished.
　　When soldiers are near, things sell dearly.

When things sell dearly, wealth is exhausted.
When wealth is exhausted, people are hard-pressed by local taxes.
Diminished strength in the heartland,
Emptiness in the households.
Of the hundred clans' resources, six-tenths is gone.
Of the ruling family's resources—
    Broken chariots, worn-out horses, ∼
    Armor, helmets, arrows, crossbows, ∼
    Halberds, shields, spears, pavises, ∼
    Heavy ox-drawn wagons— ∼
Seven-tenths is gone.

Thus the wise general looks to the enemy for food.
One bushel of enemy food equals twenty bushels of mine.
One bale of fodder equals twenty bales of mine.

§

And so killing the enemy is a matter of wrath.
Taking the enemy's goods is a matter of advantage.

§

And so in chariot battles—
    When more than ten chariots are captured,
    Reward him who first captures one.
    Then change their flags and pennants.
    When the chariots are mixed together, ride them.
    Supply the captives and care for them.
This is what is meant by "victorious over the enemy and so
        increasing one's strength."

§

And so the military values victory.
It does not value prolonging.

§

And so the general who knows the military is the people's fate star,
The ruler of the state's security and danger.

3
Strategy of Attack

Sun Tzu said:

In sum, the method of employing the military—

Taking a state whole is superior.
Destroying it is inferior to this.

Taking an army whole is superior.
Destroying it is inferior to this.

Taking a battalion whole is superior.
Destroying it is inferior to this.

Taking a company whole is superior.
Destroying it is inferior to this.

Taking a squad whole is superior.
Destroying it is inferior to this.

Therefore, one hundred victories in one hundred battles is not the
    most skillful.
Subduing the other's military without battle is the most skillful.

§

And so the superior military cuts down strategy.
Its inferior cuts down alliances.
Its inferior cuts down the military.
The worst attacks walled cities.

§

The method of attacking walled cities—
    Ready the siege towers and armored vehicles.
    This is completed after three months.
    Pile up the earthworks.
    This also takes three months.
    If the general is not victorious over his anger and sets them
        swarming like ants,

One-third of the officers and soldiers are killed and the walled
city not uprooted—
This is the calamity of attack.

§

And so one skilled at employing the military
Subdues the other's military but does not do battle,
Uproots the other's walled city but does not attack,
Destroys the other's state but does not prolong.
One must take it whole when contending for all-under-heaven.
Thus the military is not blunted and advantage can be whole.
This is the method of the strategy of attack.

§

And so the method of employing the military—
When ten to one, surround them.
When five to one, attack them.
When two to one, do battle with them.
When matched, then divide them.
When fewer, then defend against them.
When inadequate, then avoid them.
Thus a small enemy's tenacity ～
Is a large enemy's catch. ～

§

Now the general is the safeguard of the state.
If the safeguard is complete, the state is surely strong.
If the safeguard is flawed, the state is surely weak.

§

And so the sovereign brings adversity to the army in three ways—

Not knowing the army is unable to advance yet ordering an
advance,
Not knowing the army is unable to retreat yet ordering a retreat,
This is what is meant by "hobbling the army."

Not knowing affairs within the three armies yet controlling the
    governance of the three armies,
Then the army's officers are confused!

Not knowing the three armies' balance yet controlling appoint-
    ments in the three armies,
Then the army's officers are distrustful!

Once the three armies are confused and distrustful,
Troubles from the feudal lords intensify!
This is what is meant by "an army in chaos leads to victory."

§

And so knowing victory is fivefold—
    Knowing when one can and cannot do battle is victory.
    Knowing the use of the many and the few is victory.
    Superior and inferior desiring the same is victory.
    Being prepared and awaiting the unprepared is victory.
    The general being capable and the ruler not interfering is victory.
These five are a Tao of knowing victory.

§

And so in the military—
    Knowing the other and knowing oneself, ⌒
    In one hundred battles no danger. ⌒
    Not knowing the other and knowing oneself, ⌒
    One victory for one loss. ⌒
    Not knowing the other and not knowing oneself, ⌒
    In every battle certain defeat. ⌒

4
Form
―――
Sun Tzu said:

Of old the skilled first made themselves invincible to await the
    enemy's vincibility.

Invincibility lies in oneself.
Vincibility lies in the enemy.

Thus the skilled can make themselves invincible.
They cannot cause the enemy's vincibility.

Thus it is said, "Victory can be known. It cannot be made."

§

Invincibility is defense.
Vincibility is attack.

Defend and one has a surplus.
Attack and one is insufficient.

Of old those skilled at defense hid below the nine earths and
      moved above the nine heavens.
Thus they could preserve themselves and be all-victorious.

§

In seeing victory, not going beyond what everyone knows is not
      skilled.
Victory in battle that all-under-heaven calls skilled is not skilled.
Thus lifting an autumn hair does not mean great strength.
Seeing the sun and the moon does not mean a clear eye.
Hearing thunder does not mean a keen ear.
So-called skill is to be victorious over the easily defeated.
Thus the battles of the skilled are without extraordinary victory,
      without reputation for wisdom and without merit for
      courage.

§

And so one's victories are without error.
Being without error, what one arranges is necessarily victorious
Since one is victorious over the defeated.

One skilled at battle takes a stand in the ground of no defeat
And so does not lose the enemy's defeat.

Therefore, the victorious military is first victorious and after that
      does battle.
The defeated military first does battle and after that seeks victory.

§

And so one who is skilled cultivates Tao and preserves method.
Thus one can be the measure of victory and defeat.

§

As for method—
    First, measure length.
    Second, measure volume.
    Third, count.
    Fourth, weigh.
    The fifth is victory.

    Earth gives birth to length.
    Length gives birth to volume.
    Volume gives birth to counting.
    Counting gives birth to weighing.
    Weighing gives birth to victory.

§

A victorious military is like weighing a hundredweight against
      a grain.
A defeated military is like weighing a grain against a hundred-
      weight.
One who weighs victory sets the people to battle like releasing
      amassed water into a gorge one thousand *jen* deep.

This is form.

5
Shih

Ordering the many is like ordering the few.
It is division and counting.

Fighting the many is like fighting the few.
It is form and name.

The multitude of the three armies can be made to meet all enemies
without defeat.
It is the extraordinary and the orthodox.

How a military comes to prevail, like throwing a grindstone against
an egg.
It is the empty and the solid.

§

In sum, when in battle,
Use the orthodox to engage.
Use the extraordinary to attain victory.

§

And so one skilled at giving rise to the extraordinary—
As boundless as heaven and earth,
As inexhaustible as the Yellow River and the ocean.

Ending and beginning again,
It is the sun and the moon.

Dying and then being born,
It is the four seasons.

§

Musical pitches do not exceed five,
Yet all their variations cannot be heard.

Colors do not exceed five,
Yet all their variations cannot be seen.

Tastes do not exceed five,
Yet all their variations cannot be tasted.

The shih of battle do not exceed the extraordinary and the
orthodox,
Yet all their variations cannot be exhausted.

The extraordinary and the orthodox circle and give birth to
  each other,
As a circle has no beginning.
Who is able to exhaust it?

§

The rush of water, to the point of tossing rocks about. This is shih.
The strike of a hawk, at the killing snap. This is the node.
Therefore, one skilled at battle—
  His shih is steep.
  His node is short.
Shih is like drawing the crossbow.
The node is like pulling the trigger.

§

Pwun-pwun. Hwun-hwun.
The fight is chaotic yet one is not subject to chaos.

Hwun-hwun. Dwun-dwun.
One's form is round and one cannot be defeated.

Chaos is born from order.
Cowardice is born from bravery.
Weakness is born from strength.

Order and chaos are a matter of counting.
Bravery and cowardice are a matter of shih.
Strength and weakness are a matter of form.

§

One skilled at moving the enemy
  Forms and the enemy must follow,
  Offers and the enemy must take.
Move them by this and await them with troops.

§

And so one skilled at battle
Seeks it in shih and does not demand it of people.
Thus one can dispense with people and employ shih.

One who uses shih sets people to battle as if rolling trees and rocks.
As for the nature of trees and rocks—
    When still, they are at rest.
    When agitated, they move.
    When square, they stop.
    When round, they go.
Thus the shih of one skilled at setting people to battle is like rolling
      round rocks from a mountain one thousand jen high.

This is shih.

6

The Solid and Empty

One who takes position first at the battleground and awaits the
      enemy is at ease.
One who takes position later at the battleground and hastens to
      do battle is at labor.
Thus one skilled at battle summons others and is not summoned
      by them.

How one can make the enemy arrive of their own accord—offer
      them advantage.
How one can prevent the enemy from arriving—harm them.
Thus how one can make the enemy labor when at ease and starve
      when full—emerge where they must hasten.

§

To go one thousand li without fear, go through unpeopled
      ground.
To attack and surely take it, attack where they do not defend.
To defend and surely hold firm, defend where they will surely
      attack.
Thus with one skilled at attack, the enemy does not know where
      to defend.
With one skilled at defense, the enemy does not know where to
      attack.

§

Subtle! Subtle!
To the point of formlessness. ↝
Spiritlike! Spiritlike!
To the point of soundlessness. ↝
Thus one can be the enemy's fate star. ↝

§

To advance so that one cannot be resisted, charge against the empty.
To retreat so that one cannot be stopped, go so far that one cannot
      be reached.

And so if I wish to do battle, the enemy cannot but do battle with me.
I attack what he must save.

If I do not wish to do battle, I mark a line on the earth to defend it,
      and the enemy cannot do battle with me.
I misdirect him.

§

And so the skilled general forms others yet is without form.
Hence I am concentrated and the enemy is divided.
I am concentrated and thus one.
The enemy is divided and thus one-tenth.
This is using one-tenth to strike one.
When I am few and the enemy is many, I can use the few to strike the
      many because those with whom I do battle are restricted!

The ground on which I do battle with him cannot be known.
Then the enemy's preparations are many.
When his preparations are many, I battle the few!

Prepare the front and the rear has few.
Prepare the left and the right has few.
Everywhere prepared, everywhere few.

The few are those who prepare against others.
The many are those who make others prepare against them.

§

Knowing the battle day and knowing the battleground,
One can go one thousand li and do battle.
Not knowing the battle day and not knowing the battleground,
The front cannot help the rear, the rear cannot help the front,
The left cannot help the right, the right cannot help the left.
How much more so when the far is several tens of li and the near
        is several li away!

§

Though by my estimate the military of Yueh is many,
How does this further victory?
Thus it is said, "Victory can be usurped."
Although the enemy is numerous, they can be kept from fighting.

§

And so prick them and know the pattern of their movement and
        stillness.
Form them and know the ground of death and life.
Appraise them and know the plans for gain and loss.
Probe them and know the places of surplus and insufficiency.

§

The ultimate in giving form to the military is to arrive at
        formlessness.
When one is formless, deep spies cannot catch a glimpse and
        the wise cannot strategize.

Rely on form to bring about victory over the multitude,
And the multitude cannot understand.
The elite all know the form by which I am victorious,
But no one knows how I determine the form of victory.
Do not repeat the means of victory,
But respond to form from the inexhaustible.

Now the form of the military is like water.
Water in its movement avoids the high and hastens to the low.

The military in its victory avoids the solid and strikes the empty.
Thus water determines its movement in accordance with the earth.
The military determines victory in accordance with the enemy.
The military is without fixed shih and without lasting form.

To be able to transform with the enemy is what is meant by
        "spiritlike."

Of the Five Phases, none is the lasting victor.
Of the four seasons, none has constant rank.
The sun shines short and long.
The moon dies and lives.

Spiritlike essentials.

7

The Army Contending

Sun Tzu said:

In sum, the method of employing the military—

The general receives the command from the sovereign,
Joins with the army, gathers the multitude, organizes them and
        encamps.
Nothing is more difficult than an army contending.

The difficulty for a contending army
Is to make the circuitous direct
And to make the adverse advantageous.

Thus make their road circuitous
And lure them with advantage.
Setting out later than others and arriving sooner
Is knowing the appraisals of circuitous and direct.

§

A contending army brings advantage.
A contending army brings danger.
Contending for advantage with an entire army, one will not
        get there.

Contending for advantage with a reduced army, one's baggage
  train is diminished.

Therefore, rolling up one's armor, hastening after advantage day and
    night without camping, continually marching at the double
    for one hundred li and then contending for advantage—
  The commander of the three armies is captured.
  The strong ones sooner, the worn-out ones later, and one in ten
    arrives.
Going fifty li and contending for advantage—
  The ranking general falls.
  By this method half arrive.
Going thirty li and contending for advantage—
  Two-thirds arrive.
Therefore—
  An army without a baggage train is lost,
  Without grain and food is lost,
  Without supplies is lost.

§

Therefore—
  Not knowing the strategies of the feudal lords,
  One cannot ally with them.
  Not knowing the form of mountains and forests, defiles and
    gorges, marshes and swamps,
  One cannot move the army.
  Not employing local guides,
  One cannot obtain the advantage of the ground.

§

And so the military is based on guile,
Acts due to advantage,
Transforms by dividing and joining.

§

And so—
  Swift like the wind,
  Slow like the forest,

Raiding and plundering like fire,
Not moving like a mountain,
Difficult to know like yin,
Moving like thunder.

§

When plundering the countryside, divide the multitude.
When expanding territory, divide the advantage.
Weigh it and act.

§

One who knows in advance the Tao of the circuitous and direct
       is victorious.
This is the method of the army contending.

§

Therefore, the *Governance of the Army* says—
    "Because they could not hear each other, they made drums
       and bells.
    Because they could not see each other, they made flags and
       pennants."
Therefore—
    In day battle use more flags and pennants.
    In night battle use more drums and bells.
Drums and bells, flags and pennants are the means by which one
       unifies the ears and eyes of the people.
Once the people have been tightly unified,
The brave have no chance to advance alone,
The cowardly have no chance to retreat alone.
This is the method of employing the many.

§

And so the *ch'i* of the three armies can be seized.
The heart-mind of the commander can be seized.

Therefore, morning ch'i is sharp, midday ch'i is lazy, evening ch'i
       is spent.

Thus one skilled at employing the military
Avoids their sharp ch'i and strikes their lazy and spent ch'i.
This is ordering ch'i.

Use order to await chaos.
Use stillness to await clamor.
This is ordering the heart-mind.

Use the near to await the far.
Use ease to await labor.
Use fullness to await hunger.
This is ordering strength.

Do not engage well-ordered pennants.
Do not strike imposing formations.
This is ordering transformation.

§

And so the method of employing the military—
    Do not face them when they are on a high hill.
    Do not go against them with their back to a mound.
    Do not pursue them when they feign defeat.
    Leave a way out for surrounded soldiers. ∽
    Do not block soldiers returning home. ∽
This is the method of employing the many.

Four hundred sixty-five.

8

The Nine Transformations

Sun Tzu said:

In sum, the method of employing the military—

The general receives the command from the sovereign,
Joins with the army and gathers the multitude.

§

In spread-out ground do not encamp.

In junction ground join with allies.
In crossing ground do not linger.
In enclosed ground strategize.
In death ground do battle.

§

There are roads one does not follow.
There are armies one does not strike.
There are cities one does not attack.
There are grounds one does not contest.
There are commands of the sovereign one does not accept.

§

And so the general who comprehends the advantages of the nine
    transformations
Knows how to employ the military!
The general who does not comprehend the advantages of the nine
    transformations,
Though knowing the form of the ground, is unable to obtain the
    advantages of the ground!
When one orders the military but does not know the teachings of
    the nine transformations,
Though knowing the five advantages, one is unable to employ
    people!

§

Therefore—
    The plans of the wise necessarily include advantage and harm.
    They include advantage. Thus one's service can be trusted.
    They include harm. Thus adversity can be undone.

Therefore—
    Subdue the feudal lords with harm.
    Occupy the feudal lords with tasks.
    Hasten the feudal lords with advantage.

§

And so the method of employing the military—
    Do not rely on their not coming.
    Rely on what we await them with.
    Do not rely on their not attacking.
    Rely on how we are unable to be attacked.

§

And so for the general there are five dangers—
    Resolved to die, one can be killed.
    Resolved to live, one can be captured.
    Quick to anger, one can be goaded.
    Pure and honest, one can be shamed.
    Loving the people, one can be aggravated.
All five are the excesses of the general,
A calamity in employing the military.

To overturn an army and kill the general,
One must use the five dangers.
One cannot but examine them.

9
Moving the Army

Sun Tzu said:

In sum, positioning the army and scrutinizing the enemy—

In crossing mountains,
    Hold to the valleys.
    Look out at life ground and take a high position.
    Battle downhill. Do not ascend.
This is positioning the army in mountains.

In crossing water,
    One must distance oneself from it.
    When the invader approaches across water, do not meet him in
        the water.
    To order a strike when he is half across is advantageous.
    When wishing to do battle,
    Do not go close to the water to meet the invader.

Look out at life ground and take a high position.
Do not go against the current.
This is positioning the army by water.
In crossing salt marshes,
　　Be sure to leave quickly. Do not linger.
　　If one encounters an army in the midst of a salt marsh,
　　Hold to the water grass and keep one's back to the trees.
　　This is positioning the army in salt marshes.

On plains
　　Take a position on level ground.
　　Keep the high to the right and back.
　　In front, death. Behind, life.
This is positioning the army on plains.

All four are the advantages of the army, how the Yellow Emperor
　　　　was victorious over the Four Emperors.

§

In sum, the army likes the high and hates the low,
Values yang and disdains yin,
Sustains life and takes a position in the solid.
This is what is meant by "surely victorious."
The army is without the hundred afflictions.

In hills and dikes, take a position in yang.
Keep them to the right and back.
This is the advantage of the military, the assistance of the earth.

When it has rained upstream, the stream's flow intensifies.
Stop fording. Wait for it to calm.
When crossing heavenly ravines, heavenly wells, heavenly prisons,
　　　　heavenly nets, heavenly sinkholes and heavenly fissures,
One must quickly leave them. Do not go near.
When I am far from them, the enemy is near them.
When I face them, the enemy has his back to them.

When alongside the army are defiles, ponds, reeds, small forests
　　　　and dense vegetation that can conceal people,

Search these carefully and repeatedly.
They are where the devious take position.

When the enemy is near and still, he is relying on the steep.
When the enemy is far and provokes battle, he wishes the other
        to advance—
    He is occupying the level and advantageous.

§

Many trees move.
He is approaching.

Many obstacles in thick grass.
He is misleading us.

Birds rise up.
He is concealing himself.

Animals are startled.
He is launching a total assault.

§

Dust is high and sharp
Chariots are approaching.

It is low and wide.
The infantry is approaching.

It is dispersed and wispy.
The firewood gatherers are approaching.

It is scattered here and there.
He is encamping his army.

§

His words are humble and his preparations increase.
He will advance.

His words are strong and his advance is forced.
He will retreat.

Light chariots come out first and take position on the flank.
He is deploying.

He is not in difficulty yet requests peace.
He is strategizing.

They rush out to deploy.
He has set the moment.

Half of them advance.
He is luring you.

§

They lean on their weapons.
They are hungry.

Those who draw water drink first.
They are thirsty.

They see advantage but do not advance.
They are tired.

Birds gather.
It is empty.

They call out at night.
They are afraid.

The encampment is disorderly.
The general has no weight.

Flags and pennants are moved about.
There is chaos.

Officers are angry.
They are fatigued.

They feed grain to their horses and eat meat, the army does not
      hang up their water pots, and they do not return to their
      quarters.
The invaders are exhausted.

§

He repeatedly and soothingly speaks to his men in measured tones.
He has lost the multitude.

There are many rewards.
He is in distress.

There are many punishments.
He is in difficulty.

At first he is harsh and later fears the multitude.
He is utterly unskillful.

He approaches with gifts and entreaties.
He wishes to rest.

The military is wrathful and faces one for a long time without
either engaging or withdrawing.
One must carefully examine this.

§

In the military more is not better.

Do not advance in a martial way.
It is sufficient to gather strength, assess the enemy and take him—
that is all.

However, if one does not plan and takes the enemy lightly,
One will certainly be captured by him.

§

If the troops do not yet feel close kinship with one and they are
punished, they will not submit.
If they do not submit, they are difficult to employ.
If the troops already feel close kinship with one and punishments
are not carried out, do not employ them.

And so assemble them by fellowship,
Make them uniform by the martial.
This is what is meant by "certain to seize it."

If one acts consistently to train the people, the people will submit.

If one acts inconsistently to train the people, the people will not
    submit.
One who acts consistently is in accord with the multitude.

10

Forms of the Earth

Sun Tzu said:

The forms of the earth—
    open, hung, stalled, narrow, steep and distant.

I am able to go. He is able to come. This is called "open."
As for the open form—
    Be first to occupy the high and yang.
    Secure your supply routes.
    If I do battle, it is advantageous.

I can go but it is difficult to return. This is called "hung."
As for the hung form—
    When the enemy is unprepared, I emerge and am victorious
        over him.
    When the enemy is prepared, if I emerge and am not
        victorious,
    It is difficult to return.
    It is not advantageous.

I emerge and it is not advantageous. He emerges and it is not
    advantageous. This is called "stalled."
As for the stalled form—
    Although the enemy offers me advantage, I do not emerge.
        I lead my troops away.
    To order a strike when half the enemy has emerged is
        advantageous.

As for the narrow form—
    If I occupy it first, I must fill it and await the enemy.
    If the enemy occupies it first and fills it, do not pursue.
    If he does not fill it, pursue.

As for the steep form—
> If I occupy it first, I must occupy the high and yang and await
>> the enemy.
> If the enemy occupies it first, I lead the troops away.
> Do not pursue.

As for the distant form—
> Since shih is equal, it is difficult to provoke battle.
> To do battle is not advantageous.

> All these six are a Tao of the earth,
> The general's utmost responsibility.
> One cannot but examine them.

§

And so in the military there is driven off, the bow unstrung,
>> dragged down, the mountain collapsing, chaos and
>> routed.
All these six are not a calamity of heaven.
They are the excesses of the general.

Now shih is equal and he uses one to strike ten.
This is called "driven off."

The troops are strong and the officers weak.
This is called "the bow unstrung."

The officers are strong and the troops weak.
This is called "dragged down."

A great officer is wrathful and does not submit.
When he encounters the enemy,
He is filled with rancor and does battle on his own.
The general does not know his ability.
This is called "the mountain collapsing."

The general is weak and not strict.
His training and leadership are not clear.
The officers and troops are inconstant.
The formations of the military are jumbled.
This is called "chaos."

The general cannot assess the enemy.
With the few he engages the many.
With the weak he strikes the strong.
The military is without elite forces.
This is called "routed."

All these six are a Tao of defeat,
The general's utmost responsibility.
One cannot but examine them.

§

Now forms of the earth are an assistance to the military.
Assess the enemy and determine victory.
Appraise the steep and level, the far and near.
This is a Tao of the superior general.
One who knows these and employs battle is certainly victorious.
One who does not know these and employs battle is certainly
       defeated.

§

And so when according to the Tao of battle there is certain
       victory and the ruler says do not do battle, one can
       certainly do battle.

When according to the Tao of battle there is no victory and the
       ruler says one must do battle, one can not do battle.

§

And so he advances yet does not seek fame.
He retreats yet does not avoid blame.
He seeks only to preserve the people,
And his advantage accords with that of the ruler.
He is the treasure of the state.

He looks upon the troops as his children.
Thus they can venture into deep river valleys with him.
He looks upon the troops as his beloved sons.
Thus they can die together with him.

He is generous yet unable to lead.
He is loving yet unable to give orders.
He is chaotic and unable to bring order.
They are like spoiled children.
They cannot be employed.

§

Knowing my troops can strike, yet not knowing the enemy cannot
        be struck.
This is half of victory.

Knowing the enemy can be struck, yet not knowing my soldiers
        cannot strike.
This is half of victory.

Knowing the enemy can be struck, knowing my soldiers can
        strike, yet not knowing that the form of the earth cannot
        be used to do battle.
This is half of victory.

§

And so one who knows the military
Acts and is not confused,
Initiates and is not exhausted.

§

And so it is said—
    Know the other and know oneself, ◠
    Then victory is not in danger. ◠
    Know earth and know heaven, ◠
    Then victory can be complete. ◠

I I

The Nine Grounds

Sun Tzu said:

The method of employing the military—

There is dispersed ground, light ground, contested ground, connected ground, junction ground, heavy ground, spread-out ground, enclosed ground and death ground.

The feudal lords battle for this ground.
This is "dispersed."

I enter another's ground, but not deeply.
This is "light."

If I obtain it, it is advantageous. If he obtains it, it is also advantageous.
This is "contested."

I am able to go. He is able to come.
This is "connected."

Where the grounds of three feudal lords meet, the one who arrives first will obtain the multitudes of all-under-heaven.
This is "junction."

I enter another's ground deeply, with many walled cities and towns at my back.
This is "heavy."

I move through mountains, forests and swamps—in sum, roads difficult to move along.
This is "spread-out."

The way by which I exit and enter is narrow.
The way by which I pursue and return is circuitous.
His few can strike my many.
This is "enclosed."

If quick, I survive.
If not quick, I am lost.
This is "death."

Therefore—
In dispersed ground do not do battle.
In light ground do not stop.

In contested ground do not attack.
In connected ground do not cross.
In junction ground join with allies.
In heavy ground plunder.
In spread-out ground move.
In enclosed ground strategize.
In death ground do battle.

§

In ancient times those called skilled at battle were able to
        prevent—
    The enemy's van and rear from reaching each other, ⌇
    The many and the few from relying on each other, ⌇
    Noble and base from helping each other, ⌇
    Superior and inferior from coordinating with each other, ⌇
    Separated troops from regrouping, ⌇
    The assembled military from becoming uniform. ⌇

§

If it accords with advantage, then act.
If it does not accord with advantage, then stop.

§

Dare one ask,
    "The enemy, amassed and in good order, is about to approach.
    How do I await him?"
I say,
    "Seize what he loves, and he will heed you!"

§

It is the nature of the military that swiftness rules.
Ride others' inadequacies.
Go by unexpected ways.
Attack where he has not taken precautions.

§

In sum, the Tao of being an invader—

Enter deeply and one is concentrated.
The defenders do not subdue one. ∼

Plunder rich countryside.
The three armies have enough to eat. ∼

Carefully nourish and do not work them.
Consolidate ch'i and accumulate strength. ∼

Move the military about and appraise one's strategies.
Be unfathomable. ∼

Throw them where they cannot leave.
Facing death, they will not be routed. ∼
Officers and men facing death, ∼
How could one not obtain their utmost strength? ∼

When military officers are utterly sinking, they do not fear. ∼
Where they cannot leave, they stand firm. ∼
When they enter deep, they hold tightly. ∼
Where they cannot leave, they fight. ∼

Therefore, they are—
    Untuned yet disciplined, ∼
    Unsought yet obtained, ∼
    Without covenant yet in kinship,
    Without orders yet trusting. ∼

§

Prohibit omens, remove doubt, and even death seems no disaster.

§

My officers do not have surplus wealth.
It is not that they hate goods.
They do not have surplus deaths.
It is not that they hate longevity.

On the day that orders are issued,
The tears of seated officers moisten their lapels,
The tears of those reclining cross their cheeks.

Throw them where they cannot leave—
It is the bravery of Chuan Chu and Ts'ao Kuei.

§

And so one skilled at employing the army may be compared to
        the *shuai-jan*.
The shuai-jan is a snake of Mount Heng.
Strike its head and the tail arrives.
Strike its tail and the head arrives.
Strike its midsection and both head and tail arrive.

Dare one ask,
    "Can one then make them like the shuai-jan?"
I reply,
    "One can. The people of Yueh and the people of Wu hate
        each other.
    When they are in the same boat crossing the river,
    They help each other like the left and right hand."

§

Therefore, tying horses together and burying wheels
Is not enough to rely on.

Make bravery uniform.
This is a Tao of governance.

Attain both hard and soft.
This is a pattern of earth.

§

And so one skilled at employing the military takes them by the
        hand as if leading a single person.
They cannot hold back.

§

In his activity ∼
The commander is tranquil and thus inscrutable,
Orthodox and thus brings order. ∼

He is able to stupefy the ears and eyes of officers and troops,
Preventing them from having it. ∽

He changes his activities, ∽
Alters his strategies,
Preventing the people from discerning. ∽

He changes his camp, ∽
Makes his route circuitous, ∽
Preventing the people from obtaining his plans. ∽

The leader sets the time of battle with them, ∽
Like climbing high and removing the ladder. ∽
The leader enters with them deep into the land of the feudal
        lords, ∽
Pulling the trigger. ∽

Like driving a flock of sheep,
He drives them there,
He drives them here, ∽
No one knows where they are going. ∽

He gathers the multitude of the three armies
And throws them into the defile.

This is what is meant by "the activity of the commander."

§

The variations of the nine grounds,
The advantages of contracting and extending,
The patterns of human nature—
One cannot but examine them.

§

In sum, being an invader—
    Deep then concentrated,
    Shallow then dispersed.

To leave the state and go over the border with soldiers. This is
        crossing ground.

Four ways in. This is junction ground.
To enter deeply. This is heavy ground.
To enter shallowly. This is light ground.
Unyielding at the back, narrow in front. This is enclosed ground.
Unyielding at the back, enemy in front. This is death ground.
No way to leave. This is exhaustion ground.

Therefore—
    In dispersed ground I will unify their will.
    In light ground I will make them come together.
    In contested ground I will keep them from lingering.
    In connected ground I will make firm my ties.
    In junction ground I will be careful of what I rely on.
    In heavy ground I will hasten to bring up my rear.
    In spread-out ground I will advance along his roads.
    In enclosed ground I will block the gaps.
    In death ground I will show them that we will not live.

§

And so the nature of the feudal lords—
    When enclosed, they resist.
    When there is no holding back, they fight.
    When overcome, they follow.

Therefore—
    Not knowing the strategies of the feudal lords,
    One cannot ally with them.
    Not knowing the form of mountains and forests, defiles and
        gorges, marshes and swamps,
    One cannot move the army.
    Not employing local guides,
    One cannot obtain the advantage of the ground.
    Not knowing one of these four or five,
    One is not the military of the kings and overlords.

The military of those kings and overlords—
    If they attack a great state, then its multitude is unable to
        gather together.

Their awesomeness spreads over the enemy, and his allies
    cannot assemble.

Therefore—
    Do not contend for allies in all-under-heaven.
    Do not cultivate balance in all-under-heaven.
    Trust in self-interest.
    Spread one's awesomeness over the enemy.
Thus his state can be seized and his walled cities can be made
    to submit.

§

Without method's rewards, ∼
Without proper orders, ∼
Bind the multitude of the three armies ∼
As if leading a single person. ∼

Bind them with deeds. Do not command them with words.
Bind them with harm. Do not command them with advantage.

Mire them in the ground of extinction and still they survive.
Sink them in death ground and still they live.

Now the multitude is sunk in harm, ∼
Yet still they are able to make defeat into victory. ∼

§

And so conducting the affairs of the military ∼
Lies in carefully discerning the enemy's purpose. ∼
Concentrate strength in one direction. ∼
Go one thousand li and kill his general. ∼
This is what is meant by "skillful deeds."

§

Therefore, on the day the policy is initiated— ∼
    Close the passes and break the tallies.
    Do not let their emissaries pass. ∼
    Hone it in the upper court
    In order to fix the matter. ∼

§

When the enemy opens the outer gate, ∼
One must quickly enter. ∼
Make what he loves the first objective.
Hide the time of battle from him. ∼
Discard the ink line and respond to the enemy ∼
In order to decide the matter of battle. ∼

Therefore—
    At first be like a virgin. ∼
    The enemy opens the door. ∼
    Afterward be like an escaped rabbit. ∼
    The enemy will be unable to resist. ∼

12

Attack by Fire

Sun Tzu said:

In sum, there are five attacks by fire—
    The first is called "setting fire to people."
    The second is called "setting fire to stores."
    The third is called "setting fire to baggage trains."
    The fourth is called "setting fire to armories."
    The fifth is called "setting fire in tunnels."

Making fire has requisites.
The requisites must be sought out and prepared.

There is a season for setting fires.
There are days for starting fires.
The season is when heaven is dry.
The days are when the lunar mansion is the Winnowing Basket,
        the Wall, the Wings, and the Chariot Platform.
All four lunar mansions are days when the wind rises.

If fire is set inside, respond immediately from the outside.
If fire is set and his military is still, do not attack.

Rush to where the fire is calamitous.
If one can pursue them, then pursue.
If one cannot pursue, then stop.

If fire can be set outside, do not wait to set it inside.
Set it according to the season.
If fire is set upwind, do not attack from downwind.
If during the day wind is prolonged, at night the wind
        will stop.
One must know the variations of the five fires.
Use counting to watch for the time.

And so one who uses fire to aid an attack is dominant. ∼
One who uses water to aid an attack is strong. ∼
Water can be used to cut off. ∼
It cannot be used to seize. ∼

§

Now battle for victory, attack and attain it.
But if one does not follow up on the achievement, it is
        inauspicious.
One's fate is "wealth flowing away."

Thus it is said—
    The enlightened ruler contemplates it.
    The good general follows up on it.

If it is not advantageous, do not act.
If it is not attainable, do not employ troops.
If it is not in danger, do not do battle.

The ruler cannot raise an army on account of wrath.
The general cannot do battle on account of rancor.
If it accords with advantage, then employ troops.
If it does not, then stop.

Wrath can return to joy.
Rancor can return to delight.
An extinguished state cannot return to existence.
The dead cannot return to life.

Thus the enlightened sovereign is careful about this.
The good general is cautious about this.

These are a Tao of securing the state and keeping the army whole.

13
Employing Spies

Sun Tzu said:

In sum—
When raising one hundred thousand soldiers and setting out
        on a campaign of one thousand li, the expenses of the
        hundred clans and the contributions of the nation are
        one thousand gold pieces a day.
Inner and outer are disturbed.
People are exhausted on the roads.
Seven hundred thousand households are unable to manage their
        affairs.

On guard against them for years to contend for a single day's victory,
        yet, by begrudging rank and the reward of a hundred gold
        pieces, he does not know the nature of the enemy.
  He is utterly inhumane.
  He is not the general of the people.
  He is not the assistant of the ruler.
  He is not the ruler of victory.

§

And so the means by which an enlightened sovereign and a wise
        general act, and so are victorious over others and achieve
        merit superior to the multitude's—
This is foreknowledge.

  Foreknowledge cannot be grasped from ghosts and spirits,
  Cannot be inferred from events,
  Cannot be projected from calculation.
  It must be grasped from people's knowledge.

§

And so there are five kinds of spy to employ.
There is the native spy, the inner spy, the turned spy, the dead spy
        and the living spy.
When the five spies arise together and no one knows their Tao,
This is what is meant by "spiritlike web."
It is the treasure of the people's sovereign.

The living spy returns and reports.
Employ the native spy from among the local people.
Employ the inner spy from among their officials.
Employ the turned spy from among enemy spies.
The dead spy spreads false information abroad. I order my spy to
        know it, and he transmits it to the enemy spy.

§

And so, in the kinship of the three armies—
    No kinship is more intimate than that of a spy.
    No reward is more generous than that for a spy.
    No affair is more secret than that of a spy.

If not a sage, one cannot employ spies.
If not humane, one cannot send out spies.
If not subtle and secret, one cannot obtain a spy's treasure.

Secret! Secret!
There is nothing for which one cannot employ spies.

When the affairs of a spy are heard before they are under way,
The spy and those who have been told all die.

§

In sum,
The army one wishes to strike, the walled city one wishes to
        attack and the person one wishes to kill—
One must first know the family name and given name of the
        defending general, his intimates, the steward, the
        gatekeeper and attendants.
I order my spy to surely seek them out and know them.

I must seek out the enemy's spies who come to spy on me.
Accordingly, I benefit them, direct them and then release them.
Thus a turned spy can be obtained and employed.

With this knowledge the local spy and the inner spy can thus be
        obtained and sent out.
With this knowledge the dead spy thus spreads false information
        and can be sent to tell the enemy.
With this knowledge the living spy can thus be sent out on time.

One must know the matter of the five spies.
Knowing it surely lies in the turned spy.
Thus one cannot but be generous with a turned spy.

§

When Yin arose, I Chih was in Hsia.
When Chou arose, Lü Ya was in Yin.

Only if the enlightened ruler and wise general can use people
        of superior knowledge as spies will they surely achieve
        great merit.

These are essentials of the military.
The three armies rely on them and act.

Acknowledgments

THE IDEAS IN THIS BOOK are not new and are mostly not ours. We once thought they were, but our agent Joe Spieler reminded us that there aren't any new ideas, just the same old ones getting recycled in different ways every so often. That was a relief to hear.

The Rules of Victory represents a stage in a long, ongoing conversation with a very large number of people, who have contributed their wisdom and insight in many different ways. We could not possibly keep track of them all and give them all credit here, but we are deeply thankful just the same. If you run across a sentence that sounds particularly insightful, you can bet that with a little prodding we could trace it back to a conversation with a friend or the work of a colleague. So, to all who've been part of the development and evolution of these ideas, and who've taught us in many ways: we trust that you'll recognize yourself in this work and we hope we didn't embarrass you. We offer a bow and a hearty thank you.

Then there are those to whom we owe special thanks: to everyone who attended our seminars and asked tough questions; to the many readers, commenters, contributors, seminar hosts, teachers, and those who served by example, including Harry Tate, Patrick Lawler, Michael Scott, Carol Johnstone, Eric Ruby, David Frevola, Michael Carroll, Michael Chender and the folks at the Shambhala Institute, Meg Wheatley, Jon Kabat-Zinn, Erica Ariel Fox, Carolyn Rose Gimian, Judi Juskevich, and the members of the Denma Translation Group; to the staff of the *Shambhala Sun* who accommodated our work on this volume and who contributed to it; to Melvin McLeod, strategic thinker, colleague, and friend; to Joe Spieler, agent, friend, and fine actor; to Peter Turner, for his key comments and patient support, and to his colleagues at Shambhala Publications who work with skill and exertion to make books like ours succeed in a very difficult industry; to Marc Benioff, whose insight into the Sun Tzu created a remarkable ground for practice; to Adam Kahane for his incisive comments about the important stuff; to Jerry Granelli for listening practice, insights into the Sun Tzu, and the constant sound of humor; to Kidder Smith, for his deep knowledge and understanding of the text and its tradition in general, and his support and encouragement for this project in particular. Our sections on shih draw heavily from his original work, and he developed and introduced us to reading practice.

We owe a particularly large thank you and bow to our editor Eden Steinberg, who was tireless in her questions, in her trust in our instincts, and in coming up with creative solutions when we could not. We admire her skill in taking us whole in so many of those instances.

We cannot thank deeply enough Carolyn, Jenny, Judi, Anna, and Madeline, who sustain us with their loyalty and confidence, and who were unreasonably patient during the long time this project took to complete.

All gratitude and a deep bow to the lineage of sage human beings who've transmitted wisdom such as the Sun Tzu down through the centuries so that we could experience it as true, exemplified most for us by our teacher Chögyam Trungpa.

Notes

Chapter 1: What Is The Art of War?

1. Reading practice was developed by our close colleague Kidder Smith, professor in the Asian Studies Department at Bowdoin College. Professor Smith was the lead translator and codirector of the Denma Translation Group for our *Art of War: The Denma Translation*.

Chapter 2: View, Practice, and Action

1. Gyorgy Kepes, *Language of Vision* (Chicago: Paul Theobald, 1944), 46.

2. Stephen Pinker, *Words and Rules: The Ingredients of Language* (New York: Basic Books, 1999), 273.

3. Kepes, *Language of Vision*, 31.

4. John C. Maxwell, *The 21 Irrefutable Laws of Leadership Workbook* (Nashville: Thomas Nelson, 2002), 67.

5. Global Executive, "Firing Blanks?" *The Economist* website, Jan. 28, 2002.

Chapter 3: The Big View

1. Cheryl Dahle, "Natural Leader," *Fast Company*, Nov. 2000, 268.

2. Lao Tzu, *Tao Teh Ching,* trans by John C. H. Wu (Boston: Shambhala Publications, 2003), 55.

3. Daniel Gilbert, "He Who Cast the First Stone Probably Didn't," *New York Times*, July 24, 2006.

4. Maureen Dowd, "Bike-Deep in the Big Muddy," *New York Times,* Aug. 27, 2005.

5. Jerome Groopman, *How Doctors Think* (Boston: Houghton Mifflin, 2007), 40.

6. Robert A. Caro, *The Years of Lyndon Johnson*, vol. 1, *The Path to Power* (New York: Vintage/Ebury, 1983), 319.

Chapter 4: The Basic Practice

1. Ulrik Schramm, *The Undisciplined Horse* (London: J. A. Allen, 1989), back cover.

2. Edward Rothstein, "Puzzles, Origami and Other Mind-Twisters," *New York Times,* Apr. 3, 2006.

3. Colonel Peter Faber, "Four Questions and Answers on Asymmetric Warfare," Occasional Paper written for the NATO Defense College, www.ndc.nato.int/download/research/asym_war_comments.pdf (2004).

4. Steve Silberman, "The Bacteria Whisperer," *Wired,* Apr. 2003, 108.

Chapter 5: Strategic Practices

1. Max Jacobson, Murray Silverstein, and Barbara Winslow, *Patterns of Home: The Ten Essentials of Enduring Design* (Newtown, Conn.: Taunton Press, 2002), 9.

2. Nassim Nicholas Taleb, *The Black Swan: the Impact of the Highly Improbable* (New York: Random House, 2007), 284.

3. U.S. Congress, 108th Cong., 2nd sess., *Congressional Record* 150, no. 108 (2004): S 9105.

4. Arthur Zajonc, interview by Barry C. Boyce for article to appear in *Shambhala Sun* magazine, May 12, 2005, transcript, archives of Victory Communication.

5. Lucette Lagnado, "Seniors in Vermont Are Finding They Can Go Home Again," *Wall Street Journal,* Oct. 23, 2006.

6. Chögyam Trungpa, *True Command* (Trident: Halifax, 2003), 64.

7. Richard Brown, interview by Barry C. Boyce for article to appear in *Shambhala Sun* magazine, September 24, 2006, transcript, archives of Victory Communication.

Chapter 7: How to Enter This Wisdom Lineage

1. Listening practice was developed by jazz drummer, composer, and teacher Jerry Granelli and used in his innovative music teaching in the Creative Music Workshop in Halifax, Nova Scotia.

Also of Interest

IF YOU ARE INTERESTED in studying the *The Art of War* further, you might enjoy the following materials available from Shambhala Publications.

The Art of War: The Denma Translation
Most translations of *The Art of War* present the classic Sun Tzu text solely from a military, historical, or academic perspective. While the Denma translation is faithful to those perspectives, it is the only translation that presents the text's broader meaning as a wisdom text, thus enabling modern day readers to apply its insights to contemporary challenges with greater effectiveness. This edition of the *The Art of War* includes line-by-line commentary as well as in-depth essays on key themes.

The Art of War Box: Book and Card Deck
This unique book-and-card kit will help readers gain new insight into the text and the powerful philosophy that underlies it. Here, the core teachings of the Sun Tzu are presented in the form of fifty maxims displayed on beautifully produced cards with commentary on the reverse side of each. Also included is a fold-out card stand, and a paperback book that includes a full translation of the text and illuminating essays on the central ideas that have made *The Art of War* a perennial classic.

Art of War: Book and Audio-CD Set
This book-and-CD set allows Sun Tzu's words to return to their original medium—the spoken word. Included here on three CDs is a reading of the complete *Art of War*, as well as a reading of the

text interspersed with helpful commentary. The booklet features an introduction to Sun Tzu's teachings, *The Art of War* text, and in-depth essays on its key ideas.

Index

Page numbers in boldface refer to The Art of War text.

About the Authors

FOR OVER TWENTY-FIVE YEARS, James Gimian has taught seminars, corporate retreats, and leadership programs on how to effectively apply the strategies and principles of *The Art of War* in a wide range of contexts. Gimian is also the publisher of the *Shambhala Sun* magazine, and the codirector of the Denma Translation Group, which produced a critically acclaimed and best-selling translation of *The Art of War*.

Barry Boyce is a member of the Denma Translation Group and has taught seminars on *The Art of War* throughout North America and in Europe. He is a senior editor and staff writer for the *Shambhala Sun* magazine and also works as a freelance writer and writing teacher, through his company Victory Communication.

For more information, visit www.rulesofvictory.com.